The marketing case

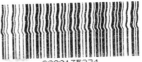
G000135274

Everyone interested in marketing should pick up this book. Packed with hundreds of mini case studies on the marketing strategies of well-known companies throughout the world, it offers a feast of real-life examples of marketing practice.

The Marketing Casebase contains brief explanations of key marketing techniques and strategies, from market analysis to the marketing mix. The book covers consumer, industrial and service marketing and is fully cross-referenced to dip into again and again. It is an invaluable hand-book for students and professionals alike.

Brian MacNamee is currently a marketing manager and **Ray McDonnell** is a marketing consultant. They have both lectured in marketing and have extensive experience in industry.

The marketing casebase

Short examples of marketing practice

Brian MacNamee and
Ray McDonnell

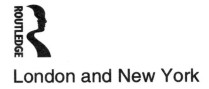

London and New York

First published 1995
by Routledge
11 New Fetter Lane, London EC4P 4EE

Simultaneously published in the USA and Canada
by Routledge
29 West 35th Street, New York, NY 10001

Typeset in Times by LaserScript, Mitcham, Surrey
Printed and bound in Great Britain by
Mackays of Chatham PLC, Chatham, Kent

British Library Cataloguing in Publication Data
A catalogue record for this book is available from the British Library

Library of Congress Cataloging in Publication Data
MacNamee, Brian, 1960–
    The marketing casebase/Brian MacNamee and Ray McDonnell.
    p. cm.
    Includes bibliographical references and index.
    ISBN 0–415–10321–5 (pbk.)
    1. Marketing – Case studies. I. McDonnell, Ray, 1962–
II. Title.
HF5415.M26746   1995
658.8 – dc20   94-31229
                                                           CIP

ISBN 0–415–10321–5

The comments pertaining to specific companies and organisations are
supported by media and/or trade opinion and are not intended to
reflect badly on those companies and personnel concerned. These cases
highlight the practices of modern marketing management and strategy.

Contents

Figures

Tables

Preface

Marketing theory today contains an abundance of concepts, techniques and principles designed to advance the study of the behaviour of markets. Similarly, within the real life business environment organisations are consistently developing new ways of implementing the marketing approach. The interaction of these two trains of activity meets in the application of marketing theory to actual market situations. This book provides 'real life' examples of marketing theories and practices among companies and organisations demonstrating the application of theory to practice.

The book is intended to make marketing theory come alive and increase its relevance by providing instances of everyday marketing management practice. While not a theoretical book, its contents follow the standard approach of most marketing textbooks.

The book is recommended for two publics. First, for use on the wide range of third-level undergraduate and postgraduate marketing courses that exist and any other courses with a marketing theme. The book will serve as a useful supplementary text for both students and lecturers alike who, we believe, will benefit from the marketing examples which relate marketing theory to the 'real-life' business environment. Here it will serve as an aid to a better understanding of the theoretical marketing textbooks that exist. Second, the book will appeal to the professional manager or would-be manager interested in the subject of marketing and who wants an 'interesting and informative read'.

The examples have been drawn from a wide variety of different sources including leading business magazines, journals and newspapers from the UK, USA and other countries. The examples deal with the consumer, industrial and, occasionally, not-for-profit markets, covering both goods and services. New developments in marketing as well as established issues are included, with examples from both large and small organisations.

Most examples presented in the book have been adapted from a variety of sources. Occasionally we have reprinted an article word-for-word, retaining its original flavour. All permissions have been obtained and in the interests of continuity all source details are in the notes sections at the end of each chapter.

It has been an interesting job to research and select the examples for this book, and we hope that readers find it of true value in developing a better understanding of marketing today.

Raymond McDonnell
Brian MacNamee

Chapter 1

The strategic planning process

INTRODUCTION

Today, strategic planning is very much of a buzz word, often misquoted and much less understood. But what does it mean? Basically, a firm that engages in strategic planning is attempting to develop a plan that uses the organisation's strengths in the most effective way to take advantage of identified market opportunities and/or minimise the effect of identified threats on the company.

In formulating its strategic plan, the organisation analyses its environment and markets for threats and opportunities, determines its own strengths and weaknesses *vis-à-vis* its competitors, formulates a mission statement or purpose for itself, sets goals (both long-term and short-term) that are consistent with its mission to capitalise on market opportunities and minimise the threats facing the company, and develops a plan to achieve these goals. The firm must be clear on how to implement the plan – for example, setting budgets, hiring staff, motivating staff, communicating the purpose and goals throughout the organisation. Performance standards that are consistent with the company goals are set for individuals, departments and divisions within the company and performance is regularly measured against these standards to ensure the company is on track. The company must continually monitor the implementation of its plan, quickly adjusting elements of it should feedback from the market suggest so. This is the strategic planning process in its simplest form.

Strategic planning is planning based on a rigorous analysis both of the firm's environment and markets (including, of course, competitors), and of itself – its own strengths and weaknesses. It focuses the firm's attention on what it is good at – where its distinctive competencies lie. The firm's energy is focused on market opportunities where its distinctive competencies could bring competitive advantages.

In this chapter, we start off with SWOT analysis – an examination of the firm's internal strengths and weaknesses and the external threats and opportunities facing it. The SWOT analysis basically addresses the question 'Where is the firm now?' A strategic market planning tool, the portfolio model is then described with reference to US company 3M. Portfolio models can be useful for multi-business firms by helping them understand the current situation of their portfolio of businesses and deciding general strategic directions for them.

Once a firm has determined its current situation, it is then in a position to develop a mission statement and set corporate goals. The importance of corporate responsibility as a goal in the 1990s is then highlighted. When developing a mission statement and setting goals the organisation must build on its strengths or 'distinctive competencies' and formulate a strategy that translates these into competitive advantage. Finally, strategy implementation is covered, describing how various firms implement their strategies. Strategies need to be evaluated on a regular basis and changes made if goals are not being realised. Setting performance standards and measuring performance against those standards is how the effectiveness of a strategy is assessed.

SWOT

SWOT (alternatively called TOWS) is an analysis of an organisation's internal strengths and weaknesses, and the external market opportunities and threats facing it. It is typically carried out before formulating strategy.

Volkswagen[1]

Volkswagen demonstrates how a successful company experienced great difficulties in the early 1970s, but then developed a strategy that resulted in an excellent market position in the late 1970s. The TOWS matrix shown in Figure 1.1 focuses on the crucial period from late 1973 to early 1975. The external threats and opportunities pertain mostly to the situation VW faced in the USA, but a similar situation prevailed in Europe at that time.

In a situational analysis as conceptualised above, one would first list and analyse the threats and opportunities in the external environment and the weaknesses and strengths of the enterprise before developing alternative strategies and tactics. However, in this illustration, to be concise, the situation and the related actions, shown in Figure 1.1, are combined.

	Internal strengths:	Internal weaknesses:
	1 Strong R.&D. and engineering 2 Strong sales and service network 3 Efficient production/automation capabilities	1 Heavy reliance on one product (although several less successful models were introduced) 2 Rising costs in Germany 3 No experience with US labour unions if building plant in USA
External opportunities: (consider risks also) 1 Growing affluent market demands more luxurious cars with many options 2 Attractive offers to build an assembly in USA 3 Chrysler and American Motors need small engines	Strengths and opportunities: 1 Develop and produce multiproduct line with many options, in different price classes (Dasher, Scirocco, Rabbit, Audi Line) (O_1, S_1, S_2) 2 Build assembly plant using R.&D., engineering, and production/automation experience (O_2, S_1, S_3) 3 Build engines for Chrysler and AMC (O_3, S_3)	Weaknesses and opportunities: 1 Develop compatible models for different price levels (ranging from Rabbit to Audi Line) (O_1, W_1) 2 To cope with rising costs in Germany, built plant in USA, hiring US managers with experience in dealing with US labour unions (O_2, W_2, W_3)
External threats: 1 Exchange rate. Devaluation of dollar in relation to Deutschmark (DM) 2 Competition from Japanese and US automakers 3 Fuel shortage and price	Strengths and threats: 1 Reduce effect of exchange rate by building a plant in the USA (T_1, T_2, S_1, S_3) 2 Meet competition with advanced design technology – e.g. Rabbit (T_2, T_3, S_1, S_2) 3 Improve fuel consumption through fuel injection and develop fuel efficient diesel engines (T_3, S_1)	Weaknesses and threats: A Overcome weaknesses by making them strengths (move towards OS strategy) 1 Reduce threat of competition by developing flexible product line (T_2, W_1) B Possible options *not* exercised by VW: 1 Engage in joint operation with Chrysler or AMC 2 Withdraw from US market

Figure 1.1 Application of the TOWS matrix to Volkswagen, covering the period from late 1973 to early 1975

Weaknesses and threats (WT)   A company with great weaknesses often has to resort to a survival strategy. VW could have seriously considered the option of a joint operation with Chrysler or American Motors. Another alternative would have been to withdraw from the American market altogether. Although in difficulties, VW did not have to resort to a survival strategy because the company still had many strengths. Consequently, a more appropriate strategy was to attempt to overcome the weaknesses and develop them into strengths. In other words, the direction was toward the strength–opportunity position (SO) in the matrix shown in Figure 1.1. Specifically, the strategy was to reduce the competitive threat by developing a more flexible new product line that would accommodate the needs and desires of the car-buying public.

Weaknesses and opportunities (WO)   The growing affluence of customers has resulted in 'trading up' to more luxurious cars. Yet, VW had essentially a one-model policy which presented a problem when the design of the Beetle became obsolete. A new model line had to be introduced to reach a wider spectrum of buyers. In order to minimise the additional costs of a multiproduct line, the building block principle was employed in the design of the new cars. This allowed using the same parts for different models that ranged from the relatively low-priced Rabbit to the higher priced Audi line.

Another weakness at VW was the rising costs in Germany. For example, in 1973 wages and salaries rose 19 per cent over the previous year. Similarly, increased fuel costs made the shipping of cars to the United States more costly. This situation favoured setting up an assembly plant in the United States. However, this also created some problems for VW because it had no experience in dealing with American organised labour. To overcome this weakness, VW's tactic was to recruit managers from Detroit who were capable of establishing good union relations.

Strengths and threats (ST)   One of the greatest threats to VW was the continuing appreciation of the Deutschmark against the dollar. For example, between October 1972 and November 1973 the mark appreciated 35 per cent. This meant higher prices for the buyer. The result, of course, was a less competitive posture. Japanese and American automakers obtained an increasingly larger share of the small-car market. To reduce the threats of competition and the effects of the unfavourable exchange rate, VW was forced to build an assembly plant in the United States.

Another strategy for meeting competitive pressures was to build on VW's strengths by developing a car based on advanced technology. The result of this effort was the Rabbit, a model with features later adopted by many other car manufacturers.

The oil crisis in 1973–74 not only caused a fuel shortage, but also price rises, a trend that has continued. To meet this threat, VW used its technological capabilities not only to improve its engines (through the use of fuel injection, for example), but also to develop the very fuel-efficient diesel engine. This tactic, which was congruent with its general strategy, helped improve the firm's market position.

Strengths and opportunities (SO)   In general, successful firms build on their strengths to take advantage of opportunities. VW is no exception. Throughout this discussion VW's strengths in research, development, engineering, and its experience in production technology became evident. These strengths, under the leadership of Rudolph Leiding, enabled the company to develop a product line that met market demands for an economical car (the Rabbit, successor to the Beetle), as well as the tastes for more luxurious cars with many available options (Scirocco and the Audi line).

Eventually the same company's strengths enabled VW to plan and build the assembly facility in New Stanton, Pennsylvania. Thus, VW could benefit from substantial concessions granted by the state government to attract VW which, in turn, provided many employment opportunities.

In another tactical move, VW manufactured and sold small engines to Chrysler and American Motors. These companies urgently needed small engines for installation in their own cars and revenues from these sales improved the financial position of VW.

FURTHER REFERENCE

Chapter 3, The Marketing Environment: Political (p. 48); Economic (p. 49)

BUSINESS PORTFOLIOS

For large multi-business firms portfolio models can be of assistance by helping them analyse the current situation of their various businesses. They can help a firm decide general strategic directions for its portfolio of businesses.

Portfolio analysis techniques such as the Boston Consulting Group (BCG) growth–share matrix[2] are a valuable strategic market planning tool for diversified multi-business organisations. The BCG growth–share matrix allows a company to classify its portfolio of businesses, be they divisions, product lines, products, or brands, in a two-by-two matrix using the dimensions of market growth rate and relative market share. Termed strategic business units or SBUs, the portfolio contains units of an organisation with its own mission, objectives and planning autonomy. The market growth rate dimension provides a measure of market attractiveness and the market share for the SBU relative to the share of the industry's largest competitor provides a measure of its strength in the market.

The classifying of businesses in this way helps top management decide which businesses to build, maintain, phase down and phase out, thus helping them allocate company resources in an efficient way. It should be emphasised that portfolio analysis techniques only assist marketers in analysing the market situation and do not provide strategic solutions, beyond a general level, to a particular problem. The BCG growth–share matrix is not a substitute for strategic decision making. Before making strategic decisions on its SBUs, a company needs to consider more factors than the market growth rate and the relative market share of the SBU. For example, market opportunities, company capabilities, overall corporate objectives, interdependence among the various SBUs and the future cash-flow projections at the individual SBU level and the aggregate firm level are all factors that must also be analysed before assigning a mission and allocating resources to an SBU.

Nevertheless, portfolio analysis techniques are useful in providing management with a picture of the current health of its portfolio of businesses and are used by many organisations as a valuable diagnostic tool.

3M[3]

In the 1980s the 3M Corporation defined twenty 'strategic business centres' (comparable to SBUs). Each strategic business centre (SBC) was composed of individual operating units – usually divisions or departments, responsible for particular products or market segments. Some SBCs covered two or more divisions – for example, Memory Media consisted of Data Recording Products and Magnetic A/V Products.

Each 3M SBC examined its portfolio of products and markets on a matrix using the dimensions of maturity and competitive position.

Figure 1.2 portrays the strategic condition of a particular 3M business by geographic market. The maturity stages affect the nature of marketing strategy. In embryonic industries, 3M businesses emphasise market or product-oriented strategies to improve their competitive position. As their industries mature, these businesses will likely emphasise integration, efficiency, and rejuvenation through innovation. In the late stages of maturity, consolidation and divestment will be considered. On the competitive position axis, each 3M business is ranked against its competitors to ascertain its relative position.

In establishing corporate strategies, the complete portfolio of the corporation, Figure 1.3, was plotted in terms of competitive position, overall maturity, market attractiveness, future growth prospects, profit and cash generation, and risk. Resources were then allocated to each SBC on the basis of corporate objectives, portfolio balance, and the merits of each SBC strategy.

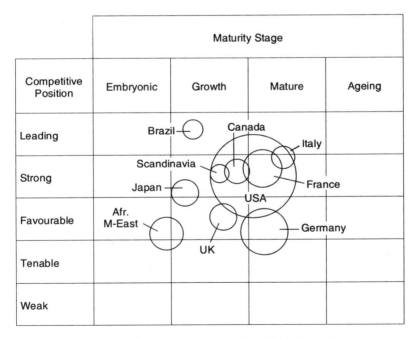

Figure 1.2 Strategic condition of a particular 3M business by geographic market

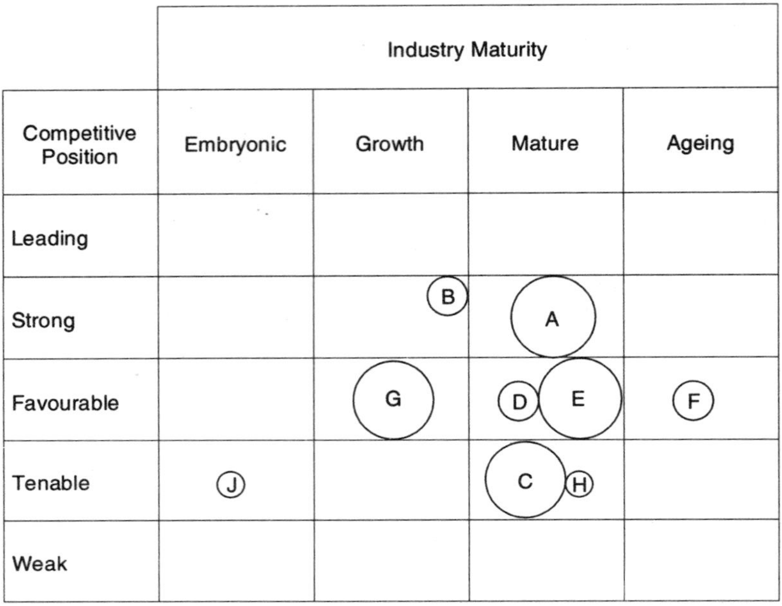

Competitive Position	Industry Maturity			
	Embryonic	Growth	Mature	Ageing
Leading				
Strong		B	A	
Favourable		G	D E	F
Tenable	J		C H	
Weak				

Figure 1.3 Corporate portfolio array (illustrative)

FURTHER REFERENCE

Chapter 15, Organisation Structures: Strategic business units (pp. 246–247)

Once a firm has determined its current situation, it is then in a position to develop a mission statement.

MISSION STATEMENTS

> A business is not defined by its name, statutes, or articles of incorporation. It is defined by the business mission. Only a clear definition of the mission and purpose of the organisation makes possible clear and realistic business objectives.[4]

The mission statement is a statement of an organisation's core corporate values providing an overall purpose and sense of direction and serving as a framework in helping the organisation prepare business plans to achieve set goals. It reveals the long-term vision of an organisation in terms of what it wants to be and who it wants to serve. It is general rather than specific, allowing the organisation a certain leeway in the strategic planning process, therefore not stifling management creativity while guiding the organisation to adhere to the fundamental values and direction outlined in the mission statement.

The mission statement should provide personnel throughout the organisation with a shared sense of direction, image, philosophy and motivation. The motivational power of a mission statement is best described by Honda's mission when overtaken by Yamaha as the number one motorcycle manufacturer in the world: 'We will crush, squash, slaughter Yamaha'. A mission statement should fuel the employees' spirit. It should be communicated throughout the organisation and understood by all personnel. For example, the UK high street retailer Debenhams has its mission statement printed on a card which employees are expected to carry with them.

Mission statements are developed with other stakeholders in mind besides employees. External stakeholders should also be considered including, for example, shareholders, suppliers, competitors and society.

Creating a new mission statement

No mission statement lasts for ever. Internal conditions within an organisation and/or environmental changes may make an existing mission statement inappropriate and force the organisation to redefine its mission.

WWF UK[5]

In 1989, WWF UK (World Wide Fund For Nature) recognised that there had been a significant change in the purpose of the organisation over the previous years and embarked on the development of a new mission statement. The original purpose of WWF was primarily to act as a fund-raising business with a secondary purpose of spending the funds raised on the conservation of nature and natural resources in an efficient manner. WWF had realised for some time that to achieve real success in the battle for the planet, it needed to influence those decision makers in whose hands the future of the planet lay – primarily decision makers in government and industry.

WWF needed to transform itself from a fund-raising organisation that raised money to give to others to undertake conservation to one of an environmental organisation supported by fund-raising. A new mission statement was drawn up to reflect this fundamental shift in emphasis.

To date, the strategic shift has been a resounding success and funds raised have increased sharply. In terms of influencing the decision makers, WWF is now recognised as having a pre-eminent position in dealing with the government and with industry. Its mission statement is thus:

WWF's Mission

WWF's Mission is to Achieve the Conservation of Nature and Ecological Processes by:

Preserving Genetic, Species and Ecosystem Diversity

Ensuring that the Use of Renewable Natural Resources is Sustainable Both Now and in the Longer Term, for the Benefit of All Life on Earth

Promoting Actions to Reduce, to a Minimum, Pollution and the Wasteful Exploitation and Consumption of Resources and Energy

WWF's Ultimate Goal is to Stop, and Eventually Reverse, the Accelerating Degradation of Our Planet's Natural Environment, and to Help Build a Future in which Humans Live in Harmony with Nature

---

General Mills

The US company General Mills has a rather short and to-the-point mission statement:

Our mission is to be a leader among corporations. We will strive to achieve excellence in any endeavours we undertake.

To fulfil this mission, we must be both responsive and anticipatory as we serve our four major constituencies: consumers, employees, shareholders, and society.

F.W. Woolworth Company

The mission statement of F.W. Woolworth Company reads:

The mission of F.W. Woolworth Company is to provide value to consumers in North America, Germany and Australia through distinctly individual but complementary retailing businesses. These businesses are being managed on a decentralised basis, to generate levels of profit that reward investors, sustain long-term growth, provide competitive rewards for employees, and benefit the communities in which they live and work.

Marks and Spencer

The mission statement of the UK high-street retailer Marks and Spencer reads:

To offer our customers a selective range of high quality well-designed and attractive merchandise at reasonable prices.

To encourage our suppliers to use the most modern and efficient techniques of production and quality control dictated by the latest discoveries in science and technology.

With the co-operation of our suppliers, to ensure the highest standards of quality control.

To plan the expansion of our stores for the better display of a widening range of goods (and) for the convenience of our customers.

To simplify operating procedures so that our business is carried on in the most efficient manner.

To foster good human relations with customers, suppliers and staff.

FURTHER REFERENCE

Chapter 1, The Strategic Planning Process: Goal formulation (p. 12)
Chapter 13, Sales Promotion and Public Relations: Public relations (p. 213)

GOAL FORMULATION

After the mission statement has been developed, the organisation can then set about setting corporate goals consistent with the mission.

The 1990s saw the emergence of corporate responsibility as a goal among many UK companies alongside the traditional goals of bottom-line profits and shareholder returns.

Unipart[6]

Unipart, the UK car parts maker bought out by its management in 1987, used to have poor relations with unions and poor relationships with suppliers when it was part of the car maker British Leyland.

After the buyout, the company set as a goal the development of co-operation among the stakeholders in the company. All Unipart staff wear the same uniform regardless of rank thus eliminating the 'us and them' demarcations between bosses and workers. Multi-skilling was introduced to train people in a variety of different jobs. This increased the self-worth of employees, reduced job boredom and helped them to understand other people's problems. Unipart began investing in staff training programmes (previously for management only) and a monthly award programme was launched to recognise outstanding service to customers. Quality Circles were encouraged and staff suggestions resulted in millions of pounds being saved.

A programme was launched to improve supplier quality and reliability and build trust and co-operation. Also, the unions were 're-recognised' in October 1991. Being a 'nice' company has resulted in sales up 50 per cent and profits doubled since the buyout.

Marks and Spencer

Corporate responsibility towards the stakeholders in a company, including staff, suppliers, the community and the environment became recognised as a way to longer-term success for many companies. A number of companies, however, had been doing it for years. Marks and Spencer (M & S), the UK high street retailer, in many ways set the standard with its excellent stakeholder relations. Staff have thorough training, subsidised canteens, on-site doctors, generous redundancy terms and out-placement counselling. Many of M & S's suppliers have been with the company for years, some for decades. Relations are excellent to the point of sister company status with M & S and its suppliers working closely together to iron out problems and provide quality products and services.

Having determined its mission and goals the organisation is then clear on where it wants to go. It should also be clear about what it is good at – its distinctive competencies – and formulate a strategy which builds on these strengths, ideally translating them into competitive advantage in the market place.

DISTINCTIVE COMPETENCE/COMPETITIVE ADVANTAGE

A business needs to be able to identify its own particular distinctive competence, i.e. some activity the company is particularly adept at compared with competitors. By capitalising on its distinctive competence, a company may develop a competitive advantage in the market place.

AEPP Automotive[7]

AEPP Automotive, a UK-based manufacturer of automotive engine pistons possesses a distinctive competence in speed of manufacturing which has translated into a competitive advantage for the firm. In 1989, it took the company 26 weeks from a customer's first enquiry to develop, manufacture, test and deliver a new design of automotive engine piston. By 1991, they had more than halved the 'time-to-market' cycle. Furthermore, it is planned to halve the cycle again, from twelve to six weeks by the end of 1993. The speed of its manufacturing cycle has given the firm a global lead ahead of its competitors.

The majority of the major car manufacturers are subcontracting more and more piston design and manufacture as they hurry to shorten their own 'time-to-market' for new cars. In January 1993, Opel, the German car maker, began to use AEPP as the sole supplier of pistons for the 1.6 litre engines used in two of Opel's top selling models. Ford of Europe are also a customer of AEPP. AEPP's sales are projected to be 16 per cent up for 1993 with a 20 per cent rise projected for 1994. The factor that has given AEPP such a lead in the market is a computer-based design and analysis process called RAPIER (Rapid Analysis of Products by Integrated Engineering Routines) which was developed by the R.&D. centre of AEPP's parent company, T & N. The process allows, for example, engineers to predict problems in both manufacture and product performance and to analyse them before they occur. This has increased design and production quality as well as reducing development costs by minimising expensive and time-consuming engine tests.

STRATEGY IMPLEMENTATION

The majority of marketing literature focuses on strategy formulation with little attention given to its implementation. It must be remembered that the most brilliant creative strategy which promises to yield a sustainable competitive advantage to a company is by itself useless unless it can be effectively implemented. The strategic plan must be effectively communicated to staff who should understand their roles and what is expected of them. Staff should also be motivated and committed to achieving the objectives of the plan. In short, staff within the company must be sold on the plan.

Staff training programmes may need to be put in place to increase capabilities and incentive schemes may be needed to generate staff motivation and reward them on the plan's attainment. Successful implementation also depends on such factors as strong leadership and direction from the top, a company culture and organisation structure that embraces change, and procedures for implementing, monitoring, evaluating and controlling the plan.

Simon Access[8]

Simon Access, the UK specialist access equipment manufacturer which produces equipment for the construction industry and the fire service, put customer service at the heart of its strategy for the 1990s in an attempt to become the global leader in its field.

In implementing this customer service strategy, the company took a number of steps. The entire workforce (with no exceptions) were taken to a major international exhibition on fire-fighting equipment in the UK. This served to make staff aware that a host of competitors existed and that to survive, the company needed to improve its products constantly. Many staff had never actually met customers and distributors so the company introduced them for the first time.

Building on the exhibition visit, the company developed a programme to help change the corporate culture into one which fosters quality and customer service. One element of the programme involved the establishment of user groups composed of customers and company staff. These user groups allow the company to better understand the needs and concerns of its customers and important product development opportunities have been identified through such groups.

Quality improvement across all stages of the business cycle from initial idea generation/product conception to after-sales service is a goal of the company and staff are made aware of progress through use of display boards showing targets and achievements to date. Extensive staff training programmes with customer service as the major theme were also implemented.

FURTHER REFERENCE

Chapter 8, New Product Development: Idea generation (p. 132)

Delta Airlines

The US airline, Delta Airlines, places great emphasis on customer service in its strategy, seeing it as a way to build customer satisfaction and loyalty. Treating its staff well and keeping them well trained and motivated is seen as translating into high productivity and superior customer service which helps to differentiate the airline from its competitors.

Implementing this strategy called for Delta to offer its staff, for example, a no-redundancy policy promising job security and creating staff loyalty to the company, flexible working practices, extensive staff training programmes and a Customer Service Awards scheme to reward staff who demonstrate an exceptional level of customer service.

Danly Machine Corporation

Danly Machine Corporation in the USA recognises the importance of communication between management and staff in helping to achieve its strategic plan. Elements of its communication programme include regular letters from senior management sent to staff keeping them abreast of business developments, regular open and frank meetings between management and staff, staff encouragement to air their problems and ideas to management through 'confidential' letters, and a telephone hotline to disseminate important information.

Successful strategy implementation calls for, among other things, regular measurement of the progress of a plan and its adjustment if the goals are going off track.

SETTING PERFORMANCE STANDARDS/MEASURING PERFORMANCE

Effective measurement of performance is an essential part of strategy. It is important not to get locked into old short-term financial indicators such as return on investment, sales growth and operating income in measuring performance against new strategies or new operating processes.

The balanced scorecard[9]

The balanced scorecard, first proposed in the January–February 1992 issue of the *Harvard Business Review* ('The Balanced Scorecard – Measures that Drive Performance'), provides executives with a comprehensive framework that translates a company's strategic objectives into a coherent set of performance measures. Much more than a measurement exercise, the balanced scorecard is a management system that can generate breakthrough improvements in such areas as product, process, customer, and market development.

The scorecard presents managers with four different perspectives from which to choose measures. It complements traditional financial indicators with measures of performance for customers, internal processes and innovation and improvement activities.

The balanced scorecard is not, however, a template that can be applied to businesses in general or even industry-wide. Different market situations, product strategies, and competitive environments require different scorecards. Business units devise customised scorecards to fit their mission, strategy, technology, and culture.

Apple Computer

Apple Computer developed a balanced scorecard to focus senior management on a strategy that would expand discussions beyond gross margin, return on equity and market share. A small steering committee, intimately familiar with the deliberations and strategic thinking of Apple's Executive Management Team, chose to concentrate on measurement categories within each of the four perspectives and to select multiple measurements within each category. For the financial perspective, Apple emphasised shareholder value; for the customer perspective, market share and customer satisfaction; for the internal process perspective, core competencies; and, finally, for the innovation and improvement perspective, employee attitudes. Apple's management stressed these categories in the following order:

Customer satisfaction   Historically, Apple had been a technology and product-focused company that competed by designing better computers. Customer satisfaction metrics are just being introduced to orient employees toward becoming a customer-driven company.

Core Competencies Company executives wanted employees to be highly focused on a few key competencies: for example, user-friendly interfaces, powerful software architectures, and effective distribution systems. However, senior executives recognised that measuring performance along these competency dimensions could be difficult. As a result, the company is currently experimenting with obtaining quantitative measures of these hard-to-measure competencies.

Employee commitment and alignment Apple conducts a comprehensive employee survey in each of its organisations every two years; surveys of randomly selected employees are performed more frequently. The survey questions are concerned with how well employees understand the company's strategy as well as whether or not they are asked to deliver results that are consistent with that strategy. The results of the survey are displayed in terms of both the actual level of employee responses and the overall trend of responses.

Market share Achieving a critical threshold of market share was important to senior management not only for the obvious sales growth benefits but also to attract and retain software developers to Apple platforms.

Shareholder value Shareholder value is included as a performance indicator, even though this measure is a result – not a driver – of performance. The measure is included to offset the previous emphasis on gross margin and sales growth, measures that ignored the investments required today to generate growth for tomorrow. In contrast, the shareholder value metric quantifies the impact of proposed investments for business creation and development.

The majority of Apple's business is organised on a functional basis – sales, product design, and world-wide manufacturing and operations – so shareholder value can be calculated only for the entire company instead of at a decentralised level. The measure, however, helps senior managers in each major organisational unit assess the impact of their activities on the entire company's valuation and evaluate new business ventures.

The five performance indicators at Apple are benchmarked against best-in-class organisations. Today, they are used to build business plans and are incorporated into senior executives' compensation plans.

Today, companies are increasingly emphasising non-financial variables and giving them equal importance as financial data in measuring a company's performance. This is demonstrated by the case of London Electricity.

London Electricity PLC

London Electricity PLC, faced with competition for the first time after privatisation of the electricity industry in 1989, has made customer satisfaction and quality important variables in its formal measurement system. Customer service lies at the heart of its strategy. Of course, financial variables such as earnings per share, return on investment and profit still remain vitally important.

The old accounting-driven performance system that existed before privatisation with its emphasis solely on reported quarterly earnings was not suitable in the new competitive market place that came into being after privatisation. A regulator was appointed to oversee the industry and set various customer service oriented standards of performance for the players. These standards of performance came into force in July 1991 and customers were to be compensated if the company failed to meet the standards. Failure to do so could ultimately result in London Electricity having its licence revoked. London Electricity also set itself standards of performance that were aimed at further improving its customer service above and beyond the level dictated by the regulator. Many of the other electricity companies did the same.

Customer satisfaction surveys are conducted periodically to measure the quality of customer service. In the early 90s, the company began taking steps to acquire the Quality Award BS 5750. Customer satisfaction survey results and details of the performance of the company against the standards set by the regulator and by itself are published in periodic reports circulated to all levels of management. The reports also compare London Electricity's performance with the other electricity companies.

CONCLUSION

This chapter has provided examples of how different organisations conduct many of the stages in the strategic planning process. Developing a strategic plan is perhaps the most important activity a firm can engage in and requires a lot of time, energy and thought. Implementing the strategic plan is a great challenge. Success also requires considering the human issues – communicating with and motivating staff. Today, more and more organisations, including charities and government departments and agencies, are recognising the value of strategic planning. This is mainly because organisations today are more cash constrained than ever before and are forced to maximise use of more limited resources.

NOTES

1   Volkswagen section, including Figure 1.1, reprinted from Heinz Weihrich, 'The TOWS Matrix: a tool for situational analysis', *Long Range Planning*, 1982, vol. 15, no. 2, pp. 54–66. Copyright 1982, with kind permission from Elsevier Science Ltd, The Boulevard, Langford Lane, Kidlington OX5 1GB, UK.

2   B. Heldey, 'Strategy and the business portfolio', *Long Range Planning*, February 1977.

3   3M section, including the figures, reprinted from *Planning Review*, 12 September 1984. Reprinted with permission of the Planning Forum, The International Society for Strategic Management and Planning.

4   Peter Drucker, *Management: Tasks, Responsibilities and Practices*, New York, Harper and Row, 1973.

5   WWF section reprinted from G. J. Medley, 'WWF UK creates a new mission', *Long Range Planning*, 1992, vol. 25, pp. 63–68. Copyright 1992, with kind permission of Elsevier Science Ltd, The Boulevard, Langford Lane, Kidlington OX5 1GB, UK.

6   Unipart section adapted from Nigel Cope, 'The vogue for looking good', *Management Today*, October 1993, pp. 69–73.

7   AEPP section adapted from the *Financial Times*, 7 April 1993.

8   Simon Access section adapted from 'Simon's customer-led commitment', *Business Marketing Digest*, 1992, vol. 17, no. 3, pp. 11–16.

9   Reprinted from Robert S. Kaplan and David P. Norton, 'Putting the balanced scorecard to work', *Harvard Business Review*, September–October 1993. Copyright © 1993 the President and Fellows of Harvard College; all rights reserved.

Chapter 2

Marketing strategies

INTRODUCTION

In formulating a strategy to achieve defined marketing objectives, a company should develop a number of alternative marketing strategies, evaluate each one and finally choose the strategy it feels will best achieve the objectives set. The marketing mix, which in its simplest form consists of the four elements – product, price, promotion and distribution – is a set of controllable variables under a company's direct control and the types of strategies that may be formulated are countless. For example, using the variables of price and distribution, one can easily observe the numerous choices available. Do we go for high price/limited distribution, low price/mass distribution or another combination? Formulating a strategy brings with it a great deal of uncertainty. No one can predict whether a strategy will be a success or a failure. Creativity is an important ingredient in formulating successful strategies and this element is observable in the strategies pursued by many successful companies today, examples of which are contained in this chapter.

This chapter provides an outline of some of the wide variety of strategies available to a firm. To reduce the uncertainty that strategy formulation brings, a number of well-known frameworks for helping a firm in strategy formulation are described – Michael Porter's generic strategies,[1] and Philip Kotler's intensive, integrative, and diversification growth strategies.[2] The chapter ends with examples of military-style strategies.

GENERIC STRATEGIES

According to Porter, for a firm to have a competitive advantage in an industry it must choose between a strategy of cost leadership and one of differentiation. Furthermore, the firm must decide whether to pursue the strategy over many industry segments or just a few, perhaps even a single market segment, within the industry. Porter describes three generic strategies: cost leadership, differentiation and focus. The focus strategy has two variants, cost focus and differentiation focus.

The cost leadership and differentiation strategies seek a competitive advantage over a broad market while the focus strategies seek cost leadership (cost focus strategy) or differentiation (differentiation focus strategy) in a narrow market.

Cost leadership

Among the companies who pursue a cost leadership strategy are Goodyear in the tyre industry, Texas Instruments in the electronics industry and Virgin Airlines.

In the tyre industry, Goodyear chose the route of becoming the lowest cost producer. Its emphasis on competing in many industry segments and aggressively pursuing volume and economies of scale formed the heart of its strategy.

Texas Instruments is a highly competitive high-tech electronics manufacturer that concentrates on increasing efficiency, enhancing technology and production volumes to lower costs and as a result can lower its prices.

Virgin Airlines, the UK airline, displays a cost leadership strategy on its North Atlantic route. This strategy was instigated to steal business away from British Airways and has been very successful.

Differentiation and differentiation focus

Morgan[3]

Morgan, the UK sports car manufacturer is the oldest private car manufacturer in the world. Its product places it in the sports car sector of the UK car market. Within this sector, Morgan occupies a specialist niche – the classic sports car segment. Morgan's strategy may be described as a differentiation focus strategy – their car is very different from any other in the market and its appeal is to the driver who requires a traditional British sports car laden with 1950s nostalgia. Morgan is still operated by the founding family.

The company lacks the technology and high performance products of other sports car manufacturers. It places little importance on reducing its high production costs originating from a labour intensive production process (each car is handmade). The company has little desire to increase output – in 1991 Morgan produced 464 cars and the figure today remains approximately 500 cars a year. As a result of these factors, the cars are expensive. However, for Morgan customers this fact is not important – Morgan cars have a waiting list of customers that can extend for four years or more.

FURTHER REFERENCE

Chapter 7, Products: Product differentiation (p. 117)

Michelin

While Goodyear pursued a cost leadership strategy (see above), Michelin, the French tyre manufacturer, emphasised R.&D. and developed the radial tyre which redefined customers' needs and eventually rendered the cross-ply tyre obsolete. Its image of progressiveness differentiates Michelin from its rivals.

FURTHER REFERENCE

Chapter 2, Marketing Strategies: Flanking (p. 36)

Bang & Olufsen

Bang & Olufsen, the small Danish manufacturer of audio-visual equipment, pursues a differentiation focus strategy in a market dominated by multinational conglomerates such as Sony, Philips and Matsushita. Its audio and television systems are very stylish, futuristic and expensive. Their prices range from £1,000 for the cheapest system to £10,000 for the top of the range. Many of their products are in the permanent design collection at the Museum of Modern Art in New York.

FURTHER REFERENCE

Chapter 7, Products: Product differentiation (p. 117)

Armstrong Rubber The US manufacturer is focused on a highly specialised customer segment and produces tyres only for aviation, agricultural and civil engineering industries.

Cost focus

Ryanair

Ryanair, the small Irish airline established in 1989, pursues a cost focus strategy offering a cheap fares/no-frills service flying passengers on the Dublin–London route. This strategy has proved a great success for the airline on one of the busiest routes in Europe and has taken valuable business away from the state airline, Aer Lingus. In 1994, Ryanair claimed it held a 30 per cent share of the Dublin–London route. In May 1994, Ryanair plans to add two new routes, Dublin–Glasgow and Dublin–Manchester, using the same low-price, no-frills strategy against its competitors on these new routes – Aer Lingus and the Isle of Man airline, Manx Airlines.

Stuck in the middle

Today *and the* Post *newspapers*[4]

The market for newspapers in the UK is composed of tabloids and broad sheet newspapers – the so-called qualities. In general, particular newspapers cater for particular segments of the population, these segments are based broadly on socio-economic and political groupings. No single newspaper can be said to cater for a cross-section of the population. In contrast, other forms of media such as main evening television news programmes attract a broad range of viewers. This was recognised by the newspaper entrepreneur Eddie Shah who believed he could produce a newspaper which would appeal to different socio-economic groups thus giving him a broader base. The *Today* newspaper which he launched combined the informed weighty editorial of the quality papers with the sensationalism of the tabloid. The paper was a failure, the generally accepted reason being that it had too wide a target market, thus not focusing on a particular segment. It tried to be all things to all people. (The paper has since been bought by News International and refocused.)

Refusing to give up, Shah carried out research into the newspaper market which showed that readers were dissatisfied with the sexist nature of some of the major tabloids. Readers surveyed conveyed they would prefer it if the so called 'smutty' sections of some of the tabloids were eliminated. In launching his more downmarket paper the *Post*, Shah maintained the sensationalist approach of the competing tabloids while dropping the smutty elements. This he called 'the breeze without the sleaze'. Once again however the paper failed, the reason being that those who wanted sensationalism in their newspaper also wanted 'sleaze'. This was provided by other tabloids but not by the *Post*, therefore they continued to buy the other tabloids. The contradiction in the market research findings can be put down to the respondents' unwillingness to admit they wanted sleaze in their paper.

INTENSIVE, INTEGRATIVE, AND DIVERSIFICATION GROWTH STRATEGIES

According to Kotler,[5] alternative growth opportunities open to a firm can be classified as intensive (opportunities within its present product–market scope), integrative (opportunities within the various stages of the value-added chain, e.g. raw material production, retailing), and diversified (opportunities outside the firm's present product–market scope).

Ansoff[6] has suggested a method for identifying intensive growth strategies in the form of a product/market expansion grid. The three means of realising intensive growth are market penetration, market development and product development.

With a market penetration strategy, the firm aims to increase sales of its present products in its present markets. A market development strategy denotes a firm attempting to sell its present products in new markets. A product development strategy represents a firm's attempts to develop new products for its present markets.

Intensive growth

Baileys Irish Cream Liqueur

R & A Bailey and Co., producer of the world renowned cream liqueur, Baileys Irish Cream, began an aggressive market penetration, market development and product development strategy for the brand in late 1992/1993.

1 Market penetration

In 1993, R & A Bailey decided to attempt to increase sales of its brand in the UK market by expanding usage of the drink, and increasing consumption against a background of increasing competition in cream liqueurs.

To expand usage, a £2 million television advertising campaign 'Baileys with Ice' was developed to reinforce the contemporary all-year round image of the drink and separate it from the 'stuffy' image of traditional liqueurs with their mainly 'after dinner' role. The appeal was to younger consumers to drink Baileys on a greater number of occasions.

To further increase consumption of the drink, sales promotional strategies pushed the one litre bottles and half bottles. Special promotional packs were developed consisting of the one litre bottle with two free cream liqueur glasses. The half bottles were promoted just after Christmas 1993 to those customers who would traditionally buy a single bottle of Baileys for Christmas and after Christmas top up their supplies of drinks.

2 Market development and product development

In 1992, 3.8 million cases of Baileys cream liqueur were sold worldwide – a similar figure to the previous year's sales. This prompted R & A Bailey to market the brand in Japan which was recognised as a potentially lucrative market.

In early 1993, Baileys was launched on the Japanese market after a period of test marketing. The regular brand was offered in addition to a specially developed premium brand for the Japanese, called Baileys Gold. Baileys Gold, made with ten-year-old malt whiskey, was developed to appeal to the Japanese taste for premium quality spirits. It was also priced at double the price of the regular brand.

R & A Bailey anticipate great sales for the two brands but also acknowledge that it will be a long time before they can judge whether their strategy has proved successful based on their experience in other foreign markets.

FURTHER REFERENCE

Chapter 13, Sales Promotion and Public Relations: Sales promotion – strategies (p. 212)
Chapter 7, Products: Product line extension (p. 112)

Master Foods[7]

Another example of a company which developed new products for its existing market is the British food company, Master Foods. The company's main product was its 'Uncle Ben' brand of rice which was targeted at the younger members of the ABC1 segment who had families but also worked. A critical factor for such individuals is convenience. The company however had a problem in that rice was not a traditional British food and compared with other countries the British consumed much less rice – on average 1.9 kg per capita, compared with 3.7 kg for France and 6 kg for Spain. One of the reasons for this was the relatively high rate of consumption of potatoes in Britain.

Furthermore, rice was usually eaten as part of a base for other food – mainly sauces such as curry, etc., therefore promoting rice alone was unlikely to significantly increase its consumption. Master Foods decided therefore to develop other foods which could be used in conjunction with rice thus providing the necessary means for consumers to purchase more rice. The answer came with the development of their own ready-to-serve wet cooking sauces, which came in jars. These new products were supplied in nineteen different varieties and four different styles: Indian, stir fry, chilli and French. The new products are heated straight from the jar and then served on a rice base. This combination provides the target ABC1's with the means of preparing a main meal in a relatively short time. The new Uncle Ben sauces captured over 50 per cent of the market worth around £47 million soon after their introduction.

As a result of the development of the sauces and other factors the consumption of rice increased by 19 per cent in 1991 and Master Food's share of the rice market increased by 2.3 per cent in the same year. The strategy adopted by Master Foods was therefore successful in developing new products for existing markets and also in penetrating their existing market for rice.

FURTHER REFERENCE

Chapter 6, Segmentation and Positioning: Behavioural – occasion of use (pp. 99–100); Psychographic/demographic segmentation (p. 102)

Volkswagen[8]

The car industry in the 1990s provides examples of companies pursuing intensive growth strategies, in particular market development and product development.

The 1990s witnessed the major American, European and Japanese car manufacturers aggressively pursuing market development strategies in the developing world – central and Eastern Europe, Latin America, Asia and the countries of the Asian-Pacific rim.

Volkswagen (VW) is the leading car maker in China, one of the world's fastest growing markets with two joint ventures in Changchun and Shanghai. Volkswagen's first joint venture in China began in 1985 and comprised a 50 per cent stake in the Shanghai-Volkswagen Automobile Company for the local production of the VW Santana. The impetus for Volkswagen was provided by the North American Free Trade Agreement, booming economies and free market policies of the developing countries together with the slump in car sales in saturated Western Europe, Japan and the USA. In Mexico, VW is producing cars for the US and Mexican markets.

It is often not enough simply to provide these markets with exact replicas of the cars in the developed world and product development may be necessary. In some cases modifying the product to meet local conditions is sufficient: for example, fitting heavier suspension for Indonesia's rough roads. In other cases, developing a new car model is necessary to meet buyers' needs precisely. Volkswagen is developing a new longer version of the Santana for China to give more backseat leg room for taxis and government vehicles.

CBS Records   Now owned by Sony, has started to market classical music to the so-called baby boomer cohort. This market was generally unfamiliar with classical music, so Sony has started to repackage pieces which are expected to be popular in a product series entitled 'CBS Master Works'. This is a new market for an existing product.

Hallmark   The UK greetings card company originally made cards for birthdays and other traditional occasions. Today, the company's product range demonstrates a large variety of circumstances in which a card could be purchased, e.g. secretaries' days, congratulations on your divorce.

FURTHER REFERENCE

Chapter 6, Segmentation and Positioning: Behavioural – occasion of use (pp. 99–100; Target marketing (pp. 102–105)

Integrative growth: forward integration

The three integrative growth strategies are forward integration (where a firm pursues opportunities upstream in the value chain), backward integration (where the firm pursues opportunities downstream in the value chain) and horizontal integration (where the firm pursues opportunities normally by acquiring competitors).

Matsushita[9]

The Matsushita Electric Company is composed of 45 different divisions and employs 12,000 people. The company owns 230 wholesalers selling only its own products. At the retail level 25,000 National stores ('National' is one Matsushita's strongest brand names) are controlled by the wholesalers, with the majority of the stores sales being accounted for by Matsushita products. A further 25,000 National stores exist, 50 per cent of whose sales are accounted for by Matsushita products. Matsushita controls these retailers through long-term contracts and through various services provided to the wholesalers. Such services include training classes in new technology, purchase rebates, management advice, sales training, collective advertising, and financial assistance in the design of premises. Matsushita's marketing department develops marketing plans for its wholesalers and provides support for retailers. The complete system is based on the company's philosophy of 'mutual prosperity', which is one of the guiding principles developed by its founder.

FURTHER REFERENCE

Chapter 10, Marketing Channels: Channel co-operation (pp. 169–171)

Texaco

The major international oil companies provide examples of companies that are highly integrated. Companies like Texaco for example, explore for oil, own oil wells, refineries, transportation networks and retailing gas stations. Texaco built company-owned service stations in the USA rather than rely wholly on independent station owners. The forward integration into company-owned and franchised service stations was due to the fact that all brands of petrol are pretty much alike and with intense competition at the forecourts between the oil companies, building brand loyalty through attractive service stations and offering a high level of customer service is the key to survival at the retailing end. Many of the service stations compare favourably with convenience stores, carrying a wide range of food products, and some even have fast food outlets attached to them.

Technology[10]

Technology, one of the UK's largest and most successful personal computer distributors, was acquired by ICL, the UK computer manufacturer in July 1992. ICL bought Technology with the aim of becoming the largest supplier of personal computers in the UK, ahead of IBM, Compaq and Dell and also because it had to find a cost-effective channel to market low-cost systems which could not command the profit margins necessary to support a direct sales force. Technology was integrated into the overall ICL company structure. For large customers who like dealing directly with the manufacturer, the ICL account team handle the sale and pass the implementation over to staff at Technology.

Vauxhall

On 1st March 1991, the UK car manufacturer Vauxhall launched the Network Q initiative for its franchised dealers. Vauxhall developed Network Q as a brand to help its dealers to sell used Vauxhall cars. Vauxhall wanted to improve the quality and image of franchised dealers' used car operations and give peace of mind to customers seeking a used car. Network Q dealers offered cars with guaranteed minimum standards which were closely monitored by Vauxhall. Vauxhall figured that used cars sold from Network Q dealers could command higher resale prices, and therefore the attractiveness of buying a new Vauxhall car was increased.

FURTHER REFERENCE

Chapter 10, Marketing Channels: Channel co-operation (pp. 169–171)

Shoe makers   The British Shoe Corporation (BSC) and Clarks between them own nearly 30 per cent of all specialist footwear retailers in the UK.

Integrative growth: backward integration

MFI[11]

MFI, the furniture retailer and manufacturer has been one of the few companies in its market to perform successfully in the recent recession. While competitors like Queensway became victims of the housing slump, MFI has become a leaner and stronger organisation. Part of the reason for the company's success has been the vertical integration of its activities.

The first action MFI took was to go up-market. In doing this they focused their efforts on the more expensive packages such as complete kitchens and bathrooms. This was possible because MFI owned Hygena, the best known quality brand in kitchens. They also introduced just-in-time manufacturing which meant that kitchens could almost be produced to order. MFI knew that consumers did not want to take delivery of their kitchen straight away (as in the previous do-it-yourself philosophy of self-service take-away kitchens on the spot). The vertically integrated structure made this strategy easier to implement.

The company also set up two distribution points for its products in Northampton covering a million square feet, thus incorporating distribution as well as production into its vertically integrated system. This has allowed them to reduce the area of the stores and also to minimise inventories. They have also increased the rate of delivery throughout the system. Many of the units are also delivered and fitted by the company without ever passing through a store, presenting further downstream integration.

Sixty per cent of the products MFI sells it makes itself. This has made it easier to control inventory and quality, and to smooth the flow of merchandise from the factory to the consumer. The introduction of flexible manufacturing systems, computer integrated manufacturing and the overall reduction of fixed costs throughout the system has given MFI a decided advantage in its operations. In many cases a factory is manufacturing to order, and the vertically integrated system eliminates the need for accounts, sales, customer service and other functions necessary in stand-alone manufacturing. Economies of scale in distribution, inventory control and raw material supply allows MFI to operate competitively in the market place.

FURTHER REFERENCE

Chapter 3, The Marketing Environment: Political (p. 48)
Chapter 6, Segmentation and Positioning: Repositioning (p. 107)

Kimball   The US company provides an example of a backwardly integrated company. Once the largest piano maker in the USA (before the onslaught of the Japanese), the company now makes most of its sales and profit from office furniture. Kimball owns its own sawmills and makes the lumber and plywood used in its furniture. The company also owns some hardwood forest land.

Integrative growth: backward co-operation

Companies are motivated to integrate backwards and take over a supplier for a host of different reasons, including to take advantage of attractive profits that are enjoyed by suppliers, to secure continuity of supply, and to have better control over the prices and quality of the supplier's products.

Often the capital requirements and/or management expertise required does not facilitate the takeover of a supplier. Often too, it may be possible to work closer together for mutual benefit. The 1990s have witnessed many instances of the forming of co-operative relationships between companies and their suppliers with the objectives of securing greater quality, reducing costs and increasing profitability for both parties in the relationship.

Motorola[12]

Motorola looks for partners that share its values. Then it sharpens their skills by teaching them its own total quality management techniques, even requiring them to take courses in cycle time reduction, customer satisfaction and so on at an education programme it calls Motorola University. But while nurturing long-term partnerships, it fans gentlemanly competition among partners by giving grades, even more often than schools give report cards.

Motorola teams tour suppliers' plants every two years, grading them on how well they stack up against their competitors on quality and timeliness. On top of that, Motorola's so-called commodity managers rate suppliers monthly on an index that combines cost and quality, once again comparing them with their competitors (listed anonymously) and showing how much of Motorola's business each competitor gets. Says Motorola procurement chief Tom Slaninka: 'The better performers should earn a greater share of our business.' In that way, the heat stays on.

Motorola gets its suppliers to help from the very start in designing a part and figuring out how to make it. Larry Groves, CEO of Targ-It-Tronics, a Florida outfit that makes flexible circuit assemblies for Motorola, explains that a supplier understands, often better than the customer, how to design specialised high-tech parts to minimise their material and manufacturing cost. It also knows how to skirt design flaws that make them apt to break.

For example, says Groves, a Motorola division new to the partnership objected that Targ-It-Tronics' bid on a particularly complex circuit was 30 per cent higher than a competitor's. Groves countered that the other supplier failed to grasp how labyrinthine the design really was. Sure enough, when Motorola went back for clarification, the other supplier hurriedly hiked its bid 20 per cent above Groves'.

Distraught, the Motorola managers came back to Grove to say they were already way over budget: could Targ-It-Tronics help? Some radical alterations of the design and the recipe for manufacture and assembly by Groves' engineers and – *voilà* – a 35 per cent cost reduction.

So much has Motorola come to value its suppliers' integrity that it has established a 15-member council of suppliers to rate Motorola's own practices and offer suggestions for improving, for example, the accuracy of production schedules or design layouts that Motorola gives them. Says Motorola's Slaninka: 'This will reduce cost, because every time we make an error it takes people at both ends to correct it.'

FURTHER REFERENCE

Chapter 14, Market Status and Competitive Moves: Market leader (p. 224)

Integrative growth: horizontal growth

Charoen Pokphand[13]

While the trend in recent years within Western economies was one of retrenchment into concentrating on the core business, diversification is still common, particularly in economies experiencing economic growth. This was the case for the Thai company Charoen Pokphand Group (C.P.) which is involved in industries from agriculture and food to motorcycles. The areas of activity of the company include agribusiness, aquaculture, wholesaling, retailing, petrochemicals, international trading, industrial processing, motorcycle manufacturing, brewing, communications and property. C.P. had a turnover of US$2.4 billion in 1988 and employed 15,000 people. They possessed a nationwide network of 100,000 growers whom they contracted to produce a wide range of food products. The original business was concentrated on animal feeds but this expanded into the range of activities identified above.

Concentric Marketing   When the company took over a motorcycle plant in Shanghai in 1985 this seemed like a radical diversification away from its business strengths. However what is not immediately apparent is that in developing economies, motorcycles are mainly used for practical transportation purposes, and in China they are widely used in agriculture. Therefore the marketing of the product is not much different to marketing feedstuffs and other agricultural products, and indeed the channels through which the products are supplied are often the same. C.P. was already involved in animal feedstuffs, breeding and rearing in China, and this development was an example of horizontal integration for the company capitalising on the marketing synergies of the existing networks.

Similarly when C.P. joined forces with British Telecom in bidding for the contract to install 3 million telephones in Thailand, this appeared to be another example of radical diversification. However as the company already possessed a network of 100,000 contract farmers throughout the country and held the strongest links with rural Thailand of any other organisation including the government, they were in the ideal position to provide ready-made access to every area of the country. The joint venture duly won the US$5.93 billion contract and will confer the right to operate and collect revenue on the installed lines over a 25-year period. This presents another example of horizontal growth, building on its existing market network.

Horizontal integration   The group's move into aquaculture, in relation to its established base in animal rearing and breeding, represented a horizontal move to integrate its operations in food production. Common techniques could be used in aquaculture as in agriculture and the target market for the final output would be similar. The particular application was the farming of shrimp, which presented strong potential, as shrimp carried a value seven times that of chicken which accounted for 25 per cent of the group's exports from Thailand. Other freshwater fish farming projects were added. The group was also able to use existing waste products from other animal and feedstuff processing operations to provide raw material for shrimp feedstuff.

Allied-Lyons

In March 1994, Allied-Lyons, the international food and drink giant whose brands include Courvoisier and Harvey's Bristol Cream, bought Spain's Pedro Domecq sherry and brandy group in an attempt to become world leader in spirits. The group is now second to IDV – Grand Metropolitan's drinks arm whose brands include Smirnoff vodka and J & B Rare Scotch. Allied-Lyons' purchase will allow it to introduce its own brands into Spain and Mexico, two important drinks markets, using Domecq's established distribution system there.

Nestlé

Horizontal integration commonly takes place through acquisitions with the acquiring company motivated by the desire to increase sales and profits by acquiring the assets, products, technical expertise or management talent of a competitor.

Examples of horizontal integration abound but one of the most public was the 1988 £2.55bn takeover of UK confectionery maker Rowntree Mackintosh by the giant Swiss multinational Nestlé. The takeover was motivated by Nestlé's desire to secure the attractive product lines of its competitor and become a big player in the UK confectionery market where it previously held a small share.

Fleming Company Inc. The largest food wholesaler in the USA, experienced terrific growth in the 1980s, much of it a result of acquiring other wholesaling firms. These acquisitions further boosted Fleming's buying power, providing economies of scale and increasing its profit margins.

Diversification .

A firm pursuing a diversification strategy may pursue opportunities related or unrelated to its present product-market domain and technology.

Sega Enterprises[14]

In 1993, Sega Enterprises Ltd, the $4 billion Japanese video-game producer, began steps to diversify into interactive entertainment, electronic toys and virtual reality theme parks, thus reinventing the amusement park. Its diversification strategy will build on Sega's expertise in video game technology, its deep understanding of the entertainment requirements of children and its expertise in marketing games and games machines to them. Sega's diversification strategy includes virtual reality theme parks, the Sega Channel and electronic toys.

Two virtual reality theme parks consisting of game machines that create the illusion of, for example, driving racing cars or flying spaceships, are planned to open in Japan in 1994 and Sega plans to have 50 in place by 1997. Sega perceives the parks as a high tech competitor to the Walt Disney parks. Sega of America has formed a joint venture with cable operators Time Warner and Tele-Communications to develop a pay-cable channel called the Sega Channel which was due on air in the summer of 1993. For a flat monthly fee, customers can have a video game downloaded into their Sega game machine at home. In February 1994, Sega introduced its first electronic toy line and further products are planned.

Bridgestone/Firestone

The Bridgestone/Firestone Corporation, one of the world's largest manufacturers of tyres and other rubber-related products is an example of a company that pursued opportunities both related and unrelated to its product-market domain and technology.

The company manufactures tyres for a variety of different markets including cars, motorcycles, buses, trucks, subway trains and aircraft. Bridgestone also exploited its expertise in rubber to diversify into such rubber products as conveyor belts, marine hoses, vibration dampers and inflatable rubber dams.

The company also diversified into businesses with great potential even though the products had no relationship with the company's existing technology, products or markets. These businesses included sporting goods, electronic equipment and bicycles.

FURTHER REFERENCE

Chapter 8, New Product Development: Commercialisation (p. 138)

GKN[15]

The British engineering group GKN has reduced its dependence on traditional industries such as heavy engineering, steel and engineering fastenings and has moved into the greater added value markets of industrial services and distribution, automotive and engineered components and military defence. The group has gone through a major transformation in that half the companies constituting the group in the 1970s have disappeared to be replaced by new ones operating in new markets.

The change was not confined to market sectors but also included geographic restructuring. Formerly dependent on the UK market, this currently accounts for only around 32 per cent of the group's total sales, while the rest of Europe now accounts for 39 per cent, America 24 per cent and Australia the bulk of the remainder. Part of the rationale for this restructuring has been to give the group a wider strategic base so that cyclical downturns in one sector or region will not adversely affect overall performance, i.e. the company will not be over-dependent on one sector or region.

MILITARY STRATEGIES

The techniques and principles of military warfare have been used to describe various approaches to marketing strategy. However, it is often difficult to define such strategies and many of the examples are often hybrids or combinations of more mainstream marketing strategies. Nevertheless, such military concepts often present apt descriptions for the approach of organisations to marketing. Some examples are presented in this section.

Flanking

Piedmont Airlines[16]

Piedmont Airlines in the USA adopted a flanking (Hub and Spoke) strategy in expanding its market share in the passenger air transport market. It started off as a commuter carrier and then identified the potential for becoming a regional and then a national airline by providing feeder services to travel hubs in Charlotte, Dayton, etc. and subsequently flying passengers on from these centres on longer flights up to 1,500 miles.

The strategy was also copied by other airlines with the result that the control of the travel hubs has become an important strategic factor for success in the market. By mapping the movement of passengers, airlines can identify niches in the form of geographic areas and locations not currently served by competitors. Control of these strategic niches allows the airline to gain competitive advantage over its competitors also allowing it to erect barriers against future entrants.

FURTHER REFERENCE

Chapter 1, The Strategic Planning Process: Competitive advantage (p. 13)

Michelin[17]

In 1975, the US tyre market was dominated by four US manufacturers – Goodyear, Uniroyal, Firestone and Goodrich. These four manufacturers supplied the original equipment market (OEM) with cross-ply tyres –

the only type available at that time. Michelin, a French tyre manufacturer developed a new type of tyre called a radial tyre and its success
was greatly helped by the oil crisis of 1973 and the resultant aftershocks
which resulted in a rise in fuel prices. The car manufacturers increasingly began to stress efficiency in order to maintain sales of their cars. It
was found that radial tyres reduced fuel consumption (and they also
lasted twice as long as cross-ply tyres) and the manufacturers began to
switch to these tyres as original equipment on vehicles. Michelin was
able to capitalise on this and aggressively entered the OEM market
capturing 25 per cent market share. For a time, the existing tyre manufacturers were unable to deal with the new technology. Michelin had
effectively out-flanked them.

FURTHER REFERENCE

Chapter 2, Marketing Strategies: Generic strategies – differentiation and
differentiation focus (pp. 21–22)

Head-on attack

Honda vs. Yamaha

In 1979 Yamaha launched an all-out campaign to overtake Honda as the
world's number one motorcycle manufacturer. As a result, it sent production levels soaring to 2 million units in 1981, in the expectation of
gaining the number one position. A major target for the Yamaha company was the US market where part of this battle was fought. However
in 1983 the US government introduced a tariff relief programme to
protect its indigenous motorcycle industry. This inhibited Yamaha severely
as it did not have an American production base, in contrast to Honda
who already had production facilities in place. Honda was therefore able
to absorb the affect of the tariff more readily than Yamaha who relied on
its US distributors.

Yamaha soon found itself with large stocks of unsold bikes as Honda
countered with direct attacks on the aggressor in the form of the rapid
introduction of new motorcycles priced below those of Yamaha, and
with appeals to different market segments backed by extensive promotion campaigns. Honda even developed a short-term mission which
was to 'Crush, Squash, Slaughter Yamaha'. Honda won the head-on
battle keeping Yamaha in second place in the market and even succeeded
in eliciting a public apology from its rival.

FURTHER REFERENCE

Chapter 3, The Marketing Environment: Environmental factors: regulatory (p. 44)

Guerrilla attack

Elements of the unorthodox approach used by Intel in marketing its microprocessors may be described as a form of guerrilla strategy.

Intel

In the latter half of the 1980s Intel was facing an uncertain future. Its original product, the dynamic random access memory (DRAM) chip was hit by reduced demand and price competition. The company decided to move into microprocessors, the first being the highly successful 386.

Some of the elements of the strategy included fierce legal resistance to clone manufacturers who attempted to introduce similar products, which also served to generate significant publicity for the company. Intel was also the first company of its kind to target end users by advertising directly to them, rather than to design engineers as was traditional in the industry. Intel conducted a guerrilla attack into Macintosh territory through advertisements in Macintosh magazines attempting to persuade Mac users to switch to PCs using Intel chips. This was partly designed to reduce the competitive threat of the newly introduced PowerPC chip designed by Apple, IBM and Motorola. Another guerrilla-like attack by Intel was its co-operative advertising agreements with computer manufacturers, unheard of before in the industry. Advertising also included point of purchase advertisements in retail stores, TV advertisements and billboards using the 'Intel Inside' slogan. A new market which the company has targeted is computer owners who want to upgrade their machines. For computer industry buyers Intel includes 'technology briefing' inserts in computer magazines focusing on different aspects of computer technology and developments. This serves to enhance Intel's standing in the industry by positioning it as being at the forefront of computer technology.

As indicated above, distribution strategy included making the products available in retail outlets, being the first company to sell off the shelf in mass merchant-type outlets. Sales to OEMs included pricing discounts or rebates for large quantities purchased.

CONCLUSION

This chapter has outlined examples of strategies pursued by different firms and has described them with reference to strategy formulation frameworks. In recent years companies have been increasingly concentrating on their core business adopting greater focus in this area. However many larger corporations pursue the range of strategies from integrative growth to diversification described in this chapter.

However, developing an effective strategy to meet clearly defined objectives calls for the marketer to develop a plan specific to the firm. Creativity becomes imperative in developing winning strategies and the examples provided in this chapter demonstrate this characteristic.

NOTES

1 Michael E. Porter, *Competitive Advantage: Creating and Sustaining Superior Performance*, New York, The Free Press, 1985.
2 Philip Kotler, *Marketing Management: Analysis, Planning and Control*, 4th ed., New Jersey, Prentice-Hall International, 1980.
3 The material in the Morgan section is adapted from: John Harvey-Jones and A. Masey, *Trouble Shooter*, BBC Books (UK), 1990, pp. 99–127; Richard Feast, 'Frozen in time: Morgan Motors', *Automotive-Industries*, June 1992, p. 41; Robert Heller, 'If you won't take advice, don't invite a trouble-shooter', *Management Today*, June 1992, p. 29; Richard Feast, 'Morgan: the man, the company, the motor car', *Automotive News*, 29 November 1982, p. 14; George Bickerstaffe, 'Morgan Motor: small is profitable', *International Management* (European edition), April 1982, pp. 25–26.
4 This section on *Today* and the *Post* is adapted from M. Cronshaw and E. Davis, 'Between two stools', *Accountancy*, December 1990.
5 Kotler op. cit.
6 Igor Ansoff, 'Strategies for Diversification', Harvard Business Review, September–October 1957, pp. 113–124.
7 This Master Foods section is adapted from 'Diversification is the key to rice growth', *The Grocer*, 25 July 1992, p. 36.
8 Volkswagen section is adapted from: Treece, Lowry Miller, K. Spindle, W. Lindorff, D. Smith, G. Hinchberger, B. Engardio, 'New worlds to conquer', *International Business Week*, 14 February 1994, pp. 32–37; 'Volkswagen expands operations in China', *Financial Times*, 17 November 1993; 'Volkswagen to expand its joint venture plant in China', *New York Times*, 10 November 1992, p. C3; John Watling, 'Volkswagen fires, rehires at Mexico plant', *Automotive News*, 24 August 1992, p. 8; 'GM parts group seeks new China deals', *Automotive News*, 1 November 1993, p. 41.
9 Matsushita section is adapted from: T. Kono, *Strategy and Structure of Japanese Enterprises*, M.E. Sharpe, Armonk, N.Y., 1985, pp. 49, 128–129, 164–173; Richard Tanner Pascale and Anthony G. Athos, *The Art of Japanese Management*, Penguin Books, London, 1986; J. Cruikshank,

'Matsushita', Harvard Business School Bulletin, February 1983; Matsushita Electric Industrial Co. Ltd Annual Reports.

10 Technology section is adapted from the *Financial Times*, 19 April 1993.

11 This MFI section is adapted from 'How the IRA changed the face of MFI's business strategy', *Business Age*, no. 21, June 1992, pp. 30–32. © 1994 Time Inc. All rights reserved.

12 This Motorola section is reprinted from Myron Magnet, 'The new golden rule of business', *Fortune*, 21 February 1994, pp. 28–32.

13 Charoen Pokphand section adapted from the following: Paisal Sricharatchanya, 'Not just chicken feed', 'Funds for a growing family' and 'Model modern hog farmers' *Far Eastern Economic Review*, 3 March 1988, pp. 58–59, 60, 60–61; Jonathan Moore, 'Feeding public interest', *Far Eastern Economic Review*, 3 March 1988, p. 61; Jonathan Friedland, 'Seeds of an empire', *Far Eastern Economic Review*, 20 April 1989, pp. 46–47; Ellen Salem, 'Against the grain', *Far Eastern Economic Review*, 20 April, pp. 47–48; Paul Handley, 'Food for thought', *Far Eastern Economic Review*, 25 October 1990, pp. 56–58.

14 This Sega Enterprises section is adapted from: Richard Brandt, Neil Gross, Peter Coy, 'Sega!', *International Business Week*, 21 February 1994, pp. 38–44; John Markoff, 'Sega links with cable providers', *New York Times*, 15 April 1993, p. D1; Rachel Powell, 'Televised give and take', *New York Times*, 25 April 1993, p. 9; Richard Karpinski, 'Sega Channel proves games not just kids' stuff', *Telephony*, 13 December 1993, p. 14; Gale Eisenstodt, 'Virtual Disney', *Forbes*, 28 February 1994, pp. 46–47; Andrew Pollack, 'Sega takes aim at Disney's world', *New York Times*, 4 July 1993, p. 1.

15 This GKN section is reprinted from: GKN PLC Reports & Accounts 1993; Charles Leadbeater, 'GKN: a multi-cultural challenge', *Financial Times*, 24 August 1990, p. 10.; Paul Betts, 'Swoop for a tempting morsel', *Financial Times*, 9 February 1994, p. 21; 'Core concerns at GKN', *Management Today*, June 1993; John Griffiths, 'Reshaping helps GKN recover its balance', *Financial Times*, 10 August 1989.

16 Piedmont Airlines section reprinted from C. Carroll, P. M. Lewis and H. Thomas, 'Developing competitive strategies in retailing', *Long Range Planning*, vol. 25, no. 2, 1992, pp. 81–88. Copyright 1992, with kind permission from Elsevier Science Ltd, The Boulevard, Langford Lane, Kidlington OX5 1GB.

17 See B. G. James, *Business War Games*, Penguin, 1985, p. 54.

The marketing environment

INTRODUCTION

The external environment within which organisations operate and the strategies they employ largely determine the marketing success or failure of that organisation. The organisation must continually monitor the external environment and adapt its strategies to suit that environment. In this chapter we identify the key external factors which may influence organisations. These environmental factors include technological, regulatory, natural, political, economic, social and cultural influences. Such factors are generally outside the control of the organisation. This chapter also investigates how organisations attempt to forecast their environment through scanning and how they might anticipate changes which may be occurring. Some organisations may attempt to influence their environment themselves; this is more relevant in the case of political, technological or regulatory influences.

Continual change in the external environment presents organisations with new opportunities and threats and the level of success with which they deal with these influences depends on their skill at analysing the environment, their strengths and the resources available to them. The vision of the organisation and its preparedness to change or take informed risks also determines success or failure in the market place.

The examples in this chapter will help you gain an understanding of these environmental forces and how organisations respond to them. We begin by identifying each major type of environmental force. These include examples of consumer and business-to-business marketing. We then lead on to examining environmental scanning, attempts at influencing the environment and anticipating environmental change.

ENVIRONMENTAL FACTORS

Technological

Electronic data interchange[1]

Electronic data interchange (EDI) is a recently developed technology used to exchange information electronically between organisations by means of computers linked directly or through an intermediary. The intermediary performs a 'post office-type' function, receiving the information from the sender and passing it on to the recipient. Specialist translation services may be required in order for data generated on the sender's system to be compatible with the recipient's system.

Because of the benefits of the technology (see below) many large organisations are now requiring their suppliers to transfer information via EDI. Small suppliers have found themselves having to adopt the technology or risk losing business, even though they may have been providing a high level of service already. In the USA Wal-Mart and GEC's aim is to conduct relevant communications through EDI. The retail sector and motor and electronics industries have been the most active in introducing EDI in the UK, while in the USA the technology is generally used in all industries and by small and large firms. More than 30 industries in the USA are heavily involved in implementing EDI.

The transactions performed through EDI include ordering, invoicing, demand forecasting, self-billing for suppliers, automatic restocking and even the arrangement of payment through banks which are now beginning to join EDI networks. Other functions include transmitting catalogues and designs. EDI is also being used by the public sector such as the Customs and Excise service. Wal-Mart stores in the USA send sales data daily to the jeans manufacturer Wrangler which are then used for restocking and planning. The Kroger retail chain in the USA uses scanner data in its stores to restock Procter and Gamble and other products through direct links with the manufacturer.

The benefits of EDI are its speed, facilitation of processes such as just-in-time manufacturing, the closer alignment between the customer's demand and product supplies to reflect the former's demand patterns (suppliers can be provided with their customers' demand forecasts/patterns) and reduction in the time between order placing and its delivery therefore allowing retailers to keep their stocks at a minimum. Labour costs and the overall costs of purchase orders can be cut.

The technology is particularly suitable where there are high numbers of low value transactions, such as in the supermarket sector where the large chains deal with a multitude of often smaller suppliers. Retailers can report daily sales to suppliers so that inventories can be minimised and slower selling items eliminated to reduce the number of price mark-downs on products and therefore free up shelf space. Closer alignment between supermarkets and their suppliers can also ensure that the produce on supermarket shelves is as fresh as possible. In the long run, data on consumer buying patterns can be shared between retailer and supplier. Tesco, for example, has built a network of over 1,000 firms using EDI and Sainsbury's conducts around 90 per cent of its ordering through EDI along with 65 per cent of its invoicing.

The growth of EDI has posed a threat for companies involved in the supply of paper-based business forms. Some such companies are now beginning to sell software for generating electronic forms. Based on their understanding of how organisations use information they are also entering the field of information consultancy. The growth of EDI therefore presents opportunities and threats within the marketing environment.

FURTHER REFERENCE

Chapter 1, The Strategic Planning Process: SWOT (p. 2)
Chapter 4, Marketing Research, Information, Forecasting and Measurement: Sales monitoring (p. 72)
Chapter 7, Products: The product life cycle (p. 122)

Fibre-optic communication[2]

A seminal event took place at the end of the 1980s in the field of global telecommunications with the completion of the first transatlantic and transpacific fibre-optic cable, linking Europe with America and California with Japan. Such links will enable the rapid transmission of information thus reducing the strategic importance of business location for organisations, particularly in the case of service industries as is demonstrated in the following cases:

- American insurance companies are using Irish workers to process insurance claims. The claims are transmitted to bases in Ireland by means of the fibre-optic communications links, processed by the Irish operatives and the completed files are returned to the USA. Ireland's advanced telecommunications network provides the necessary infrastructure to receive the information, and the highly trained work force possesses the necessary skills to carry out the operations at a lower cost than that which would prevail in the USA.

- Korean key-punch operators are used by Lexis Information Services in Dayton, Ohio to key-in legal documents and briefs on its database. The briefs are shipped to Korea, key-punched, and transmitted back to the USA by means of telecommunication networks.
- American Airlines operates a data processing centre in Barbados. All tickets lifted in its US network are then shipped to Barbados, where the data are entered and then transmitted back to the USA by means of advanced telecommunications linkages. The airline also offers this service to other organisations.

Regulatory

Solvay[3]

The development of Fluvoxamine, an anti-depressant drug, by the Belgian chemicals group Solvay, was one of the first in the world of a new generation of central nervous system drugs. In 1983 when the drug was launched, the company was a relatively small player in the pharmaceuticals industry and as a result it had great difficulty in achieving approval for the product despite its benefits. It did not have the resources to deal effectively with the regulatory authorities and was unable to quickly demonstrate to their satisfaction the drug's safety and benefits. It wasn't until eight years after the development and introduction of the drug that it gained widespread approval in Europe.

By 1992 in the USA, the largest market of all, Fluvoxamine still did not have approval. In 1989 a similar product called Prozac was launched by the US group Eli Lilly. In 1991 this product had achieved sales of around $910m, compared with Solvay's $40m. In order to strengthen its position Solvay decided to establish a joint marketing agreement with the US group, Upjohn, one of the purposes of which was to market Fluvoxamine with the aim of gaining greater access to geographic and therapeutic markets.

Domino Printing Sciences[4]

The European Community introduced legislation in 1981 which required perishable goods to be printed with an expiry date. There existed only one technology suited to the task, and this was industrial inkjet printing, primarily due to the non-contact nature of the process. The technology requires a combination of engineering, electronics and chemical expertise. The ink particles are electronically charged and may be required to print from distances of up to a few centimetres at high speeds. Other applications of the technology may involve the production of edible inks and fast drying processes.

The legislation was the major impetus behind the growth of the UK company Domino Printing Sciences, which specialised in industrial inkjet printers. The company's sales increased from £82,000 in 1980 to £7.4 million in 1984. In 1991 Domino had a turnover of over £60 million and in 1993 of over £80 million and is now one of the world's leading companies in the continuous inject printing process. Because of the wide range of materials it is necessary to print on, including aluminium, glass, paper and even egg shells, the printing equipment must possess reliability and speed as well as flexibility. Industrial inkjet offers these benefits.

The rapid growth also benefited other players which included Videojet (a GEC company), Linx Printing Technologies, Imaje of France and the Japanese giant Hitachi. Domino and Videojet are now the market leaders but the rapid growth has disappeared and the European market has become more competitive.

FURTHER REFERENCE

Chapter 3, The Marketing Environment: Environmental factors – Technological (p. 42–44)

Natural

Kyocera[5]

The Japanese company Kyocera is using the environment as a means of differentiating its product from others. The product is the Ecosys laser printer, which is marketed on its environmental performance. Kyocera's core business is ceramics, and its printer business is very small compared to the main players such as Hewlett-Packard and Canon. It therefore decided it needed a unique selling point (USP) to differentiate its product from the established brands. This USP was its environmental performance. Conventional laser printers contain a cartridge which holds the printing drum and the toner. This cartridge is thrown away when the toner is used up. This is perceived as being wasteful and harmful to the environment. However, the Ecosys printer uses a toner cartridge which is separate from the printing drum and the drum is also longer lasting than conventional drums through utilisation of Kyocera's ceramic technology. The toner is therefore the only part that has to be replaced regularly. The company also claims that the machine is more economical to run, saving on electricty and resulting in lower emissions of gases that are harmful to the environment.

The Ecosys is somewhat more expensive than equivalent printers, but is also slower. Despite this the company has met its sales targets for the product. Governmental purchasing policies are one of the driving forces for improved environmental performance of products. Government purchasers in many countries are now demanding such products as part of government purchasing. Furthermore many commercial companies are also adopting similar purchasing policies, e.g. British Telecom in the UK.

As a result of such pressures other printer manufacturers are also attempting to improve the environmental image of their products. This is attempted through improved energy efficient performance of the machines and the use of recycled materials in their production and packaging.

FURTHER REFERENCE

Chapter 7, Products: Product differentiation (p. 117–118)

Procter & Gamble[6]

The increasing use of cloth nappies, particularly in the USA, is providing more competition for the disposable nappy industry. Cloth nappies can be reused after cleaning, and are therefore perceived to be less harmful to the environment, through the elimination of the need to dispose of them in landfill sites. Traditionally the materials which produce the absorbency of disposable nappies were not always susceptible to disintegration, as these qualities have generally been incompatible. Furthermore materials used in the production of dis- posable nappies are paper based and therefore come from trees which also need to be sustained. Disposal in landfill sites is creating greater pressures on the environment. It is estimated that in the UK annual use of disposable nappies results in 7 million trees being cut down and produces 4 per cent of the landfill. In the USA it is estimated that over 4 million tons of nappies were disposed of in land fill sites at the end of the 1980s.

Companies like Procter & Gamble have responded to this trend by reducing the cubic size of the product, therefore requiring less space to dispose of them. The company also set up two schemes in the USA to recycle nappies, converting them into pulp and plastic. The plastic is reused in producing other plastic products. However new competitors in the market, such as the EFC Group in the UK has introduced flannelette washable nappies which can be washed 75 times. Called Bear Bottoms, they are 100 per cent flannelette and feature teddy bear images on the design. In the USA Family Club Inc. have begun to produce combination disposable and reusable products. One product is a reusable nappy with a disposable pad, and the other is also a reusable nappy, but with a washable pad.

Despite the reduction of pressure on landfill sites through the use of cloth nappies, the transportation and cleaning costs for provision of the service can also have an effect on the environment. This occurs through the consumption of energy and the emission of gases which may be harmful to the environment associated with such energy consumption.

McDonald's [7]

McDonald's decided to phase out its use of foam packaging in the USA in 1990, and convert to paper packaging. The familiar clamshell container for its hamburgers had become a symbol of a wasteful society to some, and its disposal in already stretched landfill sites was creating greater pressure on the environment. However the polystyrene material from which the packaging was made can now increasingly be recycled. In the UK a new plastics recycling plant built by Linpac Plastics started to recycle foamed polystyrene clamshell packs. Initially a six-month demonstration recycling plan was launched, and Linpac began receiving consumer waste from McDonald's. In the USA recycling was further boosted by the formation of the National Polystyrene Recycling Company in 1989 by the seven major polystyrene producers in the USA. Their aim was to recycle 25 per cent of all disposable polystyrene products by 1995.

Sun tan lotion [8]

Increases in the number of cases of skin cancer in Europe and the USA, and issues such as the depletion of the ozone layer, have led manufacturers of sun lotions to stress their protective value. There is a gradual move away from the traditional promotion of lotions solely as aiding 'long lasting tans' to an emphasis on sun 'care' terminology. This is reflected in the trend in sales towards higher factor lotions. In the UK, sales of suncare products are increasing overall, and in 1992 lotions of with high sun protector factors – greater than SPF 7 intensity – accounted for over 40 per cent of sales by value of all sun protection products' sales.

Nivea introduced a new range of suncare products in 1994 under the label 'sun sensitive'. The new range has been developed for sensitive skin, and consists of six different types of cream. Research carried out by Zyma Healthcare (marketers of Piz Buin in UK) and Laboratories RoC, however, indicates that people still associate sun tan with health and feeling good, i.e. 'brown is beautiful'. Manufacturers are therefore having to achieve a balance between encouraging a more responsible or safer approach to tanning (which may result in slower or paler tans) and encouraging tanning. Advertising messages promoting image and appearance are being diluted.

Political

Macy's, Pacific Bell, Northern Telecom, The Communications Workers of America Union [9]

In 1993 the US department store Macy's embarked on a new sales promotion with the telecommunications company Pacific Bell to promote that company's telephone services. Macy's offered services supplied by Pacific Bell when customers purchased Northern Telecom telephone equipment in their electronics department. These services included call waiting, screening and forwarding. Macy's however encountered union opposition with the promotion. In California, where the dispute initiated, the sale of telephone services is controlled by the California Public Utilities Commission. The Communications Workers of America Union claimed that Macy's personnel were not adequately trained to sell telephone services and demanded that the promotion be stopped. Dealing with customer enquiries on telephone services is regulated by the Commission. The Union also claimed the employment of what they believed to be inadequately trained Macy's personnel to sell telephone services would threaten the jobs of the highly trained Pacific Bell sales employees. They handed out leaflets to customers at Macy's stores to inform them of the situation, and claimed that employees posing as customers in Macy's stores have been given incorrect information.

Three months into the promotion Macy's had not issued any response to the requests by the Union and had asked the Union to take up their concerns with Pacific Bell. Pacific Bell, however, claimed the promotion would not threaten the jobs of its employees, as employment in the services selling function was rising. The offering for sale of telephone services when customers purchase telephone equipment provides the company with an ideal way of increasing sales. For customers requiring further information a free call line to Pacific Bell is available in the Macy's store. However the Union threatened further action if Macy's failed to respond to its requests.

FURTHER REFERENCE

Chapter 13, Sales Promotion and Public Relations: Joint sales promotions (p. 212–213)

British Airways   In 1991 BA re-introduced its sales promotion campaign 'Go for it America' which offered free seats on BA flights and various prizes, to encourage Americans to fly after the end of the Gulf War. The campaign was originally formulated after the US attack on Libya in 1986.

Economic

The Brazilian economy[10]

High levels of inflation in an economy has significant implications for business activities. This is particularly true for the Brazilian economy where the annual level of inflation runs at over 400 per cent. The value of money under such circumstances continually declines and consumers tend to 'invest' in tangible products. As a result many lower income groups spend their wages almost as soon as they receive them. Some retailers conduct more than half of their business in the early part of the month. Promotional methods by companies include accepting payment by means of post-dated cheques, thus allowing customers to hedge against inflation. Similarly, payment by credit card allows inflation hedging. Banks in Brazil generally clear cheques in one day.

For companies operating in this environment, cash management is a crucial part of their operations. In the case of the consumer electronics company Gradiente, cash flow management is critically important as short term operating profit can be wiped out by inflation. Other functions within the company such as R.&D., production, etc. often become secondary to cash flow management.

For Souza Cruz, a subsidiary of BAT industries, a main objective is to ensure that receipts from transactions throughout the country are transferred to its head office in Rio de Janeiro as quickly as possible. Payment terms with customers become crucial and Souza Cruz only allows up to five days for stockists to pay. Many companies put greater effort into financial operations than into other activities. The objective is to receive payment from customers and avoid paying suppliers too quickly, so that the money can be invested in the financial markets.

The instability of the Brazilian economy has also forced publishing houses to use caution when trying to secure Spanish language rights. When Brazil decreed an 85 per cent freeze on bank accounts to curb runaway inflation, publishers had less money available for Brazilian authors and were forced to cut down on foreign acquisitions.

In March 1992 an accord was made between various government ministries, the automotive industry and unions to form an economic agreement for the country. The car makers agreed to cut prices, carry out substantial investment in the sector, preserve employment and increase real wages by 20 per cent over three years. The unions agreed to increase productivity and stop striking. The automotive industry contributes significantly to the economy and the agreement was designed to introduce some degree of stability. Clearly the economic situation directly affected what is normally a key element of the marketing mix, i.e. pricing.

Such marketing activities as pricing and terms of payment are key aspects of the business process. Sales people must obtain the best terms of payment possible. The factors which determine price in lower inflation economies such as unit costs, etc. do not necessarily apply in Brazil. Research has indicated that inflationary expectations and government policies are the major factors which determine price. Price negotiations between companies and suppliers occur more frequently in Brazil. In the case of ICI, price negotiations take place monthly.

Due to the unpredictable nature of the economy, it is critically important for organisations to obtain as accurate information as possible on financial, economic and government policy matters. The situation also makes it extremely difficult to plan ahead to any significant degree.

Social/cultural

Euro Disney[11]

The reasons for the poor performance of the Euro Disney theme park outside Paris have been numerous. High prices (fuelled by the appreciation of the franc), the recession in Europe and the poor weather have all combined to make life difficult for Euro Disney. However, another factor has contributed to keeping the punters away in their droves, particularly the French, and this is culture. The experience of Euro Disney illustrates the importance of understanding the social/cultural environment of a country before launching a product or service there.

Disney executives apparently believed the Disney experience would be as successful in Europe as it is in the USA. Selling this to Europeans was to be like 'mugging Bambi'. The park was promoted as a piece of American culture and failed to inform potential customers exactly what entertainment they could expect. The corporation confidently believed that the more American the park could be made, the more the punters would like it.

The reaction of the usually sophisticated French was to describe the theme park as a 'cultural Chernobyl'. The French minister for culture Jack Lang described it as the 'culture of the lowest common denominator'. Only one third of the visitors to Euro Disney in the first three months were French. Disney Americana was transported directly into Europe. This included the policy of the organisation not to serve alcohol, which did not go down well with the wine-loving French. In June 1993 this was reversed when restaurants at Euro Disney began serving alcohol with meals. This was contrary to the 'family values' culture of Disney in the USA.

The concept of spending more than a few days at a theme park is also at odds with Europe's leisure patterns. Americans will happily spend up to two weeks or more at Disney, and spend a lot of money in the meantime, but not the Europeans. Many of the French are simply going to Disney on day trips, and the British are also not treating it as a main holiday destination. The attraction of calling into Euro Disney on the way to or from the south rather than as their main destination is more appealing to many British people.

The provision of abundant hotel accommodation on site has resulted in lower than expected bookings. Many visitors prefer to stay in cheaper hotels in Paris and visit Disney by train during the day, while picnicking in the parks outside. The architectural style of some of the themed buildings also demonstrates the clash of cultures. The Newport building designed by the post-modernist American architect Robert Stern with its giant classical columns and gargantuan wings is the antithesis of modern progressive French architecture.

Disney possesses a strong work ethic and a dedication to corporate values. It has proved far more difficult than anticipated for the corporation to instil this sort of dedication into the usually individualistic French. Staff turnover became very high. The Disney University struggled to imbue their approach into the local French. The Disney Corporation's fondness for strict standards for its staff and their conduct was also transferred to the locals. In Disney in the USA, men's couture in the case of hair is stipulated as 'Sideburns should be neatly trimmed and may be permitted to extend to the bottom of the ear lobe', while for women, 'If a yarn or hair ribbon is worn it should be no wider than one half inch, or longer than four inches when tied.' Moustaches are not allowed, nor dyed hair.

The reported story of the Finnish reindeer brought to Euro Disney to introduce a European flavour to the scene provides an interesting summing up of the experience of some with Euro Disney. When the reindeer's horns began peeling, apparently a natural process, allegedly Disney officials suggested painting them. Some even lost their horns but the suggested solution to replace them with fake horns was dashed when the glue wouldn't stick. Finally the reindeer failed to walk in line on the Christmas parade!

FURTHER REFERENCE

Chapter 3, The Marketing environment: Natural, (p. 45)

Harrison and Harrison Ltd [12]

One of the major problems faced by companies comes when the organisation, having operated for some time in a largely predictable environment, is faced with having to come to terms with a far more complex and uncertain one.

Messrs Harrison and Harrison Ltd, a small UK manufacturer of church organs, was faced with a changing social environment – namely the decline of religion within society. The result was a decline in its traditional market also reflected by a fall in church revenue. The nature of the product – long lasting and therefore infrequently in need of replacement – also reduced the opportunity for repeat order business. The company responded to this threat and now 75 per cent of turnover comes from repair, tuning and maintenance of organs already installed. The company also leases small instruments to orchestras. Another aspect of the changing society which has positively affected the company's business is the increase in vandalism. This has resulted in the destruction and damage of existing organs.

Due to the decrease in the size of the market in the UK and the existence of around 100 manufacturers of pipe organs, Harrison and Harrison have also begun to advertise for the first time. It also supplies organs for the export market, which it has done before, but mainly to former British colonies. Today's exports go to markets as diverse as Nigeria and South Korea.

ENVIRONMENTAL SCANNING

Royal Dutch/Shell [13]

The development of scenario planning at Royal Dutch/Shell required a comprehensive scanning method to ensure marketing and business plans were realistic. The sources of information scanned included secondary data and intelligence possessed by Shell employees in different countries. Among the variables analysed were the political, economic, technological, competitive and social environments. This included analysis of conditions in countries to determine such factors as the likelihood of different government policies occurring, the demand for oil as influenced by economic factors in different markets, and the technological development of alternative fuels.

The information obtained by scanning the business environment was used to generate scenarios in aiding decision making. After the oil crisis of 1973–74 a deep recession occurred and the company's scenario planning group began by observing what they called the 'predetermined' elements of the environment. These included inflation, subsequent deflation due to government policies and electoral patterns in the major economies of Japan, Germany and the USA where the occurrence of elections in 1976 were likely to cause the governments existing at that time to embark on economic growth strategies. The combination of these factors and the severity of the depression led the Shell planners to expect reflation to occur. Resulting from this understanding two major scenarios were developed – the 'boom and bust' scenario of sharp rises and falls in the business cycle and the 'constrained growth' scenario where recovery would be slower. In the event the recovery broadly followed the constrained growth scenario. Shell managers had anticipated this and planned for modest growth rates.

Reaction or influence – the impact of the business environment

Philip Morris[14]

The traditional view of marketing in relation to the environment in which an organisation operates has been that this environment is continually changing and cannot be influenced by the organisation to any significant extent. However, in certain aspects organisations can influence their environment. Japanese companies employ lobbyists in Washington to attempt to influence US political decision making. The technological environment can also be influenced through research and development and the licensing of newly developed technology to have it adopted as the industry standard.

The US cigarette manufacturer Philip Morris is an example of a company which has attempted to influence its environment from social attitudes to economic forces. With the increasing awareness of the negative affect of cigarettes on health, and the pressures on manufacturers from a variety of sources, the company has sought to adopt strategies designed to influence its environment.

One element of this strategy sought to influence the degree of prohibition on smoking in public places by advertising in particular magazines focusing on the numbers of smokers who engage in various public activities such as travelling on public or private run transport, going to sporting events, etc. Other methods used by the company included the publication of the *Philip Morris Magazine* which encouraged smokers to defend their decisions in choosing to smoke and to oppose anti-smoking pressures. When the US Congress was considering the introduction of a bill to prohibit all tobacco advertising in 1986 the company organised an essay competition with $80,000 prize money. The essay was on the subject of freedom of expression, claiming the bill would curtail individual freedom. When the US Bill of Rights had its 200th anniversary Philip Morris conducted a $30 million television advertising campaign celebrating the fact and sponsored a national tour of the Bill. Opponents accused the company of attempting to associate smoking with the freedoms inherent in the Bill.

Other aspects of the company's strategy has been the policy of making donations to the arts and various charitable and other groups since the 1970s, with no obligations on the recipients, thus seeking to gain favourable public relations within their environment. In the early 1990s Philip Morris agreed to increase its annual donations to AIDS and gay rights causes. Another element has been the various advertising campaigns which they have run. When the anti-smoking lobby sought to influence car manufacturers in excluding ashtrays from their vehicles, Philip Morris gave details to the car manufacturers of their customer segment which smoked. It published advertisements claiming that smokers owned 35 million cars and had purchased over 5 million in the preceding year. Similarly in 1988 the company embarked on a campaign which highlighted the importance of the tobacco industry to the US economy, emphasising the total expenditure on tobacco products.

These strategies represent ways in which a company has sought to influence the environment in which it operates. The success or otherwise of the strategies is open to debate, however it does counter the belief that organisations are completely powerless in influencing their environment.

FURTHER REFERENCE

Chapter 7, Products: Product life cycle (p. 122)
Chapter 13, Sales Promotion and Public Relations: Public relations (pp. 213–221)

Anticipating environmental change

Morton International[15]

In 1982 Morton International, the US chemical group, acquired Thiokol for its speciality defence, space and chemical businesses. One of the products produced by Thiokol at the time was automotive air bags, designed to provide protection to car drivers by inflating in front of the driver in the event of an accident. The product was based on a formula of highly volatile chemical explosives contained within the automobile steering wheel, and was difficult to manufacture. US legislators were examining the potential for introducing air bags into automobiles but manufacturers were opposed to bags. An additional problem was that insurance companies would not provide product liability cover for the company. This left Morton with a dilemma – to sustain the product without having any significant market, in the hope that regulation would support the technology; or stop producing it.

The decision was eased when Mercedes-Benz decided to install the bags in all cars sold in the USA from 1985. This still left Morton with only one customer; however they decided to maintain the product in the anticipation that it would eventually become a regular fitting for most cars. Furthermore they believed that its success would depend on cost and quality. Based on this decision Morton decided to invest over $100 million in plant and equipment for the product, to improve quality and reduce unit costs. High levels of quality control were introduced including the X-raying of bags to detect flaws; the company also built separate plants in case of explosions at one. This would ensure that customers were supplied.

Morton's risk paid off when Chrysler decided in 1989 to use Morton bags in all cars from 1990. This was followed in 1991 by a GM decision to install the bags and a decision by the US Congress to legislate for air bags to be phased in for all cars. Significant investment was made in the technology during this period with projected annual revenues for the product of $1 billion by 1994. Morton also formed an alliance with the engineering firm Robert Bosch to target the European market. As it has turned out air bags have now become a regular feature for the major manufacturers.

FURTHER REFERENCE

Chapter 3, The Marketing Environment: Technological (p. 42)

CONCLUSION

The environmental factors which influence an organisation's marketing and business activities must be identified and strategies put into place to deal with them where relevant. Certain factors may be influenced by the organisation itself, such as political or technological developments, but others are impossible to control. In the case of some organisations we have seen how they identified and reacted to these environmental factors; and of others, how they sought to influence their environment. Whether it is reaction, influence or planning for change, it is vital for organisations at least to identify the changes taking place in their environment.

NOTES

1 Electronic data interchange (EDI) section adapted from: Paul Taylor, 'Towards a world without paper', *Financial Times*, 13 October 1992; Stephen H. Haeckel and Richard L. Nolan, 'Managing by wire', *Harvard Business Review*, September–October 1993, pp. 122–132; Tom Lester, 'Squeezing the supply chain', *Management Today*, March 1992, pp. 68–70; Bill Saporito, 'Behind the tumult at P&G', *Fortune*, 7 March 1994, pp. 48–54; 'Computers in business', *Business Age*, 1 December 1993; Paul

Taylor, 'Technology in the office – valuable boost for efficiency', *Financial Times*, 26 October 1993; John Kavanagh, 'Big business implications', *Financial Times*, 21 September 1993, p. VII; Scott Haggett, 'Banks poised to launch electronic data system when clients are ready', *The Financial Post*, 11 September 1993, p. 19; Carl Thomas Ashley, 'The future of print', *Pulp and Paper*, January 1994; Kyung Tae Hwang, C. Carl Pegels, and Rao Raghav, 'Electronic data interchange systems – state of the art', *Journal of Systems Management*, December 1993; James Carbone, 'EDI expands its role into management', *Electronic Business Buyer*, September 1993, pp. 89–90; David Van and C. Bruce Kavan, 'Adopting EDI: when and why?', *Information Strategy*, Summer 1993; Gregory B. Harter, 'EDI becomes part of economic survival', *Business Credit*, January 1993; William C. Symonds, 'Getting rid of paper is just the beginning', *Business Week*, 21 December 1992, pp. 46–47; Daniel J. Biby, 'Who really needs EDI?', *Industry Week*, 2 November 1992; 'What is EDI?', *Transportation and Distribution*, June 1992; Jane Bird, 'Looking after the shop', Management Today, November 1993, pp. 78–81.

2 Fibre-optic communication section adapted from William H. Davidson, 'The role of global scanning in business planning', *Organisational Dynamics*, winter 1991, vol. 19, pp. 4–16.

3 Solvay section adapted from Paul Abrahams, 'Takeovers bring Solvay out of the shadows', *Financial Times*, 12 November 1992, p. 27.

4 Domino Printing Sciences section adapted from: Alan Cane, 'Fast growth for niche technology', *Financial Times*, 14 October 1992; 'Company Results: Domino Printing', *Investors Chronicle*, 2 July 1993, p. 52; Jeff Ferry, 'Domino jets ahead', *Management Today*, June 1992, pp. 62–65; 'Dabbling in the black arts', *Packaging Week*, 20 January 1994; *The Independent*, 26 January 1994; *Daily Telegraph*, 30 June 1993; *Guardian*, 31 January 1992; Alan Cane, 'Inkjet print battle leaves its mark', *Financial Times*, 2 July 1993; Alan Cane, 'Domino declines 19 per cent as US drive fails to pay off', *Financial Times*, 30 June 1993, p. 27; Domino Printing Sciences PLC, Report and Accounts 1993.

5 Kyocera section adapted from Peter Knight, 'A rebel among copycats', *Financial Times*, 3 November 1993.

6 Procter & Gamble section adapted from: Jennifer Lawrence, 'P&G advance in diaper derby', *Advertising Age*, 7 March 1994; 'P&G unwraps ultra-thin nappy', *Marketing Week*, 8 October 1993; Jennifer Lawrence, 'It's diaper D-day with P&G rollout', *Advertising Age*, 20 September 1993; Jacqueline S. Scerbinski, 'Consumers and the Environment: A Focus on Five Products', *The Journal of Business Strategy*, September/October 1991, pp. 44–47; 'Bear bottoms', *Beauty Counter*, December 1991; Diane Coyle, 'A baby boomlet brings in the business', *Management Today*, October 1992, pp. 84–86.

7 McDonald's section adapted from: 'McDonald's sticks with PS in the UK', *Modern Plastics*, April 1992; Jacqueline S. Scerbinski, 'Consumers and the environment: a focus on five products', *The Journal of Business Strategy*, September/October 1991, pp. 44–47; David T. Buzelli, 'Time to structure an environmental policy strategy', *The Journal of Business Strategy*, March/April 1991, pp. 17–20.

8   Sun tan lotion section adapted from: Helen Jones, 'Suncare's call for a cover-up', *Marketing Week*, 15 May, 1993, pp.15–16; 'Nivea warms to sun care', *Marketing Week*, 17 December 1993, p. 8; Chris Mihill, 'Sun lovers soaking up risky rays despite rise in malignant melanomas', *Guardian*, 27 July 1993, p. 6; Georgina Campbell, 'A darker shade of pale', *Guardian*, 22 July 1993, p. 15; Market Research GB, 'Sun Care', vol. 35, March 1992; Mintel Market Intelligence, 'Suncare preparations', May 1993 and 'Suncare products' 1993; Mintel Retail Intelligence, 'Suntan products', vol. 6, 1993 and 'Suntan goods', 1993; EIU Retail Business, July 1993, no. 425, pp. 56–68.

9   Macy's section adapted from Jim Nash, 'Macy's CWA in phone fight', *The Business Journal* (US), 23 August 1993, vol. 11, no. 19, p. 16.

10 Brazilian economy section adapted from: Nicole Sierra, 'A supply side jump start for Brazil's stalled economy', *Wall Street Journal* (Eastern Edition), 28 January 1984, p. A15; Peter Wilson, 'What if the music stops?', *The Banker*, June 1992; Bill Hinchberger, edited by John E. Pleunneke, 'Spotlight On Brazil: Brazil's inflation madness', *Business Week*, 28 February 1994, p. 4; Jim Rohwer, 'Survey of Brazil', *The Economist*, 7 December 1991; Christina Lamb, 'A rollercoaster out of control', *Financial Times*, 22 February 1993, p. 10; Paul S. Nathan, 'Ups and downs in Spanish rights', *Publishers Weekly*, 18 January 1991, p. 512.

11 Euro Disney section adapted from: 'Euro Disney: the problems', *Guardian*, 11 November 1993, p. 26; Deyan Sudjic, 'High rollers bet on sphinx', *Guardian*, 29 December 1993; William Langley, 'Euro-Dismal', *The Sunday Times*, 22 August 1993, p. 9 (Focus); Marion McKeone, 'Losses Rain Down on Dismal Disneyland', *The Sunday Business Post*, 24 October 1993, p. 13; 'The story so far – a question of the mouse's attraction', *Financial Times*, 13 June 1992, p. 5; Dominic Lawson, 'Just who is taking the Mickey?', *Financial Times*, 27 November 1993, p. 26; 'The not so magic knigdom: Euro Disney', *The Economist*, 26 September 1992; 'Waiting for Dumbo – no fun at Euro Disney', *The Economist*, 1 May 1993; John Mullin, 'Mickey Mouse in a mess', *Guardian*, 10 July 1993, p. 25; Rebecca Smithers, 'Rollercoaster year for Pluto and Mickey, *Guardian*, 17 April 1993, p. 33; 'A touch of the sun', *Guardian*, 9 July 1993, p. 23; 'The horns of a dilemma – Euro Disney faces winter', *The Economist*, 28 November 1992; 'Of mice and men – Euro Disney's fading fantasy', *The Economist*, 13 November 1993; 'Ducking doom – Euro Disney dismal performance', *The Economist*, 10 July 1993.

12 Harrison and Harrison section adapted from Charles Darwent, 'All's Harmony at Harrison', *Management Today*, March 1992, pp. 51–54.

13 Royal Dutch/Shell section adapted from: Peter M. Ginter and W. Jack Duncan, 'Macroenvironmental Analysis for Strategic Management', *Long Range Planning*, 1990, vol. 23, no. 6, pp. 91–100; Pierre Wack, 'Scenarios: uncharted waters ahead', *Harvard Business Review*, September–October 1985, pp. 73–89; Pierre Wack, 'Scenarios: shooting the rapids', *Harvard Business Review*, November–December 1985, pp. 139–150; Martha A. Peak, 'Europeans strive to be Number 1', *Management Review*, September 1990, p. 56; P.W. Beck, 'Corporate planning for an uncertain future', *Long Range Planning*, August 1982, vol. 15, no. 4, pp. 12–21; Adam Kahane,

'Scenarios for energy: Sustainable world vs Global Mercntilism', *Long Range Planning*, August 1992, vol. 25, no. 4, pp. 38–46; P. Schwartz, *The Art of the Long View*, Doubleday Currency, 1991; Paul J.H. Schoemaker and Cornelius A.J.M. Van der Heijden, 'Integrating scenarios into strategic planning at Royal Dutch/Shell', *Planning Review*, May–June 1992; Mason Tenaglia and Patrick Noonan, 'Scenario based strategic planning: a process for building top management consensus', *Planning Review*, March–April 1992; Toni Mack, 'Time, money and patience', *Forbes*, 21 August 1989.

14 Philip Morris section adapted from: Irwin Warren, 'Putting the First Amendment first', *Adweek's Marketing Week*, 26 January 1987; Victoria Griffith, 'Lobbyists fight smoke with fire', *Financial Times*, 3 December 1992; Freedman, 'Tobacco firms, pariahs to many people, still are angels to the Arts', *Wall Street Journal*, 8 June, 1988, p. 1; 'Philip Morris Unit to hold First Amendment contest', *Wall Street Journal*, 28 September 1986, p. 28; Jurg W. Mattman, 'On tour with the Bill of Rights', *Security Management*, December 1991, pp. 51–53; 'A boycott call for Philip Morris', *Business and Society Review*, Summer 1991, p. 13; Christopher Dauer, 'Unique package tailored for Bill of Rights tour', *National Underwriter*, 4 March 1991, p. 3; Alison Fahey and Judann Dagnoli, 'PM ready to deal with outdoor foes', *Advertising Age*, 18 June 1990, p. 3; Debra Gersh, 'Philip Morris executive defends Bill of Rights Campaign', *Editor and Publisher*, the Fourth Estate, 10 February 1990, p. 14; Barbara Lippert, 'Philip Morris reminds us of the high price of freedom', *Adweek's Marketing Week*, 4 December 1989, p. 54; 'Anti-smoking groups fuming over Philip Morris TV ads', *Marketing News*, 4 December 1989, p. 5; Dan Koeppel, 'A backfire heard round the nation', *Adweek's Marketing Week*, 20 November 1989, p. 5; 'Anti-smoking group critical of Bill of Rights TV spots from Philip Morris', *Broadcasting*, 13 November 1989, p. 90; Christine Donahue, 'Tobacco's battling the anti-smoking forces', *Adweek's Marketing Week*, 12 September 1988, p. 46; Jack Bernstein, 'Is Philip Morris blowing smoke?', *Advertising Age*, 1 August 1988, p. 33; Christine Donahue, 'Philip Morris defends smokers with ads', *Adweek's Marketing Week*, 4 July 1988, p. 22; Judann Dagnoli, 'PM's smokers ads fire up opponents', *Advertising Age*, 4 July 1988, p. 2; Steven W. Calford, 'Philip Morris force behind new council', *Advertising Age*, 4 April 1988; Judann Dagnoli, 'Tobacco giants pull smokers to their ring', *Advertising Age*, 8 February 1988, p. 12.

15 Morton International section adapted from: Jessica Skelley von Brachel, 'A high-stakes bet that paid off ', *Fortune International*, 15 June 1992, pp. 85–86; 'Morton plans to invest $30 million to set up European airbag plant', *Wall Street Journal*, 8 September 1993; Steven Ashley, 'Automotive safety is in the bag', *Mechanical Engineering*, January 1994, p. 58–64; Neil Weinberg, 'Out from the salt mines', *Forbes*, 3 January 1994, p. 115; Helen Kahn, 'Suit claims burns from bags constitute a defect', *Automotive News*, 11 January 1993; Jagannath Dubashi, 'Hot air', *Financial World*, 14 April 1992, p. 28; Marc Reisch, 'A revitalised Morton set for growth', *Chemical and Engineering News*, 6 January 1992, pp. 18–19; Jordan E. Goodman, 'Morton is worth more than its salt', *Money*, January 1992, pp. 64–65; David Greising, 'Will airbags cushion the new Morton?', *Business Week*, 8

July 1991, pp. 65–66; Marcia Berss, 'Nothing is in the bag', *Forbes*, 4 March 1991, p. 97; Christopher Palmeri, 'Redemption', *Forbes*, 7 January 1991, vol. 147, p. 307; Richard Rescigno, 'Crash-proof: makers of airbags are riding a boom in demand', *Barron's*, 24 December 1990, pp. 17–20; Jay Palmer, 'Divorce, where's thy sting? – Morton, Thiokol go their separate ways', *Barron's*, 25 September 1989, pp. 14–15.

Chapter 4

Marketing research, information, forecasting and measurement

INTRODUCTION

In business, information is often referred to as the most valuable commodity of all. Most companies today conduct market research mainly for the purpose of understanding their customers better and how the company can meet their needs more precisely. Some companies build elaborate databases from information acquired from their customers and use them as a cost effective means of selectively targeting these customers, for example informing them of new products they believe will appeal to these customers.

Information on the wider business environment – markets, customers, competitors and an organisation's internal operations – is vital to allow management to make effective business decisions and formulate business plans. Today, companies are building management and marketing information systems, collecting information on a systematic basis to aid management in daily decision making and the development of business plans.

In formulating marketing strategy, a company first needs to be able to forecast and measure the size of its markets and then to monitor sales on a continual basis to determine the effectiveness of that strategy. Again, acquiring information is the key.

This chapter starts by looking at the area of market research; then examples of databases and management/marketing information systems are presented. It ends with examples of how companies conduct market measurement, sales forecasting and monitoring.

QUALITATIVE RESEARCH

Qualitative research is used by marketers to help them understand the motivation, attitudes, intentions, expectations, and so on behind buying behaviour. The IT sector was one which realised the benefits of qualitative research. Microsoft, the US software manufacturer, began putting an increased emphasis on qualitative research in 1992 to back up its usage of secondary quantitative data.

Qualitative techniques, including projective techniques and focus group interviews, rely on expert practitioners and 'moderators' – those who manage the interviews.

Projective techniques

Panasonic [1]

Projective techniques also provide a way of collecting qualitative data. When developing its office automation products, Panasonic wanted to find out whether or not its positive image in consumer electronics would transfer over to this new product group. Panasonic recruited a group of consumers who were asked to select photographs of people they associated with IBM, Canon, Xerox, Epsom, and Panasonic products. Among the findings was the fact that respondents associated photographs of older, distinguished and affluent people with IBM and Xerox and photographs of younger professional-looking types with Panasonic.

These findings were used in Panasonic's advertising campaign for its office automation products. The campaign used people who matched consumers' perceptions of Panasonic types – young professional-looking types. These Panasonic types were portrayed as 1960s and 1970s baby boomers moving up the corporate ladder.

Personal interviews

Grand Rapids Label [2]

The US labelling company, Grand Rapids Label (GRL), used qualitative research in order to understand their key customers better – to identify their expectations, their needs and any problems they may be experiencing with which GRL may be able to help.

Personnel from different departments within each key customer organisation were interviewed. The interviewees were encouraged to talk freely through the use of open-ended questions. The information received from each customer was carefully analysed and customers were categorised according to their specific needs and expectations. As a result of the research, GRL has been able to devise carefully tailored selling and servicing strategies for each customer that address that customer's specific needs and expectations. GRL has become more responsive to customers and sales meetings regularly feature testimony from key customers and subsequent discussion among staff about the customers' comments. GRL has also become more responsive to problems customers are experiencing (even though the problem may not be to do with GRL's label) seeing problems as possible new product/ service opportunities.

Focus groups

Microsoft [3]

Microsoft recognised the need for improved information on which to base its business decisions and business strategy. Over 1992/1993, Microsoft conducted research into its channels of distribution and the end user, attempting to identify who the user is, where s/he is, how Microsoft can influence him/her and so on.

The firm identified two roles for qualitative research. The first is to use it in order to identify issues – focus groups are used as a positioning tool and the resultant data is then augmented with telephone quantitative studies. The second is to use it as a diagnostics tool, to get feedback about things that have already happened. Data are consolidated and fed in to the business planning process.

Customer panels

Lloyds Bank

Lloyds, the UK high street bank, began using customer panels in 1993 to gain a greater insight into their customers' needs and to identify any problems customers may be experiencing with banking at Lloyds branches. Most panels are held in the evening and involve 8–10 customers and key members of staff from the branch. The customer panels are held throughout the country and approximately 500 panel meetings were held in 1993.

Lloyds has received very useful feedback as a result of the panels and many improvements have been made as a direct result of suggestions from customers. One such improvement is the plan to have in place in all main branches by mid-1994 telephone service teams dedicated to dealing with all customer queries and problems received by phone. This improvement was a result of customers complaining about being 'passed on' when telephoning with a query or complaint.

Gateway[4]

The UK Supermarket group Gateway has conducted field research on an on-going basis using shopper panels since 1986. At the panels, a cross-section of up to twenty shoppers meets with a Gateway management team which always includes a board director. The panels allow Gateway to understand their customers' needs and motivations better and any problems they may be experiencing with shopping at Gateway branches. Gateway adjusts branch policies on a whole variety of things from bottle banks to product range in response to feedback from the local shopper panel.

DATABASES

The importance of developing and maintaining sophisticated customer databases has never been more important than in the 1990s. With increasing competition and the world-wide recession putting pressure on the marketing budgets of companies, it is important to carefully nurture existing customer relationships and use marketing pounds in the most efficient manner possible.

Having sales reps on the road is becoming increasingly expensive and for many companies using reps for the tasks of visiting unknown prospects and 'relationship building' calls on existing customers can prove uneconomic. The well-developed marketing database is one answer to these problems, when it can qualify prospects and keep existing customers in touch with the latest developments.

General Electric Company[5]

Like many large corporations, General Electric Company is sometimes viewed by customers as being very difficult to do business with. It's no wonder: With twelve businesses divided into more than 90 operating components, Fairfield, Connecticut-based GE is a huge, complex and very decentralised organisation.

Mindful of the need to improve customer service to its business-to-business customers, the company established its GE Business Information Center in 1984. Located in Albany, N.Y., the centre is staffed by 24 people. Over the past three years, they have handled more than 300,000 customer enquiries. And the volume is growing: the centre will receive around 160,000 calls this year, according to John F. Wilfore, its manager. 'Many of the callers don't have an assigned salesperson, so they don't know how to do business with us,' explains Mr. Wilfore. He adds that with tighter resources, GE salespeople are focused on 'chasing the big opportunities'. So the centre provides a way to serve smaller customers and prospects.

A relational database located on a mainframe computer is the heart and soul of the operation. When customers in North America call the centre's toll-free line, GE 'program managers' access the database to find answers to their questions – or a contact within GE who can help.

The database, for example, has information on 3,000 key contacts including field salespeople, service technicians, headquarters personnel and key GE distributors. In addition, program managers can tap into information on GE operating components such as their products, their key sales and services, toll-free numbers, distributors and sales locations.

Approximately 34 per cent of the calls the centre receives are sales-related inquiries. That means people seeking information on a GE product or service, or people ready to buy. When those enquiries occur, program managers interactively build the database during the phone conversation. They capture callers' names, job titles, phone numbers, company names and addresses. They also find out what market segment callers are in, as well as the product or service they desire. And they write a short synopsis, highlighting details of every call. 'We link those callers and that information back to either headquarters, field sales or distributors,' says Mr Wilfore, adding that 'our reason for doing that is to generate incremental sales'.

The Business Information Center and its database are utilised in numerous other ways to boost GE's marketing and sales efforts. For example, the centre serves as a key linkage point for GE's Take-The-Lead programme, an effort to promote sales across the company's businesses. When a salesperson identifies a customer need that could be served by another GE business, he or she calls the centre and a program manager searches the database to find the right contact. Program managers handle Take-The-Lead calls on a daily basis, according to Mr. Wilfore.

The centre also develops quarterly reports for regional sales managers in one of GE's businesses. Those provide details on calls handed off to distributors. The sales managers use that information when they follow-up with distributors to see how they handled calls.

'We can improve the quality of our distribution network by ensuring that customers' needs are being satisfied appropriately,' says Mr. Wilfore. In the future, Mr Wilfore expects that the centre will play an increasingly important role in GE's global marketing efforts.

Last year alone, program managers handled 2,000 inquiries from off-shore callers. The centre published information on those calls and sent it to GE's international sales offices. But some hurdles remain in preparing the centre for a large volume of international callers. 'We're trying to get our system acclimated to handling international data,' says Mr Wilfore. Language, cultural and time differences also present formidable obstacles.

FURTHER REFERENCE

Chapter 12, Personal Selling: Sales force strategy (p. 198); Prospecting (p. 205)

Dell[6]

Dell Computer Corporation prides itself on its sophisticated corporate database. Units across the company – including manufacturing, finance, marketing and sales – are linked to the database and continually feed it with information. The database is organised by market segment and manipulated by marketers who attempt to identify the best prospects for direct mailings. Statistical tools are used to analyse such factors as how recently customers bought a product or service, how much they spent, how frequently they buy Dell products and what payment method they use. Statistical analysis then produces a list of customers who represent the best prospects for mailing. Customers are kept constantly in touch with the latest developments, special offers, and so on, and the net result is the forming of a relationship between Dell and its customers which will hopefully encourage these customers to continue to purchase their future requirements only from Dell. This highly targeted direct mailing approach has resulted in high response rates and uses Dell's resources in a manner which is both cost efficient and effective from a marketing viewpoint.

FURTHER REFERENCE

Chapter 6, Segmentation and Positioning: Behavioural – user status segmentation (p. 98); Behavioural – usage rate (p. 100)

Marui Co[7]

The Japanese department store chain Marui Co. Ltd, one of Japan's top retail chains, gathers information from point-of-sale (POS) transactions and credit vetting procedures for in-store credit cards, to develop merchandising and marketing strategies.

Nearly all Marui customers are issued with the in-store credit card instantly. Information collected at the point-of-sale from a Marui credit card customer includes customer's name and address, total amount spent, and brands and brand sizes bought. Information is held on a sophisticated customer information system (CIS) which managers can readily access and use to acquire daily reports on sales revenue by store, floor, department or unit within a department and even of each individual product. Using this information, Marui can adapt its stores and merchandise assortments to suit the needs and preferences of its customers.

Marui uses information held on its CIS to conduct direct mailing campaigns to customers. If Marui is promoting a particular range of goods, it can select promising target customers by examining their purchasing history and so ascertain the likelihood that they will be interested in the promotion.

FURTHER REFERENCE

Chapter 6, Segmentation and Positioning: Behavioural-usage rate (p. 100)

Kimberly Clark[8]

Relationship marketing involves the employment of an information based system on current and potential customers to establish a relationship with targets and interchange information between the two parties. The relationship usually seeks to differentiate between individuals/ organisations rather than treating them as all the same.

Kimberly Clark, the manufacturers of Huggies baby products, has established an information system to provide it with the names of over 75 per cent of the expectant mothers in the USA. This information is obtained from doctors, hospitals and childbirth trainers. In the course of the women's pregnancies Huggies provide them with information on baby care. The objective of this is to build a relationship with the prospective mothers. When the baby returns home the mother is sent a coupon for purchasing the Huggies product. This coupon is coded so that when the coupon is presented to the retailer the company knows which mothers have used the product.

MARKETING INFORMATION SYSTEMS

A marketing information system (MIS) can be defined as a structure consisting of people, equipment and procedures dedicated to generating and processing information on a continuous basis to aid marketing management in decision making. An MIS is future oriented, designed to prevent as well as solve problems.

Some of the benefits accruing from an effective MIS are improved managerial performance, the ability to recognise trends more quickly, thus signalling management to adjust the marketing plan, and providing guidance in setting goals.

Today, the need for an effective MIS has never been greater. Management needs more comprehensive, accurate and more timely information to aid problem solving and decision making. Executives are expected to make faster decisions and have less time to gather and analyse information. Companies are expanding their product offerings and their markets in reaction to increasing competition, making the demand for high quality information imperative. Computers continue to improve providing management with fast and often inexpensive means of processing the masses of marketing information.

Corning[9]

Corning, the New York-based glass company, a multi-business organis-ation comprising businesses such as consumer housewares, laboratory services and fibre optics, developed a sophisticated MIS through the use of networked computers with electronic mail and software to synthesise information.

Corning realised that they needed to improve the flow of general business and competitive information across department and division lines. Nearly half of its US competitors were foreign based and world-wide competition was increasing at an enormous pace.

In developing their information network, the corporate marketing department set up a business information action team made up of rep-resentatives from most major units in the company. The team conducted an information audit by interviewing 70 key managers and executives. The main finding was that internal and external reports on markets, competition and general business, were not being shared within units and across divisions. Furthermore, employees did not want a system where raw data would be dumped on them and the need for information to be effectively synthesised and distributed became paramount. Managers wanted a system that would be easy to use, flexible and produce information that was easily accessible, accurate and timely.

The outcome was the development of the Business Information Exchange Network™, a full-text database that used the electronic mail network and software to synthesise information. The information on the database is available world-wide through Corning's electronic mail network providing the company with information on the different environments in which it operates which no doubt helps management reach better quality decisions.

Adolph Coors[10]

Adolph Coors, the US beverage producer is wholly committed to the MIS concept, gathering and analysing information on market-place trends and competitors on a systematic basis and providing a competitive intelligence capability to management to help in decision making.

Coors has developed a network of people within the organisation who contribute raw data from the field. A sophisticated computerised database exists to store this information. Coors meticulously collects, sorts and analyses government filings and news reports on each major competitor. The bits and pieces of marketing, financial, economic, regulatory, human resources, and social data are synthesised to provide strategic overviews and developments.

This combination of in-house data gatherers and well-maintained files serves to draw information from a wide variety of sources and synthesises the information providing Coors management with an intelligence capability that has served the company well over the years.

American Express[11]

American Express (AMEX) have embraced IT and the MIS concept to the point where the company is interactive with its customers, developing and evolving a frequent dialogue with customers in the market place.

Its sophisticated marketing database triggers product sales opportunities by analysing customers on a continuous basis – the same way that insurance companies, knowing a person's date of birth, can send information about a product particularly relevant to someone of that age. The AMEX product offer can be tailored for individual needs.

The Mitsubishi Trading Company This company employs over 60,000 market analysts throughout the world whose main task is to obtain relevant market information and forward it to the parent company in Japan.

MARKET FORECASTING AND MEASUREMENT[12]

Estimating market potential

The life-cycle concept of market potential is defined as the greatest number of product adoptions that will eventually occur in a particular market over the product life cycle, given expected environmental conditions and expected aggregate effects of marketing actions by the industry.

A three-step process to estimate market potential (M) is proposed:

1 estimate geographic population (G);
2 multiply the geographic population by a series of chained screening ratios to estimate the market population (P);
3 multiply the market population by the estimated long-run choice probability to estimate market potential.

Geographic population (G) is all firms, establishments, or facilities within the temporal and geographic boundaries of the market. Market population (P) is a subset of the geographic population; it is all possible buyers within the temporal and geographic boundaries of the market who will eventually make a decision to adopt or reject the new product. The screening ratio (R) is the product of the variables which affects the adoption decision ($R = r_1 \cdot r_2 \cdot r_3 \ldots \cdot r_n$). The choice probability is the proportion of potential adopters who are likely to adopt.

An example drawn from a study of the market potential for a new nickel-iron battery illustrates how industrial marketers can apply the life-cycle concept of market potential.

This new product is one of the more promising batteries currently being developed for use in electric vehicles. Because of its high energy density the battery may also have other commercial applications. The nickel-iron battery is not commercially available now, but its manufacturer and a consortium of partners may introduce it in the future. To help it plan the appropriate scale of commercial production, the consortium sponsored a market assessment to forecast the North American market potential for the new battery.

The market for rechargeable batteries is segmented by end-use categories as follows: starting, lighting, and ignition (SLI); motive power; standby power; energy storage; and miscellaneous. To estimate geographic population, each of the five macro segments is further segmented by end-use application. Electric wheelchairs are one micro segment in the motive power macro segment. Illustrated below is the life-cycle concept of market potential for nickel-iron batteries used in electric wheelchairs.

According to the 1982 *Census of Manufacturers* data, 94 establishments produce electric wheelchairs in the United States, and average annual production per establishment is 9,250 wheelchairs. Each electric wheelchair requires one battery module, and the average number of wheelchairs bought each year per business customer is estimated to be five. Consequently, it is estimated that the geographic population (G) in the wheelchair market segment is: (94 establishments) $\times$ (9,250 wheelchairs per establishment) $\times$ (0.2 business customers per wheelchair) = 173,900 US business customers that buy wheelchairs. The ratio of Canadian to US value of shipments for wheelchairs is 0.06 so, lacking better information about the Canadian market, the North American geographic population is estimated to be 173,900 $\times$ (1.06) = 184,334 business customers. The percentage of all wheelchairs sold each year that are electric is estimated by industry sources to be 20 per cent. Using this as the only screening ratio, the North American market population is estimated to be P = R. G = (0.2)(184,334) = 36,867 business customers.

Certainly the market for batteries for powering electric wheelchairs would be competitive. Currently, most electric wheelchairs use sealed lead-acid batteries. If the manufacturer introduces the new nickel-iron module in this market, 36,867 business customers may contemplate adoption, but only a fraction will adopt the new battery. A concept test with potential customers and a Delphi panel of expert judges was used to estimate the choice probability for this market segment at c = 0.201. Thus, the estimated market potential for the new battery is M = c. P, or M = (0.201) $\times$ (36,867) = 7,410 eventual adopters of the new battery. Using these numbers it was concluded that lead-acid batteries will retain (1 – c). P = (0.799) $\times$ 36,867 = 29,456 of the customers in this market for a market share of nearly 80 per cent.

Sales monitoring

Safeway[13]

Safeway, the supermarket chain in the UK, in conjunction with Nielsen, provides sales data to its suppliers on a weekly basis. This allows suppliers to assess brand performance and market developments. The data is compiled through the store's electronic point-of-sale measurement technology by Nielsen and then offered to manufacturers. The information is provided in two formats. First a 'Trading Data' report allows retailers and manufacturers to analyse their results, and second a 'Marketing' report enables them to assess the performance of brands and other market trends. The data also contributes to analysing the effectiveness of sales promotions, the influence of price changes and forecasting of future demand.

Continuous research of this kind and the associated technology allows actual sales to be monitored and can forecast trends and behaviour in the market place. Marketing strategies can also be evaluated such as promotional activities, pricing strategy, and so on. Predictive models may also be developed which forecast the effect of changes in different elements of the marketing or promotional mix on a brand's performance. The goal of continuous research and associated methods may be used to quantifiably measure marketing activity.

Information Resources Inc.[14]

In the late 1980s the US market research firm, Information Resources Inc. (IRI) introduced the 'VideOcart' – a shopping trolley with a computer screen which collected market research information and showed point-of-sale advertisements relating to the actual products on the shelves as the shopper approached them. The information collected included time spent in different parts of the store, the route taken by the shopper and certain opinions of the shopper. This information was then transferred to a terminal at the checkout by means of a radio transmitter. The information could be used to examine shopping behaviour and optimise product placement on shelves.

FURTHER REFERENCE

Chapter 11, Advertising: Point-of-purchase advertising (p. 192)

Sales forecasting

Metier Management Systems[15]

In order to forecast sales levels Metier Management Systems holds its sales representatives responsible for forecasting. The US company markets project management systems, and each month sales representatives develop a three-month forecast based on the estimated sales to each prospective customer. Each sales representative meets with the sales manager monthly to review the estimates made for each customer. In this meeting, the sales manager goes through a series of questions relating to the selling cycle. These questions include such issues as project start date, the status and number of decision makers, the competitiveness of Metier's price and the current status of the project. Should the representative not know the answer to such crucial questions, the meeting is stopped and the representative then obtains the answer by phone. In answering these questions an accurate estimate of sales can be made.

This approach ensures optimum accuracy in forecasting by the sales person in developing his/her initial three month forecasts. The sales person is compelled to gain a detailed knowledge of the account in order to be able to provide the necessary information in the meetings with the sales manager. The sales manager also conducts joint visits with the sales representative to particular accounts. Accuracy of forecasting is also a factor in the sales manager's performance evaluation and she or he is also remunerated partly on this basis. Such incentives and monitoring encourage both managers and representatives to generate accurate forecasts. Forecasts are also analysed on a historical basis to identify trends which could be applied to current forecasts. These include the identification of aberration prospects such as those who kept the sales person hanging on but not making a purchase. Such prospects were eliminated from the forecast after nine months.

FURTHER REFERENCE

Chapter 12, Personal Selling: Setting targets (p. 202–203); Supervising/directing sales representatives (p. 203–204)

Frito-Lady[16] This company supplies its sales personnel with portable computers which allow the company to monitor snack food sales and trends within a matter of a couple of days. The current level of stocking in stores can also be monitored and deliveries scheduled accordingly.

The chief executive of Pepsi Co telephones four customers per day, and senior executives regularly visit retailers.

Evaluating market opportunities

Adams[17]

A company's entry into foreign markets is often instigated by limited prospects for growth in its home market. This was a major contributing factor to the decision by Adams, the UK children's clothing retailer, to consider foreign markets. The onset of the recession in the UK market and increasing competition, along with discouraging demographic trends persuaded the company (part of Sears Childrenswear) to investigate other markets.

Desk research was initially carried out, focusing on the factors of economic and demographic growth rates and the competitive market environment. As a result of this analysis Spain emerged as the market with greatest potential. The traditional market entry route into Spain by British retailers was through a concession in one of the large department stores, usually Galerias Preciados. This was then used as a pilot for potential future stores. Adams, however, decided not to follow this route and commissioned their own market research (carried out by Research International) to determine the optimal strategy for market entry. Key factors in relation to the entry strategy were location and transferability of the Adams product range. Compatibility of the Adams range with the market was necessary to make the strategy feasible, i.e. significant product modifications would be uneconomic.

The research included an initial evaluation of the retail environment in Spain followed by a number of accompanied shopping trips. This was then supplemented by a series of extended focus groups which evaluated the total Adams retail proposition – brand, product, pricing, in-store environment, etc. The five major city regions of Spain were chosen to conduct the research – Madrid, Barcelona, Valencia, Bilbao and Seville. The potential location of stores fell into three major categories – central city shopping areas consisting of department stores and specialist shops, 'shopping leisure centres' where shopping can almost be regarded as a form of leisure activity and, finally, hypermarkets.

The Spanish consumer was also examined in relation to their purchasing behaviour and segmented according to whether they were 'modern' or 'traditional'. The former preferred newer fashions for their children while the latter was more classical in their approach. The existing competition was also analysed according to factors such as quality, price, modern or traditional in their offer, and type of appeal, i.e. emotional or rational. It was concluded that the majority of the Adams range would appeal to the Spanish consumer with only minor modifications being required. The range was expected to appeal most to the modern Spanish mother in the newer commercial centres.

Adams opened its first two outlets in Madrid and Bilbao at the end of 1992. These outlets exceeded the company's trading expectations. The third outlet was opened in Barcelona in March 1993 and a further nine outlets followed in that year.

FURTHER REFERENCE

Chapter 10, Marketing Channels: Retailing types (p. 172)

The 'Bili-blanket'[18]

The process of market opportunity analysis for emerging technologies is described as consisting of five steps:

1 identification of customer functions for the technology;
2 description of market segments for each customer function;
3 market assessment of the general conditions characteristic of the market;
4 industry/competitive analysis;
5 market programming – operationalisation of a product position statement and evaluation of each component of the marketing mix.

The technology evaluated here is that of weaving optical fibres to produce a surface or mat which is illuminated on one side. The applications identified include a wide-range of commercial and health-related uses. The specific application in this case is this technology's role in treating newborn jaundice (*hyperbili-rubinemia*). The term 'Bili-blanket' will denote the use of this new technology for the application noted.

Jaundice is relatively common, affecting 7–10 per cent of full-term infants and all premature infants. This condition is also relatively benign and, when treated properly, rarely dangerous to the baby's health. Newborn jaundice is caused by the relatively inactive nature of the liver just after birth. The most widely used treatment is phototherapy. This consists of placing the infant under a set of blue lights for two or three days until the bilirubin, the cause of jaundice, returns to a safe/normal level.

The first step thus establishes the customer function of the technology: 'an aid in the treatment of newborn jaundice'. The market, in terms of the users, is the newborn and premature infant market.

1 Market description and assessment (steps 2 and 3)

Information for steps 2 and 3 was obtained by a combination of published data and a series of informal Interviews. The market is described as general medical and surgical hospitals (SIC (standard industrial classification) 8062), specifically: (a) maternity/newborn; (b) neonatal special care; and (c) neonatal intensive care units. The American Hospital Association Annual Directory provides a comprehensive listing of hospitals broken down by bed size of facility and specialisms offered. In addition to increasing concentration of health care (growth of larger hospitals and decline in the smaller ones), trends indicate:

1   increased emphasis on cost containment;
2   increased growth in investor-owned hospitals;
3   increased growth in HMOs (Health Management Organisations)
4   increased conversion of private health insurance to prospective payment (DRG) system.

A key statistic of interest in evaluating this opportunity is the birth rate and factors affecting it. *The Statistical Abstract of the United States*, published annually by the US Department of Commerce, proved helpful in this context. Table 4.1 shows a sample of these data. In addition, *Ross Lab's Guide to Centers Providing Perinatal and Neonatal Special Care* gives an annual estimate of 500,000–600,000 infants who would receive phototherapy treatment for jaundice.

The current mode of phototherapy delivery is a line of products usually referred to as 'Bili-lights'. A typical Bili-light consists of four to six fluorescent tubes housed in a protective case which is attached to an adjustable and movable stand. For the full-term infant, the Bili-light is

Table 4.1 Newborn statistics

Year	1970	1975	1980	1985	1990	1995
Birth (*in millions*)	3.73	3.12	3.61	3.83	3.85	3.63

Source: Statistical Abstract of the United States

placed over the bassinet; for the premature infant, the unit is positioned over the incubator. The infant's eyes are masked to prevent any harmful effects of the prolonged exposure to the light source. The key buying influencers for this product include (a) the clinical neonatologist, (b) neonatal and obstetric nurses, and (c) the purchasing department. The benefits sought by this group are along two lines: (a) treatment capabilities and (b) cost of treatment. The perceived advantages and disadvantages of Bili-lights (again the result of informal interviews) are shown in Figure 4.1.

In this section what has been established is a broad description of the market, trends in the broader market and the factors likely to influence market potential for this customer function, as well as the purchasing dimension associated with this market opportunity.

Determination of market potential first focused on identifying sur-rogate measures, i.e. measures that are widely/readily available. Inter-views with four area hospitals showed a consistent ratio of births to the number of phototherapy units used. Market potential, in number of units (existing phototherapy units), is calculated overleaf in Figure 4.2.

2 Competitive analysis (step 4)

In this step it is necessary to define the industry, or the broad competitive arena for phototherapy treatment, describe the competitive environment and analyse its structural dimensions. In addition, the product currently used to perform phototherapy and its advantages and disadvantages

Advantages	Disadvantages
• Proven method of treatment	• Large and bulky
• Non-contact and hence no fear of infection	• Fear of retinal damage to the infant
• Easy to use	• Increased risk of hypothermia
• Inexpensive to purchase	• Increased risk of dehydration due to hypothermia
• Long life span	• Long treatment period (three days)

Figure 4.1 Evaluation of Bili-lights

- Interviews with three area hospitals indicated a stable ratio of *14* phototherapy units for *every* 1000 births
- The 1990s market potential is accordingly estimated at 14 × 3,850* = *53,900* units

*See table 4.1 for births data

Figure 4.2 Market potential for phototherapy units

vis-à-vis the new technology are discussed. The conclusion of this step explains the market position of the new technology.

Current producers of phototherapy units are classified under manufacturers of surgical and medical instruments and apparatus (SIC 3841). As the Bili-blanket technology is a potential replacement technology, SIC 3841 is the competitive area of interest for this market opportunity. *The census of manufacturers* and *US industrial outlook* provide aggregate industry statistics. This SIC code lists 860 establishments with 1988 shipments valued at $4.8 billion. Shipments from this industry have grown at a steady 7 per cent a year for the last fifteen years, and the next five years are forecast along the same lines. Competitive imports come primarily from the developed nations. Furthermore, unlike a substantial number of the manufacturing industries, exports from the US exceed imports by a factor of two. This industry is characterised by a relatively low level of concentration (63 per cent of the firms have less than twenty employees), and a high level of specialisation (90 per cent of the total output falls within the bounds of 'surgical and medical instruments and apparatus'). Although further research indicates that only twelve of the 860 establishments manufacture Bili-lights, a broad brush analysis of SIC 3841 is important. Should new entrants plan market entry for phototherapy, the probability is high, given their base competencies, that an existing firm in this industry would be the first to develop the technology and provide access to the market place.

Industrial directories (for example, Thomas Register) along with Dun and Bradstreet market identifiers and Wards Directory, isolated twelve manufacturers of Bili-lights. With the exception of two large publicly-owned manufacturers, most manufacturers fall into the classification of small, privately owned organisations. In terms of number of employees, they range from nine to 80, with sales levels between $150,000 and $6.3 million dollars. What is important to note is that for the ten smaller manufacturers, phototherapy and closely related accessories constitute the bulk of their sales. This focused competitive arena, along with the stagnant nature of the market, may make for intensely competitive conditions.

All current competitors use the same technology (blue fluorescent light fixtures) and rather similar designs. In addition, the technology has changed little in the last twenty years. Bili-lights are competitively priced ($900–$1,500) and are simple to operate and maintain. Functionally, these units have long lives (twenty years) with minimal down times. For a potential new entrant, in addition to the competitive factors listed above, it should be clearly noted that phototherapy, as it is presently administered, is safe, reliable, causes no discomfort to the baby, and has been the accepted mode of treatment for neo-natal jaundice for twenty years.

From the market's perspective, consolidation and growth of investor-owned health-care facilities, increased public and governmental pressure for cost containment, and a relatively flat birth rate is likely to spur price competition further for what is primarily a replacement market. In this context, we introduce the concept of the Bili-blanket, the woven fibre-optic alternative to the Bili-light. The key dimensions of the fibre technology are outlined as:

1 *Thin* – this enhances handling and comfort of the infant.
2 *Flexible* – as the emissions surface is separated from the optical power source, the infant can be treated at multiple locations.
3 *Safe* – the ultraviolet (UV) and infra-red (IR) light can be controlled.

In addition, as a product in a jacket form, the Bili-blanket can provide 360° coverage thus speeding up the treatment process and cutting down on hospital stay and hospital costs.

The Bili-blanket, however, is not without its disadvantages. Given the cost associated with this technology, even a nominal rate of return would dictate an initial selling price in the range of $8,000–$10,000. While one Bili-blanket is estimated to replace four Bili-lights, the cost of *owning* and *operating* the Bili-blanket is expected to be substantially lower; a more thorough analysis of this is outlined in the next section. A second disadvantage is with the time required for the Food and Drug Administration (FDA) approval process. Owing to its 'body contact' nature the Bili-blanket would by definition be a class III device. Class III devices undergo a substantially more complex clinical trial process owing to the fear of infection. On the other hand Bili-lights, by being non-contact devices (class II), are subject to a simpler and shorter certification process.

In spite of the obvious disadvantages noted above, the Bili-blanket has a clear life-cycle cost advantage over current methods of phototherapy treatment. At the very least the Bili-blanket will provide the same functional capability at a substantial overall saving. The market positioning, therefore, would have to emphasise two key dimensions:

1   the same capability of treatment with a better handling feature;
2   a cost effective means of providing the treatment.

3   Market programming (step 5)

The critical dimensions in designing the product package include:

1   cost documentation to show savings associated with use of the product;
2   product performance and safety trials;
3   endorsement by the medical community;
4   appearance and product design.

In addition, the need to educate potential users is important, as preliminary research indicated no dissatisfaction with the existing mode of phototherapy treatment. Given the importance of the potential cost savings of the Bili-blanket, one estimate of life-cycle costs is presented in Figure 4.3.

The computations are based on the features supplied by two local area hospitals. Life-cycle costs enable one to look at the total cost of acquiring and using a product. The value-in-use of the BB documents the theoretical maximum customers could pay for the Bili-blanket if they wished to see no change in their cost per treatment. At any price below $391,600 the Bili-blanket is a better value than the Bili-light.

Communication channels encompass the range of advertising, sales promotion, and publicity. Interviews indicate publicity and personal selling as the most effective communication tools for medical equipment. Distribution channels for phototherapy are currently direct. Should producers of Bili-blanket plan on market entry, direct selling would clearly be the most preferred channel given the need to educate the market about the new technology.

The Bili-blanket is clearly a value-creating innovation to the phototherapy user market. The long and often expensive FDA approval process, and the need to educate the market place about the new technology, clearly demand substantial development costs. The stagnant nature of the market (mostly replacement sales) and narrow and limited product lines of most competitors are likely to make for an intensely competitive

A   *Bili-light:*

– Lab charges $20 × 2.3		$ 46.00
– Mother's room $300 × 0.5 × 2.3		$345.00
– Nursery charge $200 × 2.3		$460.00
Cost/treatment		$851.00

B   *Bili-blanket:*

– Lab charges $20 × 1.3		$ 26.00
– Mother's room $300 × 0.5 × 1.3		$195.00
– Nursery charge $200 × 1.3		$260.00
Cost/treatment		$481.00

C   *Bili-light:*

– Purchase price		$3,200
– Maintenance cost (life)		$1,200
Total cost of unit		$4,400

D   Value-in-use of the Bili-blanket (VBB) (computed for a total of 1,200 treatments, the effective life of the Bili-blanket):

VBB + cost of 1,200 treatments using Bili-blanket
= cost of Bili-light + cost of 1,200 treatments using Bili-light*

- VBB + 1,200 (481) = 4.400 (4) + 12 (851)
- VBB = $391,600

*Bili-light has a useful life of 300 treatments, hence the multiplier of 4 to equate it to Bili-blanket

Figure 4.3 Life-cycle cost comparison: Bili-light versus Bili-blanket

market. In part these considerations may suggest that although this market is a viable future prospect, it currently may not be the best one to target.

FURTHER REFERENCE

Chapter 5, Buyer Behaviour: Decision making unit/buyer chain (pp. 91–93)
Chapter 3, The Marketing Environment (pp. 41–60)
Chapter 6, Segmentation and Positioning: Positioning (pp. 105–108)
Chapter 9, Pricing: Setting prices (pp. 155–158)

Abbot Laboratories Hospital Products Division [19]

In the mid-1980s Abbot Laboratories Hospital Products Division (HPD) introduced their decision support system to carry out sales forecasting, pricing analysis, new product analysis and the tracking of promotional campaigns. The system was computer based and allowed for product sales data and pricing data to be analysed for profitability. The company markets over 2000 products in the hospitals market and often needs its sales personnel to quickly determine the profitability of one product line as opposed to another which may deliver the same service, in order to switch from selling one to another. The system uses historical data to determine the projected impact on overall profitability of a proposed drop in price of the more profitable line. The analysis therefore allows HPD and its sales personnel to quickly assess the market opportunity for alternative product lines.

FURTHER REFERENCE

Chapter 4, Marketing Research, Information, Forecasting and Measurement: Marketing information systems (pp. 68–70)

CONCLUSION

Today more then ever, effective marketing is dependent upon companies having good information. Increasing competition from home and overseas demands effective marketing information for decision making and formulating strategic marketing plans. Marketing information systems in particular are increasingly being recognised as a most effective way of connecting an organisation with its external environment.

NOTES

1 Panasonic section reprinted from 'Matching face with image', *Business Marketing*, March 1989, p. 58. Reprinted with permission. Copyright, Crain Communications Inc.

2 Grand Rapids Label section reprinted from Carl Messer, Michael Lyons and James Alexander, 'Classifying your customers', *Sales and Marketing Management*, Bill Communications Ltd (US), July 1993, vol. 145, no. 8, pp. 42–44. Reprinted with permission of *Sales and Marketing Management*, 355 Park Avenue South, New York, NY 10010–1789.

3 Microsoft section adapted from Louella Miles, 'A question of quality', *Marketing Business* (UK), May 1993, pp. 19–22.

4 Gateway section adapted from 'Gateway's customers speak', *Marketing Business*, August 1989, p. 2.

5 General Electric Company section is reprinted from *Business Marketing*, May 1992. Reprinted with permission. Copyright, Crain Communications Inc.

6 Dell section reprinted from Tom Eisenhart, 'Dell, Polaroid use databases to target customers, link internal units', *Business Marketing*, May 1992, pp. 24–26. Reprinted with permission. Copyright, Crain Communications Inc.

7 Marui Company section adapted from the following: Francis Dickerson, 'Cashing in on the new Japanese lifestyle', *Trends*, June 1992, pp. 13–14; Gary Robins, 'Marui's instant cards: desktop technology eliminates credit card shuffle', *Stores*, September 1992, p. 26; Andrew Tanzer, 'James Baker, meet the Dokushin Kizoku', *Forbes*, 20 April 1987, pp. 46–48.

8 Kimberly Clark section adapted from David Shani and Sujana Chalasani, 'Exploiting niches using relationship marketing', *The Journal of Consumer Marketing*, vol. 9, no. 3, summer 1992, p. 37.

9 Corning section adapted from Gary B. Roush, 'A program for sharing corporate intelligence', *The Journal of Business Strategy*, January/February 1991, pp. 4–7.

10 Adolph Coors section adapted from Leonard Fuld, 'A recipe for business intelligence success', *The Journal of Business Strategy*, January/February 1991, p. 13.

11 American Express section adapted from 'Using IT for strategic marketing advantage', *Marketing Business*, April 1989, pp. 22–23.

12 This section on market forecasting and measurement reprinted with permission of the publisher from David L. Kendall and Michael T. French, 'Forecasting the potential for new industrial products', *Industrial Marketing Management*, 1991, vol. 20, pp. 177–183. Copyright 1991 by Elsevier Science Inc.

13 Safeway section adapted from the following: 'Safeway offers weekly monitor', *Marketing*, 9 July 1992, p. 4; 'Safeway–Nielsen link to sell store information', *The Grocer*, 11 July 1992, p. 10; Mike Penfold, 'Continuous research Art Nielsen to AD 2000', *Journal of the Market Research Society*, vol. 36, no. 1, pp. 19–28.

14 Information Resources Inc. section adapted from the following: 'VideOcart is set to roll into supermarket aisles', *Marketing News*, 7 November 1988, p. 32; 'Coming to a shopping cart near you: TV Commercials', *Business Week*, 30 May 1988, pp. 61–62; 'VideoCart shopping cart with computer screen creates new ad medium that also gathers data', *Marketing News*, 9 May 1988, pp. 1–2; 'IRI rolls into future with video carts', *Advertising Age*, 2 May 1988, p. 6.

15 This section on Metier Management Systems is reprinted from William E. Gregory Jr, 'Time to ask hard-nosed questions', *Sales and Marketing*

Management, October 1989, vol. 141, pp. 88–91. Reprinted with permission of *Sales and Marketing Management*, 355 Park Avenue South, NY 10010–1789.

16   Frito-Lady section adapted from Douglas G. Shaw and Vincent C. Perro, 'Beating the odds: five reasons why companies excel', *Management Review*, August 1992, pp. 15–19.

17   Adams section adapted from Bill Allen and Maureen Johnson, 'A new market for childrenswear – how Adams took its "Apple" to Spain', *Admap*, April 1994, pp. 12–14. NTC Publications Ltd.

18   Bili-blanket section, including figure and tables, reprinted from N. Mohan Reddy, 'Market opportunity analysis for emerging technologies', *Management Decision*, vol. 28, no. 8, 1990, pp. 10–19.

19   Abbot Laboratories section is reprinted with permission from the June 1985 issue of *Business Marketing*. Copyright, Crain Communications Inc.

Chapter 5

Buyer behaviour

INTRODUCTION

In both consumer and business-to-business markets the manner in which buyers behave and the factors which influence this behaviour must be understood by marketing decision makers. Understanding buyer behaviour plays an important part in planning marketing strategy. Selecting target markets, setting marketing objectives and developing marketing plans is influenced by the marketing decision maker's knowledge and perceptions of the behaviour of buyers in the market.

In the case of consumer markets, buyer behaviour can be strongly influenced by other factors within their environment. The strongest of these factors are often social, cultural, personal or psychological in nature. These factors shape behaviour and also produce changes which marketing decision makers must take into account. The behaviour of buyers is also critically important when companies enter foreign markets.

In this chapter we present examples from both consumer and business-to-business marketing. Examples of the impact of social/personal and cultural/psychological factors on consumer behaviour are demonstrated. The buying decision process in a business-to-business situation is covered. This includes the elements of information search, evaluation of alternatives and the decision making unit or buyer chain.

FACTORS INFLUENCING CONSUMER BEHAVIOUR

Consumer buyer behaviour may be influenced by social or personal factors. These factors may affect the needs and wants of consumers, creating new demands resulting in organisations having to adopt new ways of meeting needs and communicating their message.

Social/personal factors

Toys[1]

The increasing sophistication of children's toys and games probably reflects the earlier advancement of modern day children as opposed to their counterparts of ten or twenty years ago. Fashion consciousness is also a factor which has infiltrated children's perspectives. They are subjected to greater outside influences such as television, videos, etc. Children are increasingly watching what are deemed as adult programmes. All these factors have tended to dilute the degree of parental influence and increased the child's influence somewhat. A survey by Mintel in 1992 found that parents listen to their children when making purchasing decisions, and the influence of children peaks in the 5–11 age group. Even parents are slow to recognise the changes which have resulted in a gap between the types of toys that children want and the types that adults think children want.

A general trend has occurred whereby toys that were once suitable for older children are now suitable for younger ones. Children are adopting more complex toys at an earlier age. According to Fisher Price boys give up traditional action figures at 5 years old instead of 7 as previously. Manufacturers have introduced relatively sophisticated computer-based toys and games and have also incorporated electronics into traditional products. The market share of electronic-based games has now gained leadership with CD games being one of the biggest sellers in the UK for Christmas 1993. In the early 1990s Europe's toy market grew mostly as a result of electronic games. With European children developing more sophisticated tastes earlier in life, the time scale within which any particular toy can be sold to children is narrowing.

Traditional toys for girls such as Barbie (Mattel Toys) and Sindy dolls (Hasbro) have increased in sophistication. Mattel conducts focus groups in different countries and uses a large library of girls' magazines to monitor trends among children. When first introduced about 30 years ago Sindy was an early teenager with traditional values. Now the doll is an ambitious career girl in the late teens. Barbie has been a Mod, an airline pilot and a Unicef ambassador. To this extent the dolls reflect established trends in society as a whole.

The way in which products are now promoted has also changed. Music is assuming critical importance in current advertising, and it must also have credibility among children by using the right language. The promotion of films such as Jurassic Park and the merchandise associated with it are also big business.

Cultural and psychological factors

Marketing of Religion[2]

The falling attendances in churches clearly indicates a change in behaviour of the public in relation to religion. In some cases the traditional religions are losing 'market share' to the new evangelical churches that are attracting the young. One of the responses to this change in behaviour has been the setting up of the Churches' Advertising Network (CAN) by the traditional churches to apply marketing techniques to the problem of a fall off in the practising of religion. Advertising through the media of radio and outdoor advertising has been used to promote the various churches and religion mainly during the major religious festivals of Easter and Christmas. During Easter 1994 a campaign was conducted on radio in selected regions targeted primarily at lapsed or non-attendees. It is intended to develop such campaigns into a concerted strategy.

Unlike most traditional product or service marketing, the promotion of religion cannot promise delivery of a specific tangible benefit, and some marketing commentators maintain that the 'product' itself must be modified to bring it more up-to-date. The US evangelist church and other similar churches attempt to overcome this problem through tangibilising their message by claiming they will perform miracles at meetings of their congregations.

The needs which churches attempt to satisfy are primarily spiritual, but in terms of Maslow's 'hierarchy of needs' these may be translated into social, esteem or self-actualisation needs. In the UK a particular outdoor campaign by the Evangelical Alliance, representing mainly Pentecostalist Christians, used the themes of fear, emptiness and despair in the initial round of posters, and then hope, fulfilment and happiness in the latter round. The posters exhorted people to 'Talk to Jim' – which stood for Jesus In Me.

American Express

American Express experienced difficulty in consolidating its business in Japan because of the sense of embarrassment the Japanese felt in not paying bills with cash. Despite there being 70 million credit cards in circulation in Japan at the end of the 1980s they were not commonly used. Average credit card charge income in Japan was significantly below that in the USA. Many executives either had their bills paid directly by the company or were given cash allowances for purchasing goods and services, e.g. hotel bills, meals, taxi fares, etc. American Express was aware that Japanese executives wanted cash and a sense of security when travelling abroad. As a consequence of this, American Express offered the facility of allowing customers to withdraw over $2,000 in cash per month. This resulted in an expansion of business for American Express in Japan.

CONSUMER BEHAVIOUR

Leo Burnett[3]

'The Holy Grail of marketing', is how Josh McQueen, research director at Leo Burnett, a Chicago-based advertising agency, describes the link between what advertisers already know about consumers – their age, gender, income – and what they so desperately want to know, namely their buying habits. Surveys tell admen [sic] about consumers' attitudes towards products, but often that has little bearing on what they really do once they walk into a shop. Now the electronic scanners at supermarket checkouts are changing things. As researchers pour over the mounds of detailed data that scanners produce, a clearer picture of consumer behaviour is gradually emerging.

Few have done more pouring than Mr McQueen. With the help of IRI, a big market research company in Chicago which specialises in scanner data, he and his colleagues at Burnett have studied consumer behaviour and how it is affected by different kinds of advertising and promotion. What they have learned turns much conventional marketing wisdom on its head.

Admen [sic] usually divide consumers into two groups: those who buy their product and those who do not. The aim of marketing and advertising is to hold on to existing customers while wooing new ones.

Burnett's research shows that this view is far too simplistic. In each product category, says Mr McQueen, consumers actually fall into four different behavioural groups, each with its own 'buying strategy'. 'Long loyals' are committed to one brand regardless of price or competition. 'Rotators', too, care little about price, but for them variety does matter. They regularly switch among a handful of their favourite brands. Similarly, 'deal sensitives' switch among a small set of brands but almost always buy the one that is on special offer. Finally there are 'price sensitives', who will purchase whatever product is cheapest regardless of brand.

The percentage of consumers adopting each shopping strategy differs from one product category to the next. Ketchup buyers act differently from regular buyers of cat food or breakfast cereals. Even brands within a certain category, because of their histories and past marketing, can have a disproportionate number of consumers in one group or another. Coffee is a category dominated by rotators, but nearly all of the few long loyals buy one brand, Folgers. To complicate matters still further, few consumers adopt the same buying strategy for every product category.

Why does this matter? Because of another surprising finding from an earlier study by IRI: in cases where advertising can be shown to have increased sales of established brands, around 70 per cent of growth came not from new users but from those who already buy the product. The shopping-strategy research helps to explain how this can happen. Both rotators and deal sensitives already buy the brand, but only occasionally. With the right persuasion (for rotators, an alluring advertisement; for deal sensitives, a good deal) they can be induced to buy the brand more often at the expense of another brand in their repertoire.

As an example Mr McQueen points to Maxwell House coffee, which IRI has studied in depth. A few years ago Maxwell House's managers launched a big advertising campaign to revive its flagging brand name. The campaign prompted a 69 per cent increase in sales. Of that, less than a fifth came from sales to entirely new customers. The rest of the additional sales went to existing users and the vast majority of these were rotators.

Mr McQueen argues that, once companies realise that most sales gains are likely to come from existing customers, knowing how many of each type of consumer their brands attract becomes crucial. A firm whose brand already appeals to most of the long loyals and rotators in a market will be cutting its own throat if it slashes prices low enough to appeal to price sensitives. Conversely, a brand bought mainly by deal and price sensitives might be wise to stop advertising on television and shift spending into price-cutting promotions.

Illuminating as it is, the Burnett study raises nearly as many questions as it answers. How do shopping strategies fit together with more traditional demographic categories? Do people's buying habits change with their income, or as they grow older? So long as the answers to these questions remain murky, researchers at Burnett and elsewhere will have a lot more work to do. Back to that scanner data, Mr McQueen.

FURTHER REFERENCE

Chapter 6, Segmentation and Positioning: Behavioural (pp. 96–98)

THE BUYING DECISION PROCESS[4]

The market for building materials and architectural products in the UK is characterised by a large number of suppliers and an even larger number of potential buyers. One way in which these products are procured for formal building projects is through specification of the product by the building designer(s) at the design stage of the project. Designers, many of whom are architects, will choose a particular product for a particular function within the building. This may be an external element such as a brick or a roofing tile, or an internal element such as a door handle. In deciding on which product to use the decision maker normally goes through the process as indicated in Figure 5.1.

The process contains elements of both consumer buying models and industrial buying behaviour. The presence of consumer-type elements is probably due to the personal nature of design where the designer is creating something which is an expression of his/her own ideas. The stimulus for the process is derived from the design brief after which the decision maker commences on an elimination path within the product hierarchy. This begins with broad product family, e.g. roof: flat roof or pitched roof; then product class, e.g. pitched roof: slates or tiles; product line, e.g. tiles: clay or concrete; product type, e.g. concrete tile: shape or pattern; brand, e.g. Redland or CRH; and final item, e.g. the colour.

Figure 5.1 Decision making process

Information search

The search process varies according to the particular task at hand. Tasks fall into three types:

i)   new task
ii) repeat task
iii) modified task

New task situations require more in-depth search and evaluation as this usually involves considering new products unfamiliar to the designer. Repeat task situations are solved by a combination of applying previously used products and experience. This results in an evoked set of products which are then considered. Modified tasks are solved by a combination of experience and search for new products.

The information search generally includes a high-involvement active search. The duration and complexity is dependent on the buy-class as identified above. The sources of information include general catalogues and indices, manufacturers' literature, colleagues, the trade/professional press, and manufacturers' sales personnel.

Evaluation of alternatives

The evaluation of alternative products where visual aspects are important is largely carried out using the criteria of appearance, perceived quality, performance, availability/delivery and price. Certain minimum performance standards are taken as given and it is on this basis that products are evaluated. Designers usually possess some knowledge of price within which they can set a framework for the evaluation process. The overall approach to evaluation is in general a balanced one, with an emphasis on quality and appearance in the initial stages, but weighing up all factors simultaneously.

The main methods by which building material manufacturers/ suppliers attempt to influence this process is through advertising and personal selling. They also produce product specification information and design guidance for their materials because the designer is required to draw up a design specification for each major element of the building. Advertising is normally placed in the professional and trade press and this is bolstered by various public relations activities such as new product launches, exhibitions, etc. Personal selling is usually carried out by a geographical network of sales representatives who attempt to build working relationships with designers, providing them with product and design information.

DECISION MAKING UNIT/BUYER CHAIN[5]

The construction industry in the UK exhibits a unique process, in comparison with the manufacturing industry, in producing the final product, a building. Most construction projects must be carried out in accordance with the requirements of the clients (customers). These requirements are normally translated into a design and specification of products to be used, usually by independent architects commissioned by the client. The contractor who will eventually carry out the work takes no part in this process, and in many cases has not even been appointed at the design stage. This results in a division between the design and production stages of the project.

The complicated nature of the construction process results in a range of individuals and professions becoming involved in the decision making process for the selection of building materials. For relatively large building projects up to nine different professions could be involved in the materials selection process. These include the client, the architect, the quantity surveyor, the building surveyor, the building services engineer, the consulting engineer, the interior designer, the contractor and the official planning authority.

In many situations the architect is generally the major decision maker on material selection. The quantity surveyor often influences the decision in terms of price/cost and the client will often give final approval of the selection. Depending on the materials under consideration the other members of the buyer chain exert various influences. The contractor will often be the final 'purchaser' of the materials.

In the case of flooring products on large projects the following members often form the decision making unit: architect, interior designer, quantity surveyor, client and finally the contractor. Brick manufacturers such as Butterly Brick and London Brick target the different members of this DMU primarily through advertising and personal selling. Sales personnel seek to establish relationships with individual architects, architectural practices, interior designers, etc. Efforts are also made to target clients such as the large supermarket chains, Tesco, Sainsbury etc. The companies try to influence members of the decision making unit through sales presentations using product samples, the building of model floors, visiting previous installations with the decision maker, providing hand or computer generated drawings, or by offering specialist design services for the application of their products to the project. The service may also extend to advising during construction of the particular building element. Much effort by companies is put into the process of having their materials specified by the decision making unit, ranging from identification of the actual project and members of the decision making unit, to final advice during construction of the building.

IBM

Traditionally IBM has aimed much of its marketing and selling efforts at the information technology experts within target organisations. Sales representatives with specialist product knowledge had built ongoing relationships with these decision makers. With the advent of user-friendly software including multimedia the company has widened its target to include sales and marketing managers, financial managers and also general managers or chief executive officers. The chief executive of IBM is advocating a more service oriented and friendly approach to customers. He is leading the way by going out to meet decision makers himself. The desire is to become more customer oriented.

The understanding of multimedia technology and applications is more accessible and does not necessarily require the specialist knowledge of the information technology department, as did the mainframe and network systems. The purchase of a costly multimedia computer system can involve a number of key individuals as identified above. In many organisations it is the sales and marketing, financial management, IT management, chief executive and other departmental managers who make up the decision making unit. IBM have secured greater access to the members of this unit when offering multimedia products. This is also reflected in moves to broaden the scope of advertising to include the broader range of decision makers.

CONCLUSION

The influence of the external environment in the form of societal or cultural factors and the manner in which individuals interact with their colleagues, family or others to form decision making units have important implications for marketing decision makers. Marketers must identify these behavioural characteristics and decision making processes where relevant and develop strategies to deal with them.

NOTES

1 Toys section adapted from: Allyson L. Stewart, 'Rules of the toy game different for Europe's kids', *Marketing News*, 25 October 1993, p. 9; John Thornhill, 'Why grown men dream of a future with Barbie', *Financial Times*, 17 September 1992, p. 19; Christine McGourty, 'CD games are top in toytown; doll sales thrive as boys go electronic', *Daily Telegraph*, 27 September 1993; Ruth Nicholas, 'The kids are all bright', *Marketing Week*, 22 October 1993, p. 30–34; Matthew Grimm, 'It's time for fun', *Brandweek*, 14 December 1992, pp. 23–24; 'Children – the influencing factor 1991', *Housewares UK*, Mintel, February 1992; Charles Darwent, 'Making it tough for tots', *Management Today*, June 1992, pp. 55–58.
2 Marketing of religion section adapted from Lindsay McMurdo and Helen Jones, 'Prepare to meet thy maker', *Marketing Week*, 1 April 1994, pp. 30–33.

3 Leo Burnett section directly reprinted from 'Strategic shopping: consumer behaviour', *The Economist*, September 1992, vol. 324, no. 7778, pp. 82–83. © *The Economist*.
4 Brian MacNamee, 'The opportunity for intermediaries in the provision of information within a given market structure', Dissertation for MA Marketing, Polytechnic of Central London, 1991.
5 Brian MacNamee, op. cit.

Chapter 6

Segmentation and positioning

INTRODUCTION

Most organisations who offer a product or service to a consumer find that these consumers can be grouped into different segments with one or more distinguishing characteristics or factors which differentiate them. By identifying these factors marketers may be able to meet the needs of these different segments more closely, whether it be through increased customisation of the product or the way it promotes or distributes to each different group. By segmenting the market, an organisation may be able to tailor their marketing strategy cost effectively to the needs of the segment.

There are a number of factors which can be used in identifying segments, the most important being the behavioural, geographical, demographic and psychographic factors. Behavioural segmentation may be related to buyer/user or purchase/use characteristics. User status, occasions of use, usage rate and product benefits are the more important aspects of behavioural segmentation. Once the market has been segmented the organisation is then in a position to develop and target its marketing strategy at the segment(s) which are most attractive to it. However, within these target markets there are likely to be competitive offers, and this requires the positioning of the company's product/service within the market or segment. Furthermore, on many occasions products or services need to be repositioned because consumers do not respond to the offer in the manner expected. Product positioning may be based on some of the factors used to segment markets such as benefits or user/buyer characteristics. Other factors include quality/price and positioning in relation to competitors.

In essence positioning is how the product is perceived by the consumer and depends a lot on the image generated of the product. This action differentiates the offer from its competitors; ultimately, however, it is the consumer who positions the offer through their perception of the product.

TYPES OF SEGMENTATION AND POSITIONING

Behavioural

Behavioural segmentation is based on the behaviour of the buyer or decision making unit. This may depend on their attitudes, experiences, knowledge, reaction or response to an offer.

Girobank[1]

The UK government established Girobank in 1968 to provide a basic means of transmitting money. By the mid-1980s it had established itself as a full clearing bank. The bank conducted its business through the 20,000 outlets of the UK Post Office. In 1984 Girobank decided to expand by targeting the small business sector, defined as companies with less than £1 million turnover but big enough to be registered for VAT (not-for-profit and businesses in the agricultural sector were excluded). It was also decided not to offer banking services on a wide basis to all small businesses, but to target those customers who would gain most benefit from the bank's services and would be profitable for the bank.

Girobank decided to conduct a study of the market in order to identify customers who would meet this criteria. In order to segment the market it decided to use the criteria of products/services actually used in terms of type, for example, overdraft, opening hours, access to branch etc., and also in terms of attitudes towards banks and their services. This was because the bank only offered a limited range of services which would be of benefit to particular types of customer. The study concentrated on four main factors: overdraft facilities, financial business advice, branch convenience and interest earning facilities. It was clear that bases of segmentation such as Standard Industrial Classification or sales levels would not yield the necessary match between the bank's services and potential customers needs, as these classifications did not reflect the customer's financial behaviour. It was therefore decided to carry out a cluster analysis[2] to determine segments based on customers' attitudes and behaviour. Part of this process included the identification of factors or trends which influenced behaviour. These were found to be the following:

1 The need for borrowing facilities
2 The holding of surplus funds
3 Net users of cash
4 Advice (users)
5 Low users of cash
6 Frequent depositors
7 Saturday opening considered important
8 Branch convenience considered unimportant

Ten market segments were then identified based on these factors. These were the following:

1 *Would-be big companies*
   Relatively large, typically manufacturing and financial/property/ professional services companies. Generally heavy users of bank services and self-confident in their financial dealings.

2 *The simple life*
   Mainly retailers and other suppliers of consumer services. Smaller firms generally with a lower use of, and requirement for, banking services. Longer opening hours are more important to them than other groups, and they generally use only one bank with which they are generally content.

3 *The small builder*
   High users of bank services, credit and cash. Usually use more than one bank and not particularly loyal to one bank.

4 *The restaurateur*
   Require long opening hours and have a higher need for cash withdrawal. Characteristically work in the catering business including licensed trade and hotel/guest houses. Little requirement for night safe facilities and contain a higher proportion of small (less than £100,000 annual turnover) companies.

5 *Leave me alone, I'm all right*
   Low need for advice, and their requirement for banking services is less than average.

6 *Affluent companies not dealing with the public*
   High proportion of manufacturing and financial/property/professional services companies. Lower demand for banking services than 'would-be big companies'. Higher than average need to draw cash to pay wages.

7 *Please pay me today*
High credit demand with a larger than average proportion in the service industry. Higher than average amount of payments made by post and more common for them to use more than one bank.

8 *Neither a lender nor a borrower be*
Demand a higher level of services but lower than average use of these services. Cite branch convenience as being important but have a lower than average need to withdraw and/or deposit cash. Usually satisfied with their current provider.

9 *The small, rich shopkeeper*
Higher use of cash and higher users of night safe facilities. Maintain they want credit and advice facilities but are not actually high users of these services. Found mainly in the retail, catering and consumer services business, and a higher proportion are run by women.

10 *The northerner*
The main characteristic of this group is that they are found in the north of England.

The clusters which displayed the closest match with Girobank's services were:

1 Would-be big companies – attractive to banks with strong saving facilities.
4 The restaurateur – attractive to banks with a widespread branch network.
6 Affluent companies not dealing with the public – market penetration depended on the competitiveness of the service offer and the success of promotion.
9 The small, rich shopkeeper – key success factor was the offering of advantageous credit facilities.

Girobank entered the small business sector and established itself, with the result that the sector began to make a significant contribution to the bank's profitability.

Behavioural – user status segmentation

User status segmentation uses the status of the consumer in terms of disposition to purchase as a means of segmentation.

Fingerhut[3]

Fingerhut, the US mail-order company, uses the state of buyer readiness as one means of segmenting its market. This includes the categories of potential customers, new customers, regular customers and long-term customers. The key to the company's success is the information database it holds on customers. The company uses different types of marketing programmes to target these groups. In attempting to attract new customers, advertising in newspapers, magazines and on television is used. This is also backed by direct mailing of promotional literature and special merchandise catalogues. Once a customer responds to this promotional activity the company then attempts to determine the prospect for that customer to become a regular or long-term customer. The company uses the communication opportunity with the customer to gain more information on that customer, which helps it determine the user category the customer may fit into. By including a series of information gathering examinations in its communication with the customer, the company can determine the individual's credit risk, social status, etc. A series of offers are then made to the customer with different degrees of credit. This helps Fingerhut to determine the credit worthiness of the customer, and enables them to estimate whether they will be profitable in the long run. Credit is then set at a level that reflects the company's estimate of the credit risk of the customer.

Once the customer has been established as a good risk, Fingerhut then attempts to turn them into regular or long-term customers. By utilising the information held on the customer, offers are then tailored to that individual customer. Regular or long-term customers are further segmented according to categories such as their purchase record. Such customers may be targeted with particular speciality merchandise such as electronics, clothing, car accessories, etc. Regular and long-term customers are often given very favourable credit terms and in 1992 80 per cent of Fingerhut's revenue came from existing customers.

Behavioural – occasion of use

Occasion of use employs the criteria of the occasion on which a product or service may be used as a means of segmentation.

Timex[4]

The watchmaker Timex pursued a low price strategy in the 1970s and early 1980s. However, when Asian and European competitors began to compete on price, Timex decided to reposition its product. The company produced watches for market segments based on the occasion of the product's use. Some of the new products produced were designed to be used while pursuing leisure and fitness activities. In 1984 Timex produced the Triathlon which corresponded with the holding of the Olympics in that year. Marketing efforts were targeted at those individuals partaking in physical fitness and sports activities, with particular models emphasising benefits such as accurate time measurement for particular sports. This strategy attracted younger consumers. The Triathlon sold around 400,000 units in 1984 and by the end of the 1980s Timex held about one-third of the US watch market.

Timex is continuing its occasions of use segmentation into the 1990s with the introduction of upmarket fashion watches which it licenses under the Nautica clothes brand for men. Nautica is an upmarket casual wear brand sold through speciality stores. The product line contains thirty models aimed at men aged between 25 and 54.

FURTHER REFERENCE

Chapter 6, Segmentation and Positioning: Repositioning (p. 107)

Behavioural – usage rate

Mercury

The 1980s witnessed a revolution in the UK telecommunications industry consisting of privatisation, technological change and de-regulation. Due to certain restrictions Mercury chose to concentrate its efforts on heavy phone users. From the beginning, Mercury sought to attract business from large financial companies in the City of London. Mercury offered an attractive package to the large business – cheap phone bills and a high quality service. Extensive advertising campaigns stressed the message of cheaper calls and a reliable digital network constructed in the 1980s.

Benefit segmentation

Lone Star Industries [5]

An American company, Lone Star Industries, invented an advanced concrete named Pyrament which is much stronger than standard concrete and also cures much faster. Standard concrete takes from seven to fourteen days to cure properly while Pyrament sets in four hours. Furthermore, only 18 cm of Pyrament is needed to give the same strength as 25.5 cm of standard concrete.

In its initial marketing of the product the company identified those markets where the benefits of the product – fast curing and strength – would be of greatest advantage. One market which was identified was that of airport runway repairs, while another consisted of motorway surfacing, which is ideally carried out at times of least traffic flow, i.e. at night. The benefits of fast curing to these markets is clear – downtime periods are very costly therefore the least amount of downtime the better. This allowed Lone Star to charge a much higher price for its concrete – standard concrete costs between $50 to $75 per ton, while Pyrament could be priced at $120 to $180 per ton.

By focusing on those markets where benefit sensitivity was greatest and segmenting its market accordingly the company gained a greater return on its product.

Geographical segmentation

Nordwest Zeitung[6]

The newspaper industry is one which lends itself readily to geographic segmentation, in particular local newspapers. The Nordwest Zeitung (NWZ) in Germany developed its strategy around such an approach from its inception after the Second World War. The company recognised that people were interested in news relevant to their local area, but also wanted national and international news. The NWZ was published in a number of different areas and the paper contained four different sections. One of these sections was devoted to the local news for a particular area and the remaining sections of national/regional, international and entertainment were common to all additions.

The strategy was taken one step further when in 1950 NWZ set up a co-operative venture with another newspaper, the Ostfriesen Zeitung. This expanded with the addition of ten smaller local newspapers to the partnership. The non-local sections produced by the two larger papers were sold to the local papers who developed the local section. Each local paper was marketed *as a local paper* with the main local story on the front page. The partnership also benefited from economies in securing advertising revenue. Total advertising revenue was secured by NWZ who then allocated it to the other partners on a geographical basis. This benefited the smaller local papers with whom many advertisers and agencies would not deal with because of their size. The advertisers chose the appropriate combinations of coverage offered by the local papers. As a result of the advertising agreement, the local newspapers' advertising revenues increased by as much as 50 per cent. By the nature of the newspaper product, the sale of advertising space was also segmented on a geographical basis. By 1987 the newspaper partnership recorded circulation figures covering over 84 per cent of the market.

Psychographic/demographic segmentation[7]

Psychographic segmentation involves the use of individual's lifestyles, social class, personalities and associated interests, attitudes and opinions, as a means of segmenting markets.

Social and demographic changes in France have led to changes in the make-up of French retirees. They are more numerous, have a greater life expectation, retire with a better income, and have had more prosperous working lives. Typologically, 'active idealists' are becoming the dominant group with a concurrent decline of the 'simple and quiet' segment. These segments have been profiled in Figure 6.1.

The characteristics of these segments have implications for marketing communications with the groups. These are factors taken into account by *Notre Temps* magazine which is targeted at France's retired population. Depending on whether it is advertising or editorial the magazine adopts the approach of using rational messages in its communication, avoiding over-use of image, the suggestion of isolation and the use of models at least about fifteen years younger than the target audience. An image of 'active serenity' is also employed in communications.

TARGET MARKETING

Differentiated marketing

The firm focuses on a variety of market segments and then develops a different marketing mix for each.

The Burton Group[8]   During the 1980s the Burton Group developed a multiple segmentation strategy for its range of shops. The company targeted distinct customer groups using different types of retail outlets with different images and customer appeals – Top Shop was targeted at the teenage customer; Principles at the so-called 'style' market; Dorothy

	Active idealists	Simple and quiet
Profile	Man (49%)	Woman (66%)
	Aged under 65 (75%)	Aged over 65 (62%)
	City of over 100,000 pop. (31%) or Paris area (28%)	City under 20,000 pop. (38%) Average to modest
	Affluent	circumstances
Characteristics	The youngest of the types	Lives as quietly as possible
	Behaviour: active, go-getting, enterprising	Very traditional in her lifestyles
	His ideal: a society whose lifestyles evolve	and tastes
	He likes whatever is new but rejects	Happy with her family
	excesses	Has her house and a small bank account
Consumption	Enjoyment on a reasonable basis	Very limited (heavy emphasis on mail-order purchasing)
Bank	Has confidence in banks. Open-minded, modern: many credit cards and several bank accounts	Minimum use of banking services, but has average amount of savings
Distribution	Enjoys being a consumer. Good frequentation of distribution channels. Prefers the channels that provide enjoyment on a reasonable basis	Requires reassurance and proximity. Mail-order purchasing is the only channel of which she makes above-average use
Leisure time activities	Ranks among the senior citizens who engage in the greatest number of active sports (48%)	Does not engage in sports to any great extent
	Ranks Marco Polo where travel is concerned	Does not travel much Does not read much
	Often takes more than one trip a year	Does not do much reading of newspapers or magazines
	An intellectual: the number of his book purchases is higher than the average	Does not listen to the radio very much
	Media consumption higher than average	Her time devoted to television is greater than average

Figure 6.1 Psychographic/demographic segments

Perkins at the young female market; Debenhams at the family market and Burton at the male consumer.

This may also be regarded as a form of demographic segmentation.

Concentrated marketing

Under this approach the marketer concentrates on a highly specific market or segment.

Steinway pianos The company defines its target market as the concert and professional pianist and all marketing effort is focused on this segment. Other customer groups purchase their pianos but do not form their target market.

Undifferentiated marketing

Undifferentiated marketing is similar to mass marketing, where the company targets a broad spectrum of the marketing without tailoring the offer to particular segments.

Black and Decker In the late 1970s, Japanese competition in the power tool market forced Black and Decker to move away from a policy of customising products for each market to a policy of making a smaller number of products that could be sold everywhere with the same basic marketing approach. By the mid-1980s Black and Decker had regained its 20 per cent share of the market.

Identifying targets

ICI Europe[9]

In embarking on its direct mail campaign in Western Europe ICI Europe's objectives were to raise awareness and increase the use of its chemical formulations among individual European formulators. It also wanted to develop a database of formulators, featuring the market segment in which they work and their interests in terms of chemical formulations. ICI Europe contracted a specialist list company, IBIS, to generate the list of potential target formulators for the campaign. One option was to use lists generated by magazines in which the ICI Chemical Formulators Division advertises. However, these magazines did not have facilities for renting lists. Lists from only three publications came close to matching ICI's requirement of named individuals within particular markets. IBIS however, was part of a consortium called Business Lists Europe who were able to supply lists with named individuals but generally at general manager level. The market segment could usually be identified from these lists, but did have the drawback of different countries having different methods of categorisation. This was overcome through further refining of the lists. In cases where named individuals were unable to be identified, the mail-shot was addressed to a particular function such as 'Chief Chemical Formulator'. This was translated into the appropriate language with the help of the European partners. The letters were mailed resulting in an average response rate of about 5 per cent.

POSITIONING

When the segment(s) has been identified, the product must be positioned within the segment. However, the exercise of segmenting may also automatically position the product. Products may also be positioned by benefits, as in the case of Pyrament cement on pp. 100–101, by user as in the case of demographic and/or psychographic segmentation and user status, by occasions of use and other segmentation criteria. Some examples of positioning and repositioning are presented in the following section.

Dr Martens[10]

The original Dr. Martens footwear was based on the design of a German doctor called Maertens and was licensed by a British company Whites who began production in the 1960s. The name was anglicised to Martens. Originally produced with a steel toe, the shoe was aimed at postmen and construction workers, then in the 1960s it became associated with skin-heads and latterly as an item of fashion popular with both sexes. The 'alternative' footwear shop Red or Dead was one of the retailers to adopt the Dr. Marten as a fashion item. Some designers even used the shoes. The company has also adopted a strategy of differentiation in feeding the trends in fashion. The current positioning of Dr. Martens as a fashion item is supported through the availability of a wide variety of styles, all with the familiar air-cushioned sole.

Positioning by association (with competitors)

Ford

Companies may position their product by associating it with another product. The objective of this, however, is not always to induce the consumer to purchase the promoting company's product. The product/ service with which the positioned product is compared may be one which is regarded as one of the most superior products on the market. Ford adopted this approach with its marketing of the Ford Granada Sports Coupé. In its campaign it compared the Granada Sports with the Mercedes 450 SLC. In its advertisements Ford referred to the Mercedes as: 'the world's finest sports coupé, and a remarkable achievement in automotive engineering'. However the price of the Mercedes at $23,976 at the time left it out of reach of many Americans: 'the Mercedes 450 SLC is a possession of pride for those who can easily afford its formidable price tag'.

The advertisement contained a picture of both cars, each with the price displayed above them, and went on to outline the features of the Granada. A short table also gave comparisons for selected features of both cars, such as dimensions, engine displacement, etc. The Granada Sports Coupé was priced at $4,189, nearly six times cheaper than the Mercedes. The Mercedes was targeted more at those with high disposable incomes, and also invariably took on the role of status symbol for those who purchased it. The Granada Sports on the other hand was a more affordable purchase and was unlikely to offer the status which Mercedes customers sought. It was unlikely that the target markets crossed to any significant degree. The advertisement concluded: 'If money is really no object you should certainly consider the Mercedes 450 SLC', but urged purchasers to consider the Granada in any circumstances.

By comparing its car with the Mercedes 450 SLC, Ford was positioning it against what was regarded as a benchmark in that particular product class. The objective was not to attract Mercedes customers to switch, but was offering those who could afford the Granada a car which Ford claimed could put them in the same class as the Mercedes.

Repositioning

Guinness/Grand Metropolitan [11]

The whisky industry provides an example of a product repositioning which resulted in increased success of the product. For years, the proliferation of brands led to conflicting and sometimes poor image; in some instances it was perceived as an old man's drink and accordingly priced as a commodity item. Overproduction was a recurring feature of the industry particularly in the late 1970s and early 1980s.

Takeovers in the industry in the 1980s led to the repositioning of the product by the four main companies; GrandMet, Guinness, Allied-Lyons and Seagram. These companies, in particular Guinness, with its takeover of Arthur Bells in 1985 and the Distillers Company Ltd. in 1986, set out to reposition whisky and expand markets in Europe and internationally. At the time of the takeover Distillers had a portfolio of 150 mainly whisky brands produced by twelve operating companies. Operations including sales and marketing were organised along brand lines, with the result that brands were often competing with each other. The formation of United Distillers by Guinness initiated a change from a brand perspective to a geographic or market-place perspective, focusing on brand portfolios. The global market was divided into four marketing regions – North America, Asia-Pacific, UK/Europe and International.

Many low-end brands were discontinued and the remaining ones repositioned. To help achieve this the company carried out a major international market research project to determine the perception of the brands in the market among consumers. The findings led to the development of a positioning strategy along the lines of price and psychographic characteristics. Price levels of brands were divided into deluxe, premium and standard; and psychographic segmentation consisted of extrovert and traditional brands. Guinness also developed exclusive whisky brands akin to fine wines. These included Grand Parr Elizabethan scotch at $850 a bottle, Johnnie Walker Oldest at $120 and Johnnie Walker Premier at $85. Guinness was able to increase prices while also increasing global sales. Now the drinks business has almost become a fashion business and Guinness has built a perception of quality into their brands.

The promotional tools used in the positioning strategy included advertising, sponsorship and sales promotion. Another tool of the strategy was packaging, including bottle and box design as well as labels. Distribution was also crucial to success and co-operative distribution agreements were made between the big four companies. In the case of United Distillers the European market was given two portfolios of brands – one distributed by fmcg (fast moving consumer goods) distributors concentrating on supermarkets, etc., and the other by the more trade based organisations. In the USA, Guinness acquired Schenleys who held the distribution rights to the very successful Dewars brand in America. Guinness' control of distribution went from 25 per cent to 75 per cent within a short number of years.

In the first four years of its operation United Distillers turnover and operating profits increased significantly. Industry operating profits remain steady and the future for whisky looks secure. New markets in China, Indochina, India and Eastern Europe are now coming on stream.

FURTHER REFERENCE

Chapter 10, Marketing Channels: The distribution strategy (p. 180–182)

Mills and Boon

Towards the end of 1992, Mills and Boon – a large publisher of romantic fiction – decided to revamp the company's image and reposition the product. With the new look, Mills and Boon plans to target women aged 25–40. Mills and Boon found that a relatively high proportion of women in that age group were reluctant to read a Mills and Boon book, apparently because they perceived the characters and the plots to be out of date.

The new look launched in October 1993 featured among other things a new logo and new cover designs. The well known pink rose symbol was replaced by a white rose underlining the company name. The company also decided to reposition the whole of its range. Each of the six series was redesigned and some given new names. 'Medical Romances' became known as 'Love on Call' and the 'Masquerade' series was retitled 'Legacy of Love'.

CONCLUSION

The examples presented in this chapter show the range of factors which organisations can use to segment and position their products. The identification of these factors may be through formal market research as in the case of Girobank or simply through instinct or experience. Whatever method is used it is important that organisations get it right because of the more and more competitive nature of markets. The trend towards database marketing demonstrates the increasingly sophisticated nature of segmentation and targeting. This is demonstrated in the case of the Fingerhut example.

Where mistakes are made it is often necessary to reposition, but most marketing decision makers will agree that accurate targeting and positioning is necessary to gain maximum return on marketing investment.

NOTES

1 Girobank section adapted from Colin Roach, 'Segmentation of the small business market on the basis of banking requirements', *International Journal of Bank Marketing*, 1989, vol. 7, no. 2, pp. 10–16.

2 The placement of variables in clusters based upon the values these objects have for a set of variables. The clusters are not defined a priori but are formed by the cluster analysis procedure itself. An object is assigned a cluster in such a way that it is more associated with the other objects in its cluster than with objects in any other cluster.

3 Fingerhut section adapted from Jim Bessen, 'Riding the marketing information wave', *Harvard Business Review*, September–October 1993, pp. 156, 157.

4 Timex section adapted from the following: Barbara Lippert, 'Timex sinks to great depths for sport worth watching', *AdWeek (National Marketing edition)*, 27 January 1986, p. 1; Elaine Underwood, 'Licensing: Timex an upscale watch', *Brandweek*, 26 April 1993, p. 4; Cara Applebaum, 'High time for Timex', *AdWeek's Marketing Week*, 29 July 1991, p. 24; Christie Brown, 'Sweat chic (Timex markets sports watches)' *Forbes*, 5 September 1988, p. 96; David W. Cravens and Shannon H. Shipp, 'Market Driven Strategies for Competitive Advantage', *Business Horizons*, January–February 1991, pp. 55–60.

5 Lone Star Industries section adapted from: Gregory D. Morris, 'Lone Star gambles on super cement', *Chemical Week*, 8 February 1989, p. 14; Pamela Zurer, 'Fast-curing, stronger cement developed', *Chemical and Engineering News*, 13 February 1989, pp. 37–38; Alan J. McGrath, 'Ten Timeless Truths About Pricing', *The Journal of Consumer Marketing*, Winter 1991, vol. 8, no. 1, pp. 5–14; Tom Eisenhart, 'New product breaks the commodity mold', *Business Marketing*, January 1989, pp. 28–29; 'Cement provides quick cure', *ENR*, 29 June 1989, vol. 222, p. 32.

6 Nordwest Zeitung section adapted from Werner Ketelhohn, 'What do we mean by cooperative advantage?', *European Management Journal*, March 1993, vol. 11, no. 1, pp. 30–37.

7 Psychographic/demographic segmentation section, including Figure 6.1, reprinted from A. Moundlic, 'Communication with senior citizens', *Admap* (UK), March 1990, vol. 26, no. 3, pp. 33–35. Reprinted with permission of NTC Publications Ltd.

8 Burton Group section adapted from: David Walters and Derek Knee, *Long Range Planning*, 1989, vol. 22, no. 6, pp. 74–84; A. Palmer and I. Worthington,

The Business and Marketing Environment, London, McGraw-Hill, 1992.

9 ICI Europe section adapted from 'How two international campaigns optimised response', *Business Marketing Digest*, second quarter 1991, vol. 16, no. 2.

10 Dr Martens section adapted from: James Fallon, 'Dr. Martens launches Operation Europe', *Footwear News*, 19 April 1993, p. 23; Charles Darwent, 'Fashion Fascism and Dear old Doc', *Management Today*, April 1992, pp. 50–53; 'Red or Dead finds "easy does it", works', *Footwear News*, 17 August 1992, p. 66.

11 Guinness/Grand Metropolitan section adapted from the following: David Pearson 'When Value Topped Volume', *Director*, September 1992, p. 17; Philip Rawstorne, 'United Distillers: from whisky galore to whisky grand crus', *Financial Times*, 14 June 1990, p. 19; United Distillers promotional literature; Clive Simms, Adam Phillips and Trevor Richards, 'Developing a global pricing strategy', *Marketing and Research Today*, March 1992, pp. 3–14; Philip Rawstone, 'A successful blend', *Financial Times*, 21 January 1994, p. 17; Tony Jackson and John Ridding, 'Heady cocktail with lots of fizz', *Financial Times*, 21 January 1994, p. 17; 'Guinness PLC sees im- proved outlook for scotch whisky', *Wall Street Journal*, 8 Nov 1993; Peter Temple 'Scotch off the rocks?', *Accountancy*, October 1991, pp. 114–115; Sharon Reier, 'Getting scotch off the rocks: how Guinness gave scotch a new appeal and a new price range', *Financial World*, 6 August 1991, pp. 24–26; Hashi Syedain, 'Spirits are good for you', *Management Today*, October 1990, pp. 64–69; Hashi Syedain, 'Profile: Tony Greener', *Management Today*, September 1993, pp. 49–50.

Chapter 7

Products

INTRODUCTION

The product is the most important element in a company's marketing mix.

A product consists of certain features which the astute marketer converts into desired customer benefits. In other words, for a product to be successful, it must meet customer needs. A product may be called a bundle of benefits. Customers do not usually buy features, rather they buy what those features can do for them – the problems they solve, the money they save, the time they save, etc.

Because of the proliferation of products today and the widespread adoption of self-service retailing, branding and packaging are important in helping sell a company's product and differentiating it from competitors' offerings. Branding and packaging are often referred to as the silent salesmen for a product. Adding additional services to a company's core product (called augmenting the product) also helps to differentiate the product from competing products and increases the chances of success in a crowded market place. Augmenting the product may be as simple as offering home delivery, an extended guarantee, and so on.

Like all things in life, products too have a definite life span although in some cases products appear to be 'reborn'. Witness the continuing sales of records of the Doors and the Beatles through clever promotions. Sometimes, a product can be given a new lease of life by repositioning the product in the market place. Sometimes, eliminating the product is the only option. Many products, or at least product categories, tend to follow a life cycle leading to decline and ultimately the ceasing of production.

PRODUCT ITEM, PRODUCT LINE, PRODUCT MIX

BMW

A product item is a specific model, brand or size of a product that a company sells, for example, a BMW 320i car.

A product line is a group of closely related product items, with similar physical characteristics and/or end-use applications. For example, the BMW 3 series product line includes such models as the 316, 318i, and 320i.

A product mix is all the product lines a company sells. BMW's product mix includes, for example, the 3 series, 5 series, 7 series and 8 series cars as well as motorcycles.

PRODUCT LINE EXTENSION

Product line extension is adding products to an existing product line.

Swatch Watch, Sony Walkman

Swatch Watch, the company that manufactures cheap yet very fashionable watches aimed at 12–24 year olds provides an example of a company that is actively engaged in product line extension. New watch models are introduced four times a year with designs to suit seasonal fashions.

Similarly, Sony have added to the Walkman product line over the years. Today, the product line includes Walkmans with cassette player only, with radio and cassette and even waterproof Walkmans. Sony generally release basic versions of their new products on the highly competitive consumer electronics market and when competitors inevitably launch their own versions, Sony leapfrogs past the competition by rapidly introducing new models with additional features.

BRANDING

A brand is the product or service of a particular supplier which is differentiated by its name and presentation. Brands embrace values and provide the customer with a guarantee of quality, performance, origin, and value. They allow manufacturers to differentiate products which may otherwise be very similar.

Many companies have their brands listed as assets in their balance sheets. In the 1988 accounts of Guinness, brands were valued at £1,695 million. After all, millions of pounds are spent on advertising its brands and building up their identities. It is popularly said that the IBM brand name is worth more than the gross national product of many nations.

Companies such as Novamark International charge up to £26,000 for coming up with a single name and carrying out a world-wide search of its acceptability. Another naming company, Interbrand, has a turnover in excess of £10 million and charges an average of £15,000 for developing a new brand.

Corporate umbrella branding

Heinz

Here the corporate name, e.g. Heinz, is used to brand a wide variety of food products including Heinz mayonnaise, Heinz soups, Heinz beans and so on.

Family umbrella branding

Dunnes Stores, Marks and Spencer

Here a manufacturer already having a successful brand builds upon its brand awareness by using the brand name on other product lines. In Ireland, the retailer Dunnes Stores uses its St Bernard brand for food, clothing and household goods. Similarly in the UK, Marks and Spencer uses St Michael.

Brand extension

Mars [1]

One company that has been successful with extension of its brand name is Mars. It developed a strong brand name and image with Mars chocolate confectionery and then stretched the name into a Mars drink and Mars ice cream. The Mars bar ice cream was introduced onto the UK market in 1988, and rolled out in fifteen countries in Europe and in the USA in the following year. The company had been experimenting with ice-cream products for a number of years, finally choosing the UK as a test market for the new product. The product was priced at a premium level above then existing hand-held ice-cream products. The ice-cream concept was later applied to other Mars confectionery products, which were subsequently introduced around Europe. At the turn of the decade retail sales of Mars ice-cream in Europe were estimated at £200 million. The combined sales of the Mars bar chocolate bar and the Mars bar ice cream had increased by about one-third.

Lucozade   This company has also stretched its brand name from soft energy giving drinks to energy giving sweets.

Brand licensing

A manufacturer, after spending much time and money developing an up-market brand image and a widely known brand identity, may decide to license its name to other manufactures of widely different products that need an instant prestige image, in return for royalties.

Yves St Laurent, the Parisian couturier, and Giorgio Beverly Hills, an American perfume maker, both license their names to a watch maker. Pierre Cardin, another Parisian couturier licenses its name to a host of different products including pens, bath towels and baggage. Harley-Davidson licenses its name to chocolate, toys and cologne.

Changing a brand name

Panasonic

The Panasonic name was only recently introduced to Japan for the complete line of electronics. Before this the Technics name was used for stereo equipment, the Qasar name for televisions and the National name for most of its products sold in Asia. However, as the product range became more technologically advanced some names, particularly National, became hard to stretch. The National name became synonymous with washing machines and radios and not computers, i.e. household products and not office machines.

Procter & Gamble's 'Rely'[2]

In 1981 a scare over toxic shock syndrome developed in relation to 'Rely', a brand of tampons, with the result that the product was withdrawn from the market. However what most people did not realise was that this product was a Procter & Gamble brand. Because the name was an individual brand name Procter & Gamble were able to withdraw it and in 1984 reintroduce it to the same market under the new individual brand name of 'Always'.

Ingredient branding

The value of branding has also been recognised by many suppliers who produce ingredients or components that are incorporated into final products. These input suppliers promote their ingredient to the final users of the product – the consumer. If successful, this strategy causes the consumer to pull the input product through the manufacturer of the end product.

Suppliers may be motivated by the opportunities to achieve non-price differentiation for their input, to build long-term relations with manufacturers and hopefully as a result to earn higher profits.

NutraSweet[3]

G.D. Searle, manufacturer of the artificial sweetener NutraSweet, aggressively promotes its product to consumers to build awareness of and preference for the product and consequently persuade food and beverage manufacturers to use the artificial sweetener in their products. NutraSweet has had tremendous success with its strategy to the extent that many food and beverage manufacturers are now seeking out the recognised brand to use as a key input in their final product.

These manufacturers are seeking to benefit from the quality image of and consumer preference for NutraSweet and promote the use of the ingredient in their product. Some manufacturers may use the ingredient to revitalise stagnant sales of brands. General Foods used NutraSweet in two of their products, Jell-O brand gelatine and Kool-Aid brand powdered drink mixes with this objective in mind. Sales volume increases followed effective promotion of the products with NutraSweet. Therefore, it is not only suppliers who benefit from ingredient branding but manufacturers as well.

PACKAGING

With the proliferation of brands in retail outlets today, packaging is increasingly becoming a major element in the marketing mix for a product. As well as performing a sales role, well developed packaging can reinforce the brand's image and positioning. Packaging can also provide a company with an opportunity to differentiate its product from competitors' offerings.

Vidor Batteries[4]

In 1992, the American battery manufacturer, Rayovac, used packaging as a major marketing mix element for the relaunch of its Vidor range of batteries in the UK. 'Smart Packs' consisted of four or eight batteries in a multipack and were similar to the packaging of market leaders Ever Ready and Duracell but with one exception – the Vidor multipacks came in cardboard as opposed to blister packaging. They were targeted at the heavy battery user household leaving blister cards for the light user of batteries.

The packaging offered benefits to retailers and customers alike. The customer got an alternative to the blister pack, which once opened could create storage problems, and for the retailer the packs generated higher volume per sale. Retailers were offered elaborate point-of-sale displays to show off the multipacks and these allowed the retailer to stock 89 per cent more batteries per square foot.

The multipack packaging proved successful in the USA where in 1992, Vidor had a 39.9 per cent share putting it ahead of Ever Ready and Duracell, which had 29.5 per cent and 24.7 per cent respectively.

FURTHER REFERENCE

Chapter 11, Advertising: Point-of-purchase advertising (p. 192–193)

Nurofen[5]

Crookes Healthcare, the UK manufacturer of Nurofen, an over-the-counter painkiller, used packaging to communicate the brand's uniqueness and help differentiate it from competitors' offerings.

Nurofen was launched in 1983 into a market dominated by analgesics with blue packaging. The blue packaging was associated with standard-strength analgesics such as Disprin and Panadol. Stronger analgesics such as Veganin and Codis were often in red boxes.

Nurofen was a unique product in that it contained Ibuprofen, which until then was only available on prescription. To communicate this uniqueness and Crookes' image of being a leader in pharmaceutical technology, Nurofen was launched in a silver box. The product was a tremendous success and inspired many lookalikes. Crookes continued to invest in design to further improve the product's on-shelf impact and set it apart from competitors' offerings. In 1993, Nurofen had a 12 per cent value share of the £160 million UK analgesics market, compared with leader Anadin's 17 per cent, and spent £5 million advertising the brand.

FURTHER REFERENCE

Chapter 7, Products: Product differentiation (p. 117–118)

PRODUCT DIFFERENTIATION

In the face of increasing competition, companies are increasingly attempting to focus their efforts on meeting customers' needs more precisely. This has led in some cases to increased product differentiation in the form of products tailor-made for every single buyer. The traditional manufacture of tailor-made products by craftspeople possesses the drawback of being expensive and time consuming. However many companies are now trying to develop 'mass customisation' with the aim of reproducing the benefits of a tailor-made product using a mass production approach. This represents a scale of product differentiation never achieved before.

Melbo[6]

One company which has adopted a mass customisation approach to a traditional craft is the Melbo clothing company in Japan. The company manufactures men's suits and followed a strategy of positioning itself as an exclusive supplier. Part of this strategy required offering a wide choice of styles, but this often resulted in large quantities of unsold stock at the end of the season. Rather than selling this merchandise at discount prices which would dilute the brand image, Melbo was forced to take back unsold stock from retailers. In 1978 the company embarked on a new strategy designed to produce suits to the customer's exact fitting specifications and reduce the time taken to make a suit from six days to one day. The service offered was called the 'Ready-Made Order System', with the result that when a customer entered a Melbo shop their measurements are taken and a suit designed by exclusive names is individually made to suit them.

The customer's details are faxed to the company's factory and then entered into the CAD/CAM system which controls the cutting process. The machines cut only one suit at a time which opposes the traditional objective in the clothing trade of cutting as many suits as possible with the objective of reducing production time and costs. It was necessary therefore for Melbo to increase the number of cutting machines and reduce setting up time for each operation, thus keeping the time taken to a minimum. Another method used to reduce production time is the processing of different parts of the suit at the same time, with the result that they come together in final assembly. This requires a highly co-ordinated production process.

Melbo however has not yet achieved its goal of producing a suit in one day, but has reduced the time to three days. From the time the customer orders a suit, delivery can be made within one week. In 1991 the company had sales in excess of ¥ 18 billion.

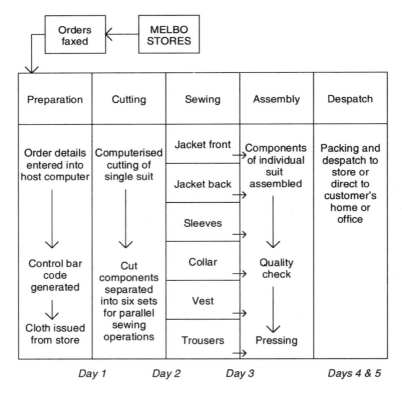

Figure 7.1 Melbo's mass customisation plant

PRODUCT AUGMENTATION

A company's basic product typically consists of features that translate into desired customer benefits, a brand name, attractive packaging and quality characteristics. It is standard for products to come with warranties and financing arrangements are also commonplace.

Today, there is increased pressure on companies to add further to their product offerings – this is the concept of product augmentation. Augmenting a product basically means adding to it in order to increase the distinctiveness of the product and hopefully secure a competitive advantage. Augmentation could take the form of offering, for example, an extended warranty, delivery arrangements, free installation.

Volvo[7]

The Swedish company Volvo was the first in the highly competitive truck industry to offer free Driveline cover across its product range for either one or two years beyond the normal warranty period. The precise length of the extended warranty period depends on whether service and maintenance is carried out by Volvo or by the vehicle owner. Driveline covers the cost of repair or replacement and reasonable costs of recovery, when failure is due to either the faulty manufacture of or the use of faulty materials in the engine, gearbox, rear axle or prop-shaft. The extended warranty enhances Volvo's image of reliability and durability in the market place.

Rank Xerox

In December 1990, Rank Xerox introduced the 'Total Satisfaction Guarantee' scheme where it unconditionally guarantees Rank Xerox office equipment for a period of three years. The customer is free to replace the item with no questions asked any time during the period. This guarantee was unique in the office equipment market at that time providing Rank Xerox with a competitive advantage.

MAHO

Another form of product augmentation is the guaranteed buyback, a product benefit that is particularly valuable in selling major items of capital equipment. In 1991, MAHO, a UK machine tool manufacturer, developed its 'new for old' scheme whereby a used MAHO universal

CNC mill can be exchanged for a new one with the purchaser obtaining for their old machine virtually the same price that they paid for it. A profitable market in second-hand MAHO machines allows the company to offer this enticing product benefit which generates valuable repeat sales.

Service augmentation

Service companies can also augment their service offering to differentiate it from competitors.

InterRent[8]

The InterRent Corporation based in Sweden, one of the country's top car rental companies, was faced with increasing competition in the mid-1980s and a perception among travel agents and customers that the offerings of all the car rental companies were more or less the same. InterRent set about differentiating/augmenting its service offering by developing three service guarantees which would hereafter form part of its service package:

1 A 'get to the destination' guarantee

Should the customer's car break down, InterRent guaranteed to have that customer on their way again to their destination within 45 minutes. InterRent engaged a subcontractor to operate a 24-hour rescue service.

2 A 'lowest price' guarantee

InterRent invested in improving its existing nation-wide computer system so that the lowest possible price could always be given immediately to the customer.

3 A 'trouble-free' service guarantee

InterRent allowed the customer to pick up the car at any InterRent location or promised to deliver it to company addresses, hotels or railway stations. Furthermore, the firm promised to deliver the car not later than five minutes after the time agreed upon – the penalty for failure was no billing for the customer. Also, under the guarantee, the customer with a reservation was guaranteed a car, either of the category booked or a superior one. Also, the customer could return the car to any InterRent location.

The new service launched in September 1986 enhanced the image of trustworthiness and reliability of InterRent and the 'new product' was a success, resulting in greatly increased sales.

PRODUCT CANNIBALISATION[9]

Miller Lite and Miller High Life

Miller High Life was positioned as the 'champagne of bottled beers' while Miller Lite was assumed to be associated with a watered-down taste. During the 1980s sales of Miller Lite declined substantially from 21 per cent to 12 per cent (1978–86) while those for Miller High Life grew from 9.5 per cent to 19 per cent in the same period. This can be said to be as a result of cannibalisation.

Gillette's 'Good News!'

Gillette had a strong shaving cream brand – 'Right Guard' – and wanted to attack Barbasol with a low-end entry. Gillette's 'Good News!' line of razors was already positioned as a low-end line and Gillette developed 'Good News!' shaving cream. It took sales from Right Guard because consumers felt that they could save money by buying Good News! and still get a Gillette product.

PRODUCT COUNTERFEITING

The Anti-Counterfeiting Group suggests that counterfeits make up between 3 and 6 per cent of all market trade. The record industry is estimated to lose $1 billion per annum. The European motor parts industry loses some $200 million per annum, perfume companies $70 million, the Swiss watch companies $750 million and drug companies $50 million. Seventy per cent of all drugs sold in Africa are counterfeit.

Paco Rabanne [10]

For about five years, the expensive men's aftershave Paco Rabanne had its European markets flooded with cheap counterfeits produced from a factory in Brazil. The identity and location of the counterfeiter were already established but stopping them was another matter. The Brazilian government was not only backing the counterfeiting operation but had even helped to fund a brand new factory. It had also given the counterfeiter incentives to export the product. In such a climate the Paco Rabanne lawyers in Rio de Janeiro had met with resounding failure. Vincente Garratu of Garratu International (intellectual property 'consultant') was appointed to investigate the situation. He visited the factory and within four days had succeeded in persuading the counterfeiter to take him on as 'export director'. He was soon established as 'Uncle Vince', friend of the family and trusted colleague.

His position gave Garratu access to all the information he required: 'We hit everyone of the companies which had purchased the stuff.' The factory's export trade was ruined and such a fuss resulted that Paco Rabanne was able to petition the Brazilian Embassy. Clearly embarrassed by the situation, the government withdrew its support and the factory closed down. The company was investigated for fraud and for bringing disrepute to the Brazilian government.

THE PRODUCT LIFE CYCLE

The concept of the product life cycle has been the source of much debate since its inception. Nevertheless, in many markets it provides at minimum a framework for creating awareness among marketers that no product or service has an unlimited lifetime demand. Under the traditional model, a product (typically a product category) goes through the four stages of introduction, growth, maturity and decline.

The concept of the product life cycle provides some explanation of why the continuous introduction of new products is necessary for many companies to maintain and improve their position in the market. Some companies such as Rubbermaid, the US household goods manufacturer, has a policy of requiring that one-third of its revenues should come from products introduced in the previous five years. This can result in products, for which demand still exists, being taken off the market, therefore minimising the life cycle of the product.

Stages of the product life cycle

1   Introduction (and concurrent decline)

Compact disc and LP record[11]

The introduction of the CD player and compact disc software itself and the resultant decline in the LP record and player illustrates products in the growth and decline stages of the product life cycle respectively. The compact disc format was introduced in 1982 as a result of a joint development between Philips and Sony. A key factor in the success of the new format displacing the old LP record format was the ownership by Sony of CBS in the USA and Philips of Polygram in Europe, two of the biggest music software companies in the world. This contributed to the new format establishing itself as the industry standard. In Japan the decline of the LP record format and the growth of the CD format occurred in the 1980s as demonstrated in Figure 7.2.

Sony established itself as the market leader in the supply of music software in Japan with a 19.3 per cent share of the market. The company also built disc production facilities in Japan, Europe and the USA, giving it the largest capacity in world markets. It also manufactures for other software suppliers. There were however a number of barriers to the adoption of the new format. Firstly the price of discs and players were relatively high, and potential users already had invested in LP record collections. As a result of these and other factors the sales of the new format were not as high as expected.

In 1984 Sony made a concerted effort in promoting the CD in Japan. This included the introduction of a new CD player the 'Discman' at half the price of existing models and with improved portability and smaller size. In 1985 the Discman had over 30 per cent share of the CD player market. The CD format was also introduced to the radio cassette and car

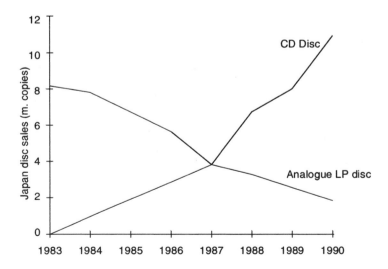

Figure 7.2 Audio products' life cycles

audio systems, thus expanding the market further. Sony also decided to market key components of the CD technology to other manufacturers, including optical pick-up, laser diodes and CD drive assemblies. In conjunction with the lower priced Discman and the other applications, this succeeded in expanding the market for the CD format and establishing it as the standard format in the market place.

2 Growth

Mobile phones [12]

Mobile telephones in the UK may be said to be in the growth stage of the product life cycle. The market for mobile telephones was instigated in 1985 with the granting of licences to operate the networks on which the calls are made to two companies, Cellnet and Vodafone. The total number of subscribers rose from almost half a million at the end of the first year of operation in 1988 to almost 2 million estimated for 1993. This represents an increase of almost 400 per cent. In 1993 it is estimated Vodafone had about 1 million subscribers and Cellnet over 800,000. Table 7.1 shows the growth in subscribers.

The reduction in growth rates in 1991/92 can be accounted for by the UK recession.

Prices were initially high for subscription and call charges, as well as for hardware. A handset in 1985 cost a few thousand pounds, whilst in 1995 they can be bought for less than £100. Call charges have also fallen significantly. Because of the high prices at the outset, the service was targeted primarily at the business market, but now the franchise of the mobile phone has reached a wider public. Both Cellnet and Vodafone now offer much cheaper connection and rental charges, and a third network operator, Mercury, entered the market in 1993 (Hutchinson

Table 7.1 Total UK cellphone subscribers, 1988–1993

	1988	1989	1990	1991	1992	1993[e]
Subscribers (in thousands)	478	869	1,156	1,233	1,397	1,900
Growth (%)		81.1	33.0	6.7	13.3	36.0

Source: Euromonitor PLC, Market Research GB, January 1994

Note: e = estimated

Microtel has become the fourth licensed operator). Both Mercury and Hutchinson provide what are termed personal communication networks (PCNs) operated through a large number of base stations due to the limited range of the signal.

Mercury is targeting the domestic user and introduced its One-2-One service which offers low charges and free local calls during off-peak period. Such pricing strategies will serve to further penetrate the market. If the market is to grow significantly it is the domestic segment which must fuel it. Mercury appears to have succeeded in further stimulating this segment with over half of its initial customers being domestic and 80 per cent first-time users. The ultimate challenge for the mobile phone will be to replace the fixed phone system. This will require further advancements in technology and reduction in costs.

The market is divided into three levels. First the network operators who operate the network, second the service providers who manage the lines and the subscribers, and third the retailers (and manufacturers) who sell the phones. Both Vodafone and Cellnet are also involved in service provision. The market is now experiencing increased competition among network operators and phone manufacturers, despite the relatively high levels of concentration. A total of seven manufacturers account for 95 per cent of the market, who along with the remaining manufacturers offer more than 60 different telephone models. Motorola and Nokia have the largest shares with 25 per cent and 23 per cent respectively.

Products are also more widely available through a range of outlets. Initially the equipment was only available through specialist outlets, but now it is available in high street shops such as Dixons, Currys and other stores. This wider availability probably resulted in a further stimulation of the market with more people becoming aware of the possibility of purchasing a mobile telephone.

Sales promotion activity is increasing as well as advertising spend. Schemes such as cashback arrangements on the purchase of handsets are increasing. Companies are currently subsidising the price of the handsets to the tune of £100–£200. Also combinations of free connection, free airtime or free rental may be offered. In 1992 almost £30 million was spent on advertising, with the aim of building awareness and interest in the mass market. It is estimated Mercury spent £10 million in promoting its One-2-One service.

In the future the most important source of growth will be the domestic consumer. It is not inconceivable that a majority of households will have a mobile telephone. With a total of 20 million households in the UK it is estimated that penetration of this market will reach 10 per cent by the year 2000. Mercury planned to cover 25 per cent of the domestic market by April 1994, the majority of these in the south east. In 1993 there was a total of 200,000 private subscribers. Forecasts estimate a total of over 1 million units the turn of the century. All in all further growth in the sector is inevitable.

FURTHER REFERENCE

Chapter 2, Marketing strategies: Integrative growth – forward integration (p. 27)
Chapter 3, The Marketing Environment: Technological (p. 43)
Chapter 13, Sales Promotion and Public Relations: Sales Promotion (pp. 210–213)

3 Maturity and decline – using the PLC concept

Quarterdeck office systems[13]

Quarterdeck Office Systems, a small computer software firm in Santa Monica, California, makes a tidy living serving a niche created by a larger firm, Microsoft.

The niche is so precise that the company's software is dedicated to enhancing only one of Microsoft's products, the immensely successful MS-DOS – the operating system that powers almost all IBM-compatible personal computers.

Quarterdeck's success began with a single product, Desq, a software enhancement for DOS that permitted PC users to switch from one program to another. Later, Quarterdeck launched Desqview, which allowed users to open up 'windows' to view one program while working on another. (At that time Microsoft's DOS didn't offer these features.) Next, Quarterdeck introduced enhancements, such as QEMM, software that expands memory beyond the limits of DOS.

Then the inevitable happened. Microsoft launched Windows 3.0, a product that incorporates the features of both Desqview and QEMM. Such aggressive action by a larger company can devastate a smaller competitor, but that didn't happen to Quarterdeck.

What saved the smaller company's neck? The firm's sales and marketing managers' knowledge and canny use of product life cycles. For a long time before Windows came on the scene, they had been observing computer users' behaviour in purchasing new software and hardware. They identified the various life-cycle stages of their products

– introduction, growth, and maturity or decline – and constantly evaluated the strategies Microsoft was following.

The Quarterdeck managers observed, for example, that QEMM worked more efficiently with older computer models that run DOS, and for users who struggle to learn new programs or resist trading up to new hardware. They also found that this segment of users was substantial.

They saw that, in contrast, Microsoft's Windows worked better with newer computer models and with software requiring more memory.

Based on these observations and on the fact that Microsoft was aiming Windows at the introduction and growth stages of the computer life cycle, Quarterdeck's managers devised a strategy to position its products at the mature and declining life cycle stages. Defining which stage each company's products occupied in the computer life cycle delineated different market segments. By carving out a narrowly defined niche in the mature and declining life cycle stages, which the market leader was likely to avoid, Quarterdeck identified its only real chance to succeed.

FURTHER REFERENCE

Chapter 6, Segmentation and Positioning: Target marketing (p. 102–105)
Chapter 14, Market Status and Competitive Moves: Market nicher (pp. 231–233)

Extending the product life cycle

The National Dairy Council[14]

In the UK milk had traditionally been delivered direct to households. In 1980 almost 90 per cent of households had their milk delivered, exemplifying a market which had matured. With the change in shopping practices in the 1980s and with competition from supermarkets, the percentage having milk delivered fell to 69 per cent by 1990. It was estimated that the service was losing one million customers per year, and between January 1990 and April 1991 the milk delivery share of the market was declining at a rate of 0.43 percentage points per month. If the trend continued the market would be non-existent by the turn of the century. It was clear that the milk delivery service was in the decline stage of the product life cycle.

The National Dairy Council, which promoted milk on behalf of the dairies and other interests, decided to launch a campaign to stem the decline in direct deliveries to households. The campaign used TV advertising and was designed to influence those customers who were at the point of switching from delivered milk to buying it in the supermarket. Invariably such customers had already begun purchasing some of their milk requirements from retail outlets. The price of milk was cheaper in the supermarket though it was concluded that for these 'drifting' customers price was not the major factor in the decision. Therefore the possibility of influencing them through advertising appeared strong.

The advertisements emphasised the benefit of convenience from the milk delivery service as opposed to having to carry it from the supermarket or shop. As a result of the campaign the decline in milk deliveries was all but eradicated for the period, with the decline falling to 0.01 percentage points per month during the period of the campaign from May to December 1991.

FURTHER REFERENCE

Chapter 11, Advertising: Communication objectives (pp. 184–186)

Pfizer

A product for treating rheumatism, backache, and other pains was patented in Paris towards the end of the nineteenth century; its name was Ben-Gay. In the early 1980s it had taken on a new application by Pfizer who began promoting it as a supplement before undertaking exercise. In the late 1980s Ben-Gay was one of the market leaders in pain killers.

CONCLUSION

Today, customers expect companies to develop products that meet their needs precisely. The successful marketers are those who develop such products knowing failure to do so will result in rejection and customers turning to competitors' offerings. In this chapter, we have seen examples of successful products. Differentiating a product against competitors' offerings will become increasingly important as self service retailing is almost the norm for several product categories. For example, computers, television and hi-fi systems are now being sold on a self service basis in warehouse clubs, such as Costco. Increasing competition and fragmentation of markets are also factors that put pressure on companies to differentiate their products through, for example, branding and packaging. At some stage, a product will reach the end of its life and the product life cycle concept is a useful tool for marketers to at least make them aware that this is so and may even have use in suggesting strategies applicable at the various stages. Here, however, the concept should be used with care and not taken as given because the life cycle of a product can be influenced by a firm's marketing strategy.

NOTES

1 Mars section adapted from the following: Barry Jones and Roger Ramsden, 'The global brand age', *Management Today*, September 1991, pp. 78–80; Patrick Barwise and Thomas Robertson, 'Brand portfolios', *European Management Journal*, September 1992, vol. 10, no. 3, pp. 277–285; Hajo Riesenbeck and Anthony Freeling, 'How global are global brands', *McKinsey Quarterly*, 1991, no. 4, pp. 3–18.

2 Procter & Gamble section adapted from C.J. Roberts and G.M. McDonald, 'Alternative naming strategies: family vs. individual brand names', *Management Decision*, 1989, vol. 27, no. 6.

3 NutraSweet section adapted from Donald G. Norris, 'Ingredient branding: a strategy option with multiple beneficiaries', *The Journal of Consumer Marketing*, summer 1992, vol. 9, no. 3, pp. 19–29.

4 Vidor batteries section adapted from 'Boosting battery sales need not be all hard sell', *The Grocer*, 1 August 1992, p. 42.

5 Nurofen section adapted from Emma Hall, 'Keep making the tablets', *Marketing Week*, 1 October 1993, p. 59.

6 Melbo section, including Figure 7.1, reprinted from Roy Westbrook and Peter Williamson, 'Mass customisation: Japan's new frontier', *European Management Journal*, 1993, vol. 11, no. 1, pp. 38–45. Copyright 1993, reprinted with kind permission of Elsevier Science Ltd.

7 Volvo section adapted from 'How extended warranties can widen the ring of confidence', *Business Marketing Digest*, 2nd quarter 1991, vol. 16, no. 2, pp. 47–52.

8 InterRent section adapted from Christian Gronroos and Hans Ake Sand, 'A winning service offer in car rental', *Management Decision*, 1993, vol. 31, no. 1, pp. 45–51.

9 Product cannibilisation section adapted from D. Baker, 'Brand exclusions: the good, the bad and the ugly', *Sloan Management Review*, June 1990, vol. 30, pp. 47–56.

10 Paco Rabanne section adapted from H. Kay, 'Fakes Progress', *Management Today*, July 1990, p. 55.

11 Compact disc and LP record section, including Figure 7.2, reprinted from Takashi Shibata, 'Sony's successful strategy for compact discs', *Long Range Planning*, 1993, vol. 26, no. 4, pp. 16–21. Copyright 1993, reprinted with kind permission of Elsevier Science Ltd.

12 Mobile phone section adapted from: Market Research GB, *Euromonitor*, January 1994; Anil Bhoyrul, 'Power to the people' and 'Muddled but profitable' and 'Happy to be rich', *Business Age*, April 1994, pp. 60–62, 65–66, 68–69; Peter Haynes, 'The personal touch – in search of a mobile

volksphone', *The Economist*, 23 October 1993; George Black, 'Survey of International Telecommunications – prices are crucial', *Financial Times*, 18 October 1993; Ian Channing, 'Survey of Mobile Telecommunications – service providers come under threat', *Financial Times*, 8 September 1993; Paul Taylor, 'Survey of Mobile Telecommunications – the street-wise take to Telepoint', *Financial Times*, 8 September 1993, p. VI; Andrew Adonis, 'Sharp rise in subscribers to Vodafone', *Financial Times*, 6 May 1993, p. 7; Paul Taylor, 'Survey of Mobile Telecommunications – drive for the mass consumer market', *Financial Times*, 8 September 1993, p. iii; 'A way of life', *The Economist*, 30 May 1992; Malcolm Brown, 'Slow march of the mobiles', *Management Today*, December 1993, pp. 54–57.

13 Quarterdeck Office Systems section reprinted from Norton Paley, 'A strategy for all ages', *Sales and Marketing*, January 1994, p. 51. Reprinted with permission of *Sales and Marketing Management*, 355 Park Avenue South, New York, NY 10010–1789.

14 The National Dairy Council section is reprinted from the following: Diane Summers, 'Gambling on a gut-feeling', *Financial Times*, 24 February 1994, p. 22; Chris Baker (ed.), *Advertising Works 7*, Chapter 1: National Dairy Council – The Milkman Relaunch, NTC Publications Ltd., pp. 3–22, UK 1993; Liquid Milk Report 1993 – *Towards 2000*, National Dairy Council, 1993; 'Doorstep v Shop, It's a two-way street – Doorstep Delivery Service 1993', National Dairy Council.

Chapter 8

New product development

INTRODUCTION

Today more than ever, innovation is the key to survival in companies. Innovating by developing new or improved products is vital in markets characterised by rapidly changing consumer needs and desires. Increased competition, technological advances, and shorter life spans for products put pressure on companies to strive constantly for improvement or face demise.

However, in spite of its necessity, new product development is expensive, time-consuming and carries a huge risk of failure. Common reasons for new product failure include products failing to meet customer needs, lack of distinctiveness of a product which may be seen as a copy of an existing superior product, or simply bad timing. As a result, much new product development work results in brand extensions rather than innovative new products because this way the company can capitalise on existing brand awareness and brand values.

The new product development process typically consists of eight stages: idea generation, screening, concept development and testing, business analysis, product development, test marketing, and commercialisation. A product may be dropped at any of these stages but obviously it is important to filter out a poor product at the earlier stages before a lot of time and money have been spent.

This chapter provides examples within many of the stages and covers the new product development process followed by R & A Bailey (maker of Baileys Irish Cream) when developing their recent new liqueur, Sheridan's, launched in 1993.

Finally, examples are provided of management structures for new product development.

IDEA GENERATION

Customers

Customers can be a good source of new product ideas. By listening to its customers, a company may identify an unsatisfied need that has great potential for that company.

United States Surgical[1]

In any ten-day period, United States Surgical sales representatives visit every one of the 5,000 American hospitals where surgery is performed. They gown up and march right into operating rooms to coach surgeons in the use of the complex instruments the company makes. They listen to what the doctors like and don't like, need and don't need. Getting right in there under the operating room lights with the customer increased revenues sharply last year and nearly doubled profits. Most of the growth is in laparoscopic instruments, used to do a variety of procedures through minute incisions. Security analysts see that as a $3 billion market by 1996; US Surgical has roughly an 85 per cent share.

United States Surgical's close connection to customers made it quick to pick up on early experiments with laparoscopy. In 1989 an employee who had graduated from the company's demanding sales training programme met a surgeon who was using a jury-rigged clip to remove gallbladders laparoscopically. The US Surgical woman carried word back to headquarters, and by early 1990 the company had a basic laparoscopic stapler ready to go.

Then its sales force, the most aggressive in the industry, took both the technique and the instrumentation out to surgeons. The result: a boom in laparoscopy, which works by inserting a tiny TV camera into the body along with slim, long-handled instruments like clips and staple guns. It's safer, cheaper, and less painful than open surgery. In 1990 no more than 30 per cent of gallbladders were removed laparoscopically; in 1991, 60 per cent were.

FURTHER REFERENCE

Chapter 12, Personal Selling: Sales force strategy, (pp. 198–199)

Employees

Employees are another great source of new product ideas.

Rubbermaid[2]

The US company Rubbermaid, manufacturer of everyday household items including plastic buckets, dustpans, sandwich boxes and washing-up mops, introduces new products at the rate of more than one a day. The company demands that one-third of its revenue comes from products introduced in the last five years. In 1994, Rubbermaid was voted the most admired corporation in the USA by Fortune magazine because of its remarkable rate of innovation and consistently good earnings growth and profitability over many years.

New product ideas are generated by employees, suppliers and customers. Business teams are set up within the company containing a wide range of personnel, e.g. representatives from marketing, manufacturing, finance and other functional areas. Each business team focuses on a specific product line and is responsible for ensuring the profitability of the line. This means that each team is constantly evaluating its product line, adding new products and dropping unprofitable ones to ensure the line is growing and adding to company profits. Besides the specialised business teams, all other employees are encouraged to submit their ideas for new products. Suppliers provide a good source of ideas, as do customers, and the company fosters a culture which welcomes change and is receptive to new ideas, whatever their source. In 1993, sales hit $1.8 billion with profits of $184.2 million. An amazing 90 per cent of new products succeed and all without any test marketing.

Raytheon   The US defence and electronics group developed a New Products Center which concentrates solely on the untested ideas of employees. Its New Product Centre has generated many millions of dollars in incremental sales over the years.

Honda R. &D.   Recruits go through an extensive one year duration in-company 'training' program. They spend three months making cars, three months selling them at dealers, and six months rotating through a variety of R.&D. jobs. Honda believes this process fosters idea generation.

Market research

New product ideas may originate from market research.

Hitachi

In 1987, Hitachi launched a quiet washing machine with a lower noise level than conventional models. Hitachi's continuous market research on the changing lifestyle of housewives revealed a market for a quiet washing machine. Research indicated that as a result of an increase in the numbers of working housewives, washing times were increasingly taking place at night or in the early morning and having a noisy machine was an obvious problem. Hitachi's new product was an answer to the housewives' worry about noise and became a tremendous success.

CONCEPT DEVELOPMENT AND TESTING

At this stage, the potential consumer is presented with a proposed product and attitudes and intentions to buy are carefully measured to determine enthusiasm and, of course, demand.

There is no tangible product at this stage and the customer is simply reacting to a picture, written statement or even an oral description of the product. Customer opinions on features, price to be charged and design (for example, colour) may be sought.

An example of the lengths some marketers go to with consumer research in new product development is provided by the detergent manufacturer who before launching a new brand of detergent interviewed 30,000 consumers for one and a half hours each about their emotional relationship with washing powder.

An outline of a basic marketing strategy is usually developed concerning product features/benefits, price, promotion and distribution.

Canon [3]

Canon's PC-10 and PC-20 maintenance-free cartridge type personal copiers were introduced in 1982 and were regarded as revolutionary new products which became trendsetters in the world copier market.

During the 1960s and 1970s the plain paper copier was widely used in large-scale offices such as those of the government, big companies, and so on. The price of the cheapest copier at the time was more than $2300. This was considered too expensive for the small office. Conventional copiers had to be serviced by professional service engineers, which, again for reasons of cost, limited the copiers to larger offices. After considering both the external and internal environment of the copier business, Canon were eager to realise their 'dream' of a unique, innovative copier that would cost $1000. The product concept was described as follows: the most compact and the lightest in the world (under 20kg); a market price of less than $1000 in the US market; maintenance – exchange of disposable parts from time to time; new functions – functions to ensure that the machine is easy and enjoyable to use.

From the product concept to the sales launch, it took three years to develop the personal copier.

FURTHER REFERENCE

Chapter 10, Marketing Channels: The distribution strategy (pp. 180–182)
Chapter 9, Pricing: Setting prices (pp. 155–158)

Mazda, Little Tikes

A method used for testing new product concepts called 'antenna shops' is being adopted by a number of well known companies. The method, originating from Japan, consists of effectively placing an R.&D. laboratory in the market place, where new product concepts can be tested on consumers. Computer generated concepts of the new product are often used in interactive interviews with consumers. Such research involves both technical and marketing personnel. Consumer perceptions can be ascertained and different product attributes can be tested for their contribution to the overall benefits of a new product. Standard methods of assessing product attributes such as conjoint analysis are also used.

The Mazda Motor Corporation has established what it called its antenna shop, consisting of a design studio, laboratory and office. The centre was given the name M2 Incorporated and is planned to be established as a separate company. The objective of the centre is to obtain input from the target market to enable the company to develop a product that meets the needs and wants of the target group. Among the other Japanese companies which have developed antenna shops are Matsushita, NEC, Canon, Sony and Ricoh.

In the USA another example of an antenna shop is that of Little Tikes which uses its child-care centre established for employees' children as a 'laboratory' to test new product concepts. In California a number of Japanese companies have set up consumer electronics antenna shops.

Commonly such establishments act as retail outlets while providing a testing facility for new product concepts.

One of the objectives of the antenna shop is to involve the consumer in the product development process at an early stage.

PRODUCT DEVELOPMENT

Up to now, the new product idea has usually remained just that, an idea. At the product development stage, the product concept is developed into a tangible product. Several prototypes may be developed before the company is happy with the final product. Potential customers have also to be happy with the product and so much attitude and usage testing is conducted to ensure that the product is a perfect tangible expression of the product concept meeting their needs and desires. The company also faces the challenges inherent in manufacturing a new product which may call for developing new manufacturing and engineering systems.

The earlier marketing strategy developed in the concept development and testing stage will be refined and encompass branding and packaging for the new product.

Cars

Car makers traditionally conduct extensive prototype development and testing and consumer attitude and usage testing for their new cars. Cars are put through extensive tests to, for example, increase safety and reduce drag. Cars are bombarded with microwaves to test electrical systems, driven over simulated bumpy roads to test suspension, and doors are opened and closed thousands of times by robots.

Customers are surveyed about car features, including for example, the firmness, width and colour of seating, the upholstery, the comfort of driving including visibility, smoothness and manoeuvrability. For example, Chrysler built a $1 billion technology centre for new vehicle development.

Gillette

When Gillette was developing its Sensor razor for men, a twin-blade razor that gives a closer shave by reacting to the contours on a face through tiny springs that moves the blades up and down, new manufacturing systems needed to be developed. For example, one of the early manufacturing challenges was trying to fit springs to the blades at a fast enough rate to facilitate mass production. Although the first prototype was developed in 1979, it was not until seven years later that lasers were developed to weld the springs onto the blades.

FURTHER REFERENCE

Chapter 8, New Product Development: Commercialisation (p. 138)

TEST MARKETING

Before launching a product nationwide, a company may decide to launch the product in a single region or a number of regions in the country. Test marketing a product allows the company to test all elements of its marketing mix before committing greater resources to a national launch. A marketer who engages in test marketing will want to know answers to several questions including:

- Is the product well perceived by the trade and consumers in the test area?
- Are any product modifications necessary?
- How effective are our advertising and sales promotion techniques?
- What is the level of trial and repeat sales? This helps the company to forecast sales nationwide for the product.
- Is our distribution system effective?

Test marketing is usually carried out on new products that involve considerable investment and/or create new product categories.

Coca-Cola[4]

In 1981 Coca-Cola began testing a new formula for its soft drink, Coke. The final formula for 'new Coke' was achieved in 1984 and tested on 40,000 people in thirty US cities. Under predominantly blind tests, respondents favoured the new formula. As a result of these favourable tests the original Coke was replaced by new Coke on 23 April 1985. This produced a consumer outcry and within three weeks the original product was re-introduced under the name Coca-Cola Classic. It immediately began outstripping sales of new Coke. It is widely agreed that the company made one major mistake in its market testing: it did not test the effect of replacing Coca-Cola with a new product formula on a *named basis*. The emphasis of the research was on *blind* testing. The Coca-Cola product had become a virtual national institution and almost part of the American heritage, and tampering with this was regarded as akin to heresy.

Sheridan's Liqueur

In early 1992, a new Irish liqueur – Sheridan's – developed by R & A Bailey and Co. Ltd (maker of Baileys Irish Cream) was test marketed in selected supermarket outlets in Dublin before launching the product nationwide in December 1992. Test marketing was felt desirable because the product concept was different or unusual to any other liqueur on the market. The bottle is divided in two with one side containing a chocolate and coffee liqueur and the other side containing a cream liqueur. Pouring the product involves first pouring the chocolate and coffee liqueur into a glass and topping up with the cream liqueur.

In-store tastings and promotions were used to entice customers to try the product and careful attention was paid to the level of repeat sales. The product was launched internationally on a phased basis in 1993.

Fisher-Price[5]

US toy manufacturer Fisher-Price test markets its new toys by inviting children into its play laboratory. The new toys, along with competitors' toys, are left with the children, who are observed through one-way mirrors. Children's reactions to, and acceptance of, the new toys are monitored. Based upon the results from the play laboratory, the decision is taken to launch or delete the product.

COMMERCIALISATION

This stage of the product development process involves launching the product with its marketing mix into the market place. Advertising and promotional expenditure will usually be very large at this stage to generate awareness, encourage sampling and generate high sales as soon as possible and so build market share.

Bridgestone[6]

Companies are often faced with the dilemma of having to develop unique new products which are highly specialised in order to maintain a competitive advantage in the market. However, the very fact that the new product may be highly specialised can often limit its market application. The Bridgestone Corporation, manufacturers of tyre and rubber related products, attempt to overcome this problem by establishing 'New Business Units' (NBUs) within which the new product/ technology is commercialised. The NBUs contain the new product/ technology which acts as the core for the unit and is supported by complementary or allied products/technologies which broaden the market for the core product/technology. This was the strategy the company used in developing 'Calmzone' a special sound-proofing unit which forms a barrier to the transmission of sound. One of the unit's first applications was to provide a sound barrier for the Japanese bullet train.

The product acted as the core of an NBU consisting of sound-proofing materials including vibration damping products and noise absorbing products. The establishment of the NBU is evaluated in the early stages of the new product development process, i.e. in the planning stage. The feasibility of establishing an NBU is therefore evaluated before the process begins. This helps co-ordinate R.&D. activity and business strategy and gives direction to the former. NBUs can also be

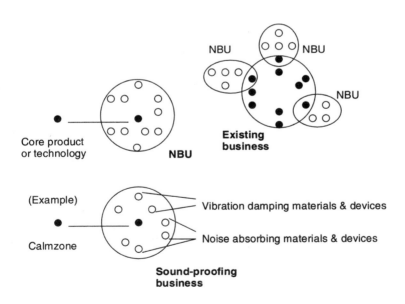

Figure 8.1 Building new business units

established around an existing product/technology from another business area, or even from outside technologies.

Gillette[7]

Gillette's Sensor razor for men is widely acknowledged as being one of the most successful launches of a consumer product. In fact, shortly after launching the product in 1990, the company was forced to withdraw its television advertising campaign temporarily because production could not keep up with demand. Sensor was launched throughout America and Europe simultaneously using the same television commercial (apart from language) in each market. The total launch costs amounted to $175 million.

Pre-launch publicity was used to prepare the way for Sensor. In 1989, an extensive corporate-image campaign was launched to promote the Gillette name throughout the USA and Europe with the slogan: 'Gillette – the best a man can get'. Other pre-launch initiatives included securing publicity in magazines and even on the CBS evening news in America.

FURTHER REFERENCE

Chapter 8, New Product Development: Product development (p. 136–137)

Spillers Foods[8]

When Spillers launched the first breakfast cereal for dogs, Goodlife Breakfast, in late 1993, approximately 2 million free trial packs were given away to dog owners at point-of-sale and through attaching trial packs to selected magazines. Other launch efforts included presentations to the major retailers, mailing to vets with details of the nutritional qualities of the product and breakfast launches for the press. These activities and more besides to build awareness and encourage sampling of the product were concentrated over a two- to three-month period and in all, the launch cost Spillers approximately £3 million.

FURTHER REFERENCE

Chapter 13, Sales Promotion and Public Relations (p. 209–223)

ORGANISATION STRUCTURES

IBM

In 1981 IBM developed a new policy of allowing small venture teams to be formed by groups of its employees to work on new product ideas, and other areas of opportunity. It referred to such units as 'companies within the company', and regarded itself as the 'venture capitalist'. These 'independent business units' (IBUs) administer their own manufacturing, marketing and finance, while the so-called 'special business units' (SBUs) depend on IBM to manage one or more of these functions. Areas of activity for these units included mainstream personal computers – IBM's first personal computer was developed by an SBU; computer aided design equipment – another SBU achieved second in the market behind leader Computervision; scientific work stations – an IBU was instrumental in IBM's challenge on DEC and Hewlett Packard in the minicomputer sector. The main advantages for IBM in this policy are first, it allows increased flexibility in innovation, reducing corporate control which often stifles activity in this area; and second, that it provides a lower risk means for IBM to enter new and emerging markets. However, the 'parent' company has experienced some resistance in incorporating these units into the main company, and has had to tread carefully in providing autonomy which it intends to eventually incorporate fully into the parent company.

FURTHER REFERENCE

Chapter 15, Organisation Structures: Strategic business units (p. 246–247)

Parallel processing/concurrent engineering

The success of the Japanese in reducing the time taken to bring new products to market has put pressure on manufacturers in other countries to find ways to reduce the time element of their product development processes.

Traditionally, the marketing department would identify a market opportunity through market research, the design or R.&D. department would put together a suitable product that met customers' needs and manufacturing would then produce it. This process, where work was passed from one department to another, had the danger of delays translating into higher costs. Too often minimum consultation occurred between departments which increased the probability of product failure. One of the keys to successful innovation lies in developing better organisational arrangements for handling new-product ideas.

Lloyds Instruments[9]

In 1993 Lloyds Instruments, a small UK manufacturer of materials testing equipment, achieved a rapid reduction in the time taken to bring its new products to market by getting departments such as production and marketing to co-operate more closely. It installed a network of computers at its factory so that engineering, design and production departments had instant access to the latest drawings and the company farmed out more design work to suppliers. The name given to this technique is parallel processing or concurrent engineering. Marketing and purchasing would be involved in a fully developed system.

This process fosters team-work. Lloyds holds regular product development meetings led by the engineering department and involving the managing director, senior design staff and representatives of sales and production.

Platform teams

Chrysler[10]

With the 1989 introduction of platform teams – autonomous groups that consist of all the professionals required to design and produce a new car or 'platform' – Chrysler pioneered a novel organisational structure. When Chrysler acquired American Motors in 1988, it decided to keep AMC's corps of 700 engineers intact. Rather than assign them to functional departments, such as steering or powertrain, it put them to work *en masse* developing the 1993 Grand Cherokee. Until then, industry practice called for designers to draw, engineers to fabricate, and manufacturers to tinker – performing their operations in isolation and in sequence.

Chrysler's innovation was to put all the engineers and designers assigned to a specific project together on a single floor, along with representatives of marketing, finance, purchasing, and even outside suppliers – hundreds of people in all – and grant them considerable autonomy. The Dodge and Plymouth Neon, an $11,000 subcompact that went on sale in January 1994, required just 31 months to develop from product approval to the start of production and cost $1.3 billion, a relative bargain.

The process worked so well that by 1991 Chrysler dissolved most of its functional groups and reassigned the members to four platform teams – small car, large car, mini-van and Jeep/truck. Chrysler put a corporate vice-president at the head of each.

Land Rover

Land Rover's highly successful jeep, Discovery, took just three years to design, develop and launch. The speed of its development was largely attributed to Land Rover's organisation of the product development team. Representatives from manufacturing, engineering, marketing, production and finance were all placed in one building. This allowed abundant and effective communication between the functions and it fostered a strong team spirit.

The development of Sheridan's liqueur[11]

In May 1993, a new Irish liqueur – Sheridan's – named after Irish writer Thomas Sheridan, was launched nationwide in Ireland by R & A Bailey and Co. Ltd. (makers of Baileys Irish Cream). Its success at home has led to its export throughout the world which is still continuing at the time of writing this chapter.

The idea for the product came from a regional director of Baileys. He saw a market opportunity for the unique liqueur, which consists of a bottle divided in two with one side containing a chocolate and coffee liqueur and the other side containing a cream liqueur. Pouring the product involves first pouring the chocolate and coffee liqueur into a glass and topping up with the cream liqueur. The end result resembles a miniature glass of Guinness.

Screening the product idea consisted of much internal discussion within Baileys. It was particularly important for the product to be special, original, innovative, have a unique taste, a package that stood out on the shelf, and have a premium image. Everything about the proposed new product was recognised as being both unique and inno-vative and this was in harmony with Baileys' progressive and open-to-new-ideas philosophy. Approval was given by the chief executive for his regional director to assume the role of product champion – a phil-osophy that runs through the organisation – and become responsible for driving the product through the development process to commercialisation. A small tightly focused team was put together dedicated to bringing the product to market. Management believed they had a potential winner on their hands and resources were dedicated to pushing the idea forward to evaluate both its technical feasibility (could such an unusual product be produced) and commercial feasibility (would it be commercially successful).

Baileys is part of International Distillers and Vintners (IDV), a UK international group which markets spirits and liqueurs world-wide, and in turn is owned by UK conglomerate GrandMetropolitan.

IDV have a new product development centre in the UK and Baileys used this resource to work on many aspects of the new product idea including formulae for the two liquids to produce a delicious unique flavoured liqueur, the blending of liquids (how to achieve the white liqueur floating on the black liqueur), packaging advice, and bottle design.

Baileys had a clear idea of the product concept, an all-year-round, all-occasion drink, rather like Baileys Irish Cream. The team did not want Sheridan's to become trapped with a traditional liqueur image – prized for slow sipping after dinner by a roaring fire. Instead, it was important to broaden the brand and position it with all-occasion spirits. A premium but moderately priced drink with a contemporary image was the target. Positioning would be done through advertising where imagery would play on spirit rather than liqueur image, for example, drinking on social occasions, group gatherings, etc. This would provide greater volume and growth for the product.

No rigorous business analysis was conducted on the product in terms of projecting sales, break-even points, costs, cash flow and profits. A tough financial appraisal would have probably rejected the idea. For example, the twin-bottle was expensive and logistically difficult to produce, fill and run down a bottling line. Production called for new and expensive technology. What was important is that management felt sure they had a winner and trade and consumer feedback were now beginning to back their idea.

Consumer groups were used during concept testing and product development to evaluate many aspects of the product, particularly taste and packaging. Also key buyers from major Irish retail outlets and the pub trade were brought in to gather their opinions on the product. Suggested improvements were incorporated into the product.

A rough marketing strategy that would be continually refined at later stages as more and more market feedback came in, was outlined at this point. The product would have a delicious unique taste, in a unique package and look like a miniature glass of Guinness when poured. The pricing would be moderate for a premium product. Promotion would be used in two ways: to build awareness and trial through tastings and in-store displays; and to secure adoption and repeat sales of the product through building a brand image and brand personality by advertising. Distribution was straightforward and Sheridan's would simply lock into Bailey's extensive distribution system.

Developing the product involved overcoming numerous hurdles and as mentioned above these included bottle manufacture and filling the bottles on a bottle line. Other hurdles included producing and attaching the labels which were both expensive and difficult to produce.

In early 1992, test marketing of Sheridan's began in Dublin. Retail outlets representative of the Dublin market as a whole were chosen. Some representatives of these outlets had been used in the earlier stages of developing the product, providing important input along the way. In a way, they were sub-champions of the product, members of the extended Sheridan's team, and therefore committed to providing abundant and constructive feedback from the test marketing.

It was recognised that success in Dublin was essential before launching the product nationwide and then rolling out on a country-by-country basis.

Useful information was picked up from the test marketing including the need to reduce the sugar content, the fact that customers liked Sheridan's on ice, that the pouring instructions needed to be made clearer, that twist-off caps were preferred to corks and labelling needed to be sharper. Bar staff needed to be shown how to pour the drink and special measuring cups were needed. It was also found that tastings and in-store displays were great for generating awareness and trial usage and drove sales initially.

A limited amount of consumer panels were held and one of the results revealed that 60 per cent of consumers would repurchase.

Test marketing was done in other countries before making a nationwide launch decision. For example, in the UK Sheridan's was test marketed in Cambridge before launching nationwide.

Although the product was originally filled and labelled by hand for test marketing, commercialisation called for adding a manufacturing facility for the product. Sheridan's is currently being rolled out on a country-by-country basis subject to successful test marketing in the countries. The brand cost approximately £6 million to develop and this investment has been quickly recouped. Although not expecting the world-wide success of Baileys Irish Cream, the company will be more than happy if Sheridan's can secure 20–25 per cent of that brand's sales in the long term, giving it another tremendous Irish success story.

FURTHER REFERENCE

Chapter 4, Marketing Research, Information, Forecasting and Measurement: qualitative research – Customer panels (p. 63)
Chapter 6, Segmentation and Positioning: Positioning (p. 105–106)
Chapter 8, New Product Development: Concept development and testing (pp. 134–136)
Chapter 11, Advertising: Communication objectives (p. 184)

CONCLUSION

This chapter has provided examples of how different companies have executed many of the stages in the new product development process. We have also seen how effective organisational arrangements are important for ensuring success in new product development. Although it is expensive, time-consuming and risky, new product development is vital for a firm's long-term success. Successful execution of new product development carries great rewards as shown by the example of Sheridan's liqueur.

NOTES

1 United States Surgical section reprinted from Jennifer Reese, 'Getting hot ideas from customers', *Fortune*, 18 May 1992, pp. 60–61. © 1992 Time Inc. All rights reserved.
2 Rubbermaid section adapted from the following: Richard Tomkins, 'Low tech, high yield', *Financial Times*, 11 March 1994, p. 11; 'Best and worst corporate reputations', *Fortune*, 7 February 1994, p. 58; Alan Farnham, 'America's most admired company', *Fortune*, 7 February 1994, pp. 50–52; 'Rubbermaid: breaking all the molds', *Sales and Marketing Management*, August 1992, p. 42; Jon Berry, 'The art of Rubbermaid', *Marketing Week*, 16 March 1992, pp. 22–25; James Braham, 'The billion-dollar dustpan', *Industry Week*, 1 August 1988, pp. 46–48.
3 Canon section reprinted from Teruo Yamanouchi, 'Breakthrough: the development of the Canon personal copier', *Long Range Planning*, vol. 22, no. 5, pp. 11–21. Copyright 1989, with kind permission from Elsevier Science Ltd.
4 Coca-Cola section adapted from the following: Mark Prendergrast, *For God, Country and Coca-Cola*, George Weidenfeld & Nicholson, London, 1993; Jaclyn Fireman, 'How Coke decided taste was it', *Fortune*, 27 May 1985, p. 54; Anna Fisher, 'Coke's brand loyalty lesson', *Fortune*, 5 August 1985, pp. 40–42; 'Old Coke is it', *Fortune*, 5 August 1985, p. 6.
5 Fisher-Price section adapted from: Kate Fitzgerald, 'Fisher-Price toys go back to roots', *Advertising Age*, 21 May 1990, p. 12; Keith H. Hammonds,

'They can make or break a toy with a giggle', *Business Week*, 19 December 1988, p. 60.
6   Bridgestone section, including Figure 8.1, is reprinted from Tokuya Urakawa, 'How Bridgestone creates new businesses through new research', *Long Range Planning*, 1993, vol. 26, no. 2, pp. 17–23. Copyright 1993, with kind permission of Elsevier Science Ltd.
7   Gillette section adapted from the following: 'The best a plan can get', *The Economist*, 15 August 1992, pp. 57–58; Nikki Tait, 'Innovation in a cut-throat world', *Financial Times*, 28 September 1993; David Willey, 'The rollout', *Journal of Business Strategy*, May/June 1993, pp. 32–33.
8   Spillers Foods section adapted from Hester Thomas, 'Launching pad', *Marketing Business*, April 1994, pp. 41–42.
9   Lloyds Instruments section adapted from *Financial Times*, 20 April 1993.
10 Chrysler section reprinted from Alex Taylor III, 'Will success spoil Chrysler?', *Fortune*, 10 January 1994, pp. 46–50. © 1994 Time Inc. All rights reserved.
11 Sheridan's section based upon an interview with Patrick Rigney, International Brand Director, Sheridan's R & A Bailey Ltd.

Chapter 9

Pricing

INTRODUCTION

Price is determined by the interaction between the value gained by the buyer and the value offered by the seller. Companies use different methods for setting prices, ranging from the highly sophisticated to the relatively arbitrary. The straight accounting methods for setting prices do not take other factors such as market competition into account. For this reason particular pricing strategies may be adopted to meet the corporate financial and marketing goals of the organisation while at the same time taking other business and market environmental factors into account. Price is therefore a key element of marketing strategy.

The major cost-based pricing methods range from marginal cost pricing to standard costing. These methods establish a basis for covering costs and contributing to profits. Particular pricing strategies such as penetration, skimming or premium pricing take consideration of demand and competitive forces. In the case of penetration pricing, the aim is usually to offer a low price to achieve market share. Premium pricing on the other hand is closely connected with positioning the product or service at the top end of the market through perceived quality and relatively high price. Companies may also charge different prices to different customers based on quantities sold or factors such as geographic location. The aim of this strategy is normally to maximise returns over and above those that would have prevailed if a single price was charged.

In this chapter we present examples of the different approaches companies use for pricing their products or services.

PRICING METHODS

Marginal cost pricing

Marginal cost pricing occurs when the fixed cost content in the selling price is reduced in order to make the price more competitive, resulting in increased volume. This is often found in the case of companies possessing technological advantages over competitors, allowing them to reduce costs. Such was the case with Henry Ford when he introduced mass production techniques in the form of the moving assembly line. In implementing such an innovation Ford was able to increase his market share by reducing unit costs and lowering prices accordingly

Standard costing/pricing[1]

The engineering industry in the USA in the 1970s generally employed the standard costing technique in setting their prices. Many of these firms started out supplying nuclear power plants with components. During this period, however, the Atomic Energy Commission introduced increased standards for such components, with closer tolerances and tighter specifications. Many of the suppliers nevertheless continued to cost nuclear components in the same way as they had costed standard components. As business from the nuclear sector increased such companies were returning lower profits or even losses. It was only when such a stage was reached that the suppliers began to realise that production costs for nuclear components were much higher than for standard applications even though both types of components were going through the same engineering processes. In the case of the nuclear components, costs such as engineering, drafting, quality, reworking and shipping were well above those for other commercial applications. This resulted in prices for nuclear components having to be increased by allocating the direct cost element of the additional work, instead of allocating the cost elements through an overhead rate on the number of production hours as they had been doing.

PRICING STRATEGIES

Penetration pricing

Penetration pricing consists of setting introductory prices at levels designed to gain maximum market share. These will usually be lower than the average price of competitors, and lower than that which consumers might expect to pay.

Wal Mart[2]

The results of a survey in 1993 of prices in discount stores in six US cities revealed that Wal Mart offered the most competitive non-sales promotion prices. The survey found that when Wal Mart entered a new market where competition already existed it adopted a penetration pricing strategy in order to establish itself as the lowest price retailer. When Wal Mart opened a store in Middletown, New York, it was found that prices on the items examined were about 20 per cent lower than the two existing competitors, Caldor and Bradlees. Similarly in Las Vegas and Berlin, New Jersey, where Wal Mart had recently established itself, prices were set lower than the competition in order to quickly gain a share of the market. In the case of Berlin the total price for a basket of items was more than 9 per cent lower than the average price of that basket in competitor shops.

In many markets Wal Mart is the price leader, setting the lowest prices and forcing the other players to follow. One of the company's major objectives is to be the lowest priced retailer in the market where competition is present. Wal Mart strives to achieve low prices through low operational costs and stringent control on expenses.

In general Wal Mart continues to offer competitive prices in established markets where it also competes with other discounters such as K-Mart, Target and Smittys. However in markets where competition is not so strong Wal Mart generally prices according to the market. The Wal Mart store in the Sun City Centre in Ruskin, Tampa Bay, is located in a relatively wealthy area with no strong immediate competition and was found to have higher prices than other Wal Mart stores where competition was greater.

FURTHER REFERENCE

Chapter 10, Marketing Channels: Retailing types – discount superstores (p. 172–173)

Skimming

This involves setting a price level designed to secure custom from the top segment of the market, i.e. those who are disposed to pay a relatively high price.

Hewlett Packard

The pricing strategy followed by Hewlett-Packard with the introduction of its laser printer for personal computers is characteristic of a skimming pricing strategy. The introductory price for the printer was set high, on average at $4,000. It was initially targeted at business users for whom the benefits of high quality printing, speed, and high levels of usage were greatest. The printers were distributed on a selective basis using dealers' personnel trained in the technical aspects of the product, who could provide expertise and support to the user. The high price was sustainable as there was no other comparable product on the market.

When competitors began to offer substitute printers, HP lowered the price and augmented the product with additional features. At this stage its pricing strategy was also supported by other elements of the marketing mix, such as increased advertising and wider distribution through mail-order, thus bringing in new segments of the market.

Price discrimination/bundling

Price bundling is the practice of offering combinations of products, or 'bundles', at a single price. Price discrimination occurs when different prices are charged to different customers.

Xerox [3]

Up to 1962 Xerox rented its photocopiers, setting the price on the basis of the number of copies per month. For a minimum of 2,000 copies per month Xerox charged a fixed rental of $25 plus 3.5 cents per copy. Customers consuming a greater number of copies per month paid the same fixed rental. As a result the cost per copy for a low consuming organisation was much greater than that for a high consuming organisation. This is demonstrated by the example in Table 9.1.

The price per copy was more expensive for the small user than the large user.

Xerox also charged different prices according to the number of copies per original. Usage charge was lower for copying many copies per original than for few copies per original. This was because at the beginning photocopiers were also competing with printers. Printers could produce multiple copies of a single original as cheaply as photocopiers, therefore the cost of photocopying multiple copies had to be competitive with the cost of using a printer. However printer costs for

Table 9.1 Cost per photocopy for small and large users

	A	B
No. of copies per month	2,500	25,000
Total cost of copying p.m.	$87.5	$875.0
Rental per month	$25.00	$25.00
Total cost p.m.	$112.5	$900.00
Cost per copy	$0.045	$0.036

Note: A = small user, B= large user

few copies of an original were high, due to the set-up costs, therefore allowing Xerox to charge a higher price for copying that required only few copies of the original. Such users were prepared to pay higher prices than those who required multiple copies. The copy machine was designed with a cover such that the number of copies per original could be counted.

The reason for charging different prices was due to the different price sensitivities of the different users. However Japanese competitors began offering relatively cheap machines to low volume users building up their market position until they were in a position to challenge Xerox in the large volume segment.

FURTHER REFERENCE

Chapter 6, Segmentation and Positioning: Types or segmentation and positioning – benefit segmentation (pp. 100–101)

Premium pricing

Apple Computer[4]

In 1983 Apple Computer decided to set the price of its personal computer well above prices of competitors' machines in the USA. Apple computers used their own unique operating system unlike most other PCs which used an 'open' operating system whereby machines from different manufacturers could be substituted for each other. This contributed to high development costs for the company. But Apple believed their machines were easier to use than DOS machines because of their 'windows' system and mouse driven capability. The company therefore decided to maintain their premium pricing policy. Gross margins on the product were held at around 50 per cent for most of the 1980s, compared to about 25 per cent for other PC manufacturers.

In 1987 the improved Mac SE and Macintosh II range were launched which were also targeted at the corporate market. The Mac IIs were popular with certain users such as graphic designers, and the 'home' market, but did not have wide appeal in the business market. Apple claimed their machines required less training to use and therefore were competitive with IBM compatible machines in terms of total costs. This was another reason why they felt they could charge a premium price. However, for new users to switch to Macs they would have to write off their existing machines, because Macs could not be easily linked into existing networks.

Meanwhile, due to the open-systems in which IBM-compatible machines could be linked into each other, the market expanded producing greater competition and also enabling greater economies of scale, resulting in prices being pushed down. One market where Apple was particularly strong was the schools market. In 1989 however it was overtaken by IBM in this market, a situation which many recognise as being a result of the premium pricing policy. Furthermore, because the market for PCs was much larger, software development companies concentrated their efforts on developing software for PCs and not Macs, resulting in a wide range of software becoming available. Finally, when Microsoft developed Windows with similar properties to Apple's software system, this further eroded the unique benefits of the Mac. Towards the end of the 1980s a colour Macintosh II with hard drive cost about twice as much as an equivalent PC. The company's share of the US PC market fell from 15 per cent in 1987 to 9 per cent in 1990.

In the autumn of 1990 Apple decided to respond to the changing conditions and introduced low-cost Macs and cut prices on existing products. Sales increased significantly as a result, but mainly at the lower end of the range. The bottom of the line model, the Macintosh Classic, carried a suggested retail price of just under $1,000 in the USA, and was intended to replace the Mac Plus at $1,799 and the SE at $2,698. The new low price strategy is also being complemented by increased flexibility of Apple hardware and software, enabling them to be linked into other PC systems and read each other's software. Such a strategy inevitably reduces the uniqueness of Apple products, and whether or not it will result in erosion of the features and benefits which differentiated it from bulk standard PC producers is a risk which the company will need to address.

FURTHER REFERENCE

Chapter 9, Pricing: Pricing strategies – Price and quality (below)

Pricing on performance

Contract Energy Management

An organisation's use of energy is in most cases an overhead, but also a necessary input to carry out the core activity which they are involved in. In the case of most organisations energy bills could be reduced by using the energy resource more efficiently. However, they do not generally devote the time or investment to achieve this reduction. Contract energy management (CEM) companies offer to manage an organisation's energy use with the aim of reducing its expenditure on energy. The customer organisation signs a contract with the CEM company without having to outlay any payments, but agrees to give the CEM company a certain percentage of the savings achieved under the contract. The 'price' charged by the contractor is therefore negotiated with the host organisation prior to the contract being signed. Under this situation the customer organisation pays a pre-negotiated 'price' to the contractor at the end or during stipulated periods of the contract.

Discrete pricing

In many organisations, particularly public organisations, purchasing agents are given certain limits or budgets for purchasing certain items, so that below these limits they possess the authority to purchase without having to seek further approval from superiors. As a result sellers often pitch their price at or near these levels thus giving them freedom to deal directly with a single decision maker.

PRICE AND QUALITY

Superdrug and perfumes[5]

The sale of fine perfumes is characterised by profit margins of between 60 per cent to 100 per cent for manufacturers and retailers. This regime however was upset by the health and beauty chain Superdrug, who began offering up-market perfumes at discounted prices in selected stores in 1991. The perfumes were sold at special counters within the store and prices were discounted by up to 30 per cent. In the areas where the strategy has been piloted, prices in competing retailers such as Boots, Littlewoods and Tesco have also been reduced.

The fragrance houses pursue a selective distribution strategy by only selling through 'authorised retailers'. The houses are resisting the move by Superdrug by not granting the chain authorised status to sell their products and refusing to supply. However the company has secured supply on the grey market. The maintenance of a high price for perfumes contributes to their image of exclusivity, in this way price is associated with perceived quality or image. In this sense a high price can be part of the satisfaction which the product offers. Superdrug's research indicated that consumers would purchase more products if prices were reduced. But in the eyes of the manufacturers a reduction in price and a consequent increase in sales would dilute the image of the product. Superdrug's attempts to advertise in some women's magazines were also refused. Magazines refusing included *Elle* and *Vogue*.

The margins on perfumes are particularly high. On average distributors' margins are about 70 per cent and retailers' 60 per cent. The case was examined by the Monopolies and Mergers Commission (MMC) in 1993 and the perfume manufacturers were cleared of unfair pricing policies. They are therefore free to continue their strategy of using high prices to confer an image of quality and exclusivity on their product.

FURTHER REFERENCE

Chapter 9, Pricing: Pricing strategies – premium pricing (pp. 152–153)
Chapter 10, Marketing Channels: The distribution strategy – selective distribution (p. 181–182)

SETTING PRICES

Netex[6]

A major agrochemical company planned to sell a new insecticide called Netex to different market segments in different countries. The company had to reconcile a number of different interests in the pricing process. The financial people favoured a cost plus approach, focusing on unit costs and associated margins. The marketing and sales people wanted a low penetration price, while counterbalancing a competitive price with one which would provide acceptable commission for sales personnel. Senior management were tending to come down in favour of price mark-ups but at levels lower than the accountants. This was a complex situation which required a comprehensive market and competitive analysis.

Among the different issues which the analysis had to take into account were consumer needs and preferences, competitor performance and competitive environment, the marginal costs of competing products and the potential level of sales. The company collected primary data through interviews with potential consumers and dealers in different countries. The study used techniques such as conjoint and regression analysis and multidimensional scaling. The process contributed to a rational discussion of the price setting decision. The result was a price structure that reflected the complexities of the markets, with a range of differentiated price systems.

In one market the perceived value of the Netex product was greater. This allowed a premium price to be set, with a slight modification in the product and its renaming as Netex-Forte, as it was not possible to sell the standard product at different prices. In some developing countries the perceived value of the product and consequent willingness to pay was much lower than the average. The result was that the product was not made available in these countries. In other markets they decided to sell Netex along with a much cheaper additive which saved farmers from having to make an additional spraying, thus giving them greater value for money. The combined package was called Netex-combi and carried a premium price for the company. The study also found that light users were less price sensitive than heavy users with the result that a significant rebate and a bonus system were offered to heavy users.

Setting price through conjoint analysis

Conjoint analysis is a means of providing quantitative measures to particular attributes or benefits of a product.

Automobiles[7]

A German car manufacturer was planning to introduce a new model to the market. The company decided the most important attributes of the car were the brand itself, price, the top speed of the car, and its petrol consumption. These attributes were then assigned characteristics as a means of measuring the comparative preference for the attributes. A questionnaire was then developed to collect data in order to be able to compare the attributes. The study sought to test three brands – the company's own brand, a Japanese brand, and another German brand;

three top speeds – 200, 220 and 240 km/hour; three rates of fuel consumption – 12, 14, and 16 litres per 100 km; and three price levels – DM 50,000, DM 60,000, and DM 70,000. From the data collected through the questionnaire nine possible product profiles were chosen. The profiles were then presented in pairs to potential customers, as shown in Table 9.2.

Numerical values were assigned to the preference for different attributes. Called 'preference contributions' these allowed the preference for different attributes to be compared. Preference contributions allow you to compare a change in the level of one attribute with that of another, e.g. improving fuel consumption by a particular amount may create the same increase in preference as reducing the price by a particular amount. In relation to a particular attribute the greater the difference between the lowest and highest preference contribution, then the more important is this attribute. The difference between preference contributions are then assigned weights based on percentages which quantify the differences in importance. The percentages all add up to 100.

The company found the following results:

Brand	35 per cent
Maximum speed	30 per cent
Price	20 per cent
Fuel consumption	15 per cent

This demonstrated that potential customers were more sensitive to brand and maximum speed than price and fuel consumption. By using the attribute levels for its new model, the company was able to project market shares and profits for different prices. The optimal price was found to be DM 70,000.

Table 9.2 Attribute comparison

Attribute	Profile A	Profile B
Brand	New model	Japanese
Max. speed	200	240
Fuel consumption	12	16
Price	50,000	70,000

Source: Hermann Simon, 'Pricing opportunities – and how to exploit them', *Sloan Management Review*, winter 1992.

Japanese price setting

Many Japanese companies adopt an approach to determining price which is in contrast to that carried out in the West. In general the Western approach to the pricing of new products is to set prices after design, engineering and prototype development of a new product has been carried out. Analysis of how much the new product will cost is then carried out. If the cost is too high the product is reworked to bring the price down. A simplified description of the Japanese approach on the other hand is to identify the product concept and then decide the planned selling price for the product. The required profit is then deducted from this resulting in the target product cost. The development process then works to this target cost. The elemental costs of the product are negotiated with suppliers or departments within the company to produce the product within the target cost. This process is facilitated by the close relationships between Japanese companies and their suppliers.

PRICE WARS

Cigarettes[8]

The continuous decline in per capita consumption of cigarettes in the USA led the major companies to diversify into new markets. The decline however also led the major players to invest in high equity brand names particularly in the 1980s. The Marlboro brand of Philip Morris (PM) was a case in point. In the 1990s discount brands began challenging the position of the established brands, with Marlboro's share declining from a high of 26 per cent down to 20 per cent. Early in 1993 the price of Marlboro was cut by 15 per cent. The other main competitor, R.J. Reynolds (RJR) reacted by cutting the price of its premium brand, Winston. PM again reacted by announcing that it would freeze prices on its premium brand cigarettes and offer promotions that would reduce premium brand prices indefinitely and also compete more vigorously than before in the discount cigarette market. The premium brands' price cut was to include the Marlboro, Merit, Benson & Hedges, Virginia Slims and Parliament brands.

The intention of PM in pursuing this strategy may have been to steal market share from other premium brands, particularly RJR, and not a move to bring back those who had switched to the discount brands. RJR was already the leader in the discount brands, but its premiums, which included Camel, were behind PM's in market share. This is where the greatest profit was to be made, so by gaining market share in the premiums and increasing prices eventually, greater long-run profitability could be achieved.

The battle was extended, however, when Liggett announced a cut in the price of Chesterfield, Eve, Lark and L&M brands with a heavy couponing promotion. Lorillard, Brown & Williamson Tobacco and American Tobacco also agreed to cut the prices of their premium cigarettes.

At the same time the price of lower positioned brands was actually increased by both PM and RJR, as well as the American Tobacco Co.'s Private Stock, Prime and Summit brands. This was intended to prevent switching from the 'premium' to the 'discount' brands. The cut in the price of premium brands affected distributors' and retailers' margins and resulted in an increased convergence in the positioning of cigarette brands. This convergence also made it difficult for the cigarette companies to increase the price of their premium brands again. Cannibalisation of the premiums by the discount brands within the same product line was a major risk.

However the position was redressed when RJR told distributors in November 1993 that it was raising prices on most of its cigarette brands including Camel and Winston by four cents a pack. The net effect of the price war was a drop in earnings for the tobacco firms in the last quarter of 1994.

FURTHER REFERENCE

Chapter 7, Products: Product cannibalisation (p. 121)

CONCLUSION

Pricing is a key element of a company's marketing mix. It is the only element that directly generates income. In this respect it must be set to meet the company's profit objectives. However, it is also very important for marketing objectives. Skimming and penetration pricing are both critically important for the competitive position of the firm, but are found at opposite ends of the spectrum. The examples presented in this chapter demonstrate the factors which companies are faced with when deciding on price: ranging from the competition faced as in the case of Wal Mart, to product positioning as in the case of perfumes. The pricing strategy chosen must therefore balance the financial and marketing objectives of the firm. In this respect pricing is often unique.

NOTES

1 Standard costing/pricing section adapted from Thomas S. Dudick, 'Pricing strategies for manufacturers', *Management Accounting*, December 1989, pp. 30–37.

2 Wal Mart section adapted from 'Studies reveal dual pricing strategies', *Discount Store News*, 7 June 1993, vol. 32, no. 11, pp. 57–9. Reprinted by permission from *Discount Store News*. Copywright Lebhar-Friedman, Inc., 425 Park Avenue, New York, NY 10022.

3 Xerox section adapted from the following: Erwin A. Blackstone, 'Restrictive Practices in the Marketing of Electrofax Copying Machines and Supplies: The SCM Corporation Case', *Journal of Industrial Economics*, March 1975, vol. 23, pp. 189–202; Thomas T. Nagle, *The Strategy and Tactics of Pricing*, Prentice Hall, 1987; Hermann Simon and Martin Fassnacht, 'Price Bundling', *European Management Journal*, December 1993, vol. 11, no. 4, pp. 403–411; 'Trying to duplicate the success of Xerox', *Business Week*, 22 October 1966, pp. 66; 'Supplying Copiers: a key to profit', *Business Week*, 12 October 1968, pp. 144; 'Xerox selling rental model, cuts price on two others', *Wall Street Journal*, 24 February 1969, p. 10.

4 Apple Computer section adapted from: *The Economist*, 24 August 1991; Thomas R. King, 'Apple to dish up saucy new campaign', *The Wall Street Journal*, 3 October 1990, p. B10; G. Pascal Zachary, 'Apple Peels Prices of its New Models', *The Wall Street Journal*, 3 October 1990, p. B1, B11; Barbara Buell, Richard Brandt, Jonathan B. Levine, and Neil Gross, 'Apple: new team, new strategy', *Business Week*, 15 October 1990, pp. 40–46; Brenton R. Schlender, 'Yet Another Strategy for Apple', *Fortune*, 22 October 1990; David Manasian, 'Four friends, four rivals – a tale of three winners and one big loser', *The Economist*, 27 February 1993.

5 Superdrug and perfumes section adapted from the following: 'Perfume price not unfair', *Manufacturing Chemist*, November 1993, p. 7; Jenny Rees, 'Perfume houses win fight with cut-price shops', *Daily Telegraph*, 12 November 1993, p. 5; Helen Slingsby, 'Superdrug kicks up a fine stink', *Marketing Week*, 2 May 1992, pp. 15–16; 'MMC investigated perfume house meeting', *The Independent* (UK), 22 August 1993, p. S1; 'Perfume war gathers pace', *Manufacturing Chemist*, March 1993, p. 13; Matthew Cole, 'Image conscious retailers put brands before bands', *Music Week*, 24 October 1992, p. 10; 'Scenting a profit with discounts', *The European*, 25 October 1992, p. 45; 'Adverts for cheap perfumes blocked', *The Independent* (UK), 5 October 1992, p. 11; 'Superdrug not budging on cheap perfume stance', *Manufacturing Chemist*, June 1992, p. 11; 'Superdrug create a stink over perfume prices', *Chemist and Druggist*, 9 May 1992; Fine Fragrances: A report on the supply in the United Kingdom, HMSO 1993.

6 Netex section reprinted from Hermann Simon, 'Pricing opportunities – and how to exploit them', *Sloan Management Review*, Winter 1992, pp. 55–65. Reprinted by permission of the publishers. Copyright 1992 by the Sloan Management Association. All rights reserved.

7 Cars section also adapted from Hermann Simon, op. cit.

8 Cigarettes section reprinted from the following: Richard M. Petreycik and
   Kevin P. Francella, 'Uncertainty clouds latest cigarette war', *U.S.
   Distribution Journal*, 15 June 1993, vol. 220, no. 6, p. 6; Maria Mooshil,
   'Tobacco firms to show earnings drop for fourth quarter'', *Wall Street
   Journal*, 10 January 1994, pp. B5D; Michael Janofsky, 'Increase by RJR
   may end a cigarette price war', *New York Times*, 10 November 1993, p. D4;
   Ira Teinowitz, 'Liggett couponing move may extend cigarette price war',
   Advertising Age, 2 August 1993, p. 2; Eben Shapiro, 'New price move by
   Philip Morris intensifies war', *Wall Street Journal*, 21 July 1993, p. B1;
   Subrata N. Chakravarty and Amy Feldman, 'Don't underestimate the
   champ', *Forbes*, 10 May 1993, pp. 106–110.

Chapter 10

Marketing channels

INTRODUCTION

Developing a sound distribution strategy for a product is imperative to help ensure that product's success in the market place – to ensure the product can be bought by the right people, at the right place and at the right time.

The marketing intermediaries a firm uses to reach its target market is a critical marketing decision and one that cannot easily be changed. An effective distribution system can take years to build as one is usually talking of building long-term relationships with outside companies. When formulating a distribution strategy, a firm can choose between several types of channel to reach its customers. It may even develop its own distribution channel, becoming vertically integrated. Many of the different types of channel are outlined with examples of companies that successfully use them.

Managing the channel is vitally important. Someone must be prepared to lead the channel. Channel members must be motivated and close co-operation between the channel members is desirable to achieve optimum results. Conflict must be eliminated to keep the channel working smoothly and on track towards the achievement of profits and customer satisfaction. Finally, competition within the channel and/or between different channel types can be healthy, motivating channel members and providing greater choice to customers. Examples are provided of companies that demonstrate effective channel management.

Retailing is the final link of many channels. In the UK, there is a wide variety of retailing forms. New types of retailer continue to evolve in response to changing customer demands and market conditions, e.g. growth of discounters and warehouse clubs in the 1990s' UK as customers become more price-sensitive in a tougher economic climate.

The main types of retailer found in the UK are described with examples of each type. The Wheel of Retailing – a theoretical model used to explain the evolution of retailing institutions – is described using examples of retailers that conform to this model.

Wholesaling is covered briefly as this area, although important, has witnessed few developments in comparison with retailing over the years. Finally, the three types of distribution strategy a firm may pursue are described.

SELECTING CHANNEL TYPE

Deciding on the type of marketing channel to use in order to reach the end-user is one of the most critical marketing decisions a company faces. There are a host of alternative ways of getting a company's goods from the producer to the end-user. For example, the company can sell directly to end-users, or use a number of middlemen including, for example, wholesalers, retailers and sales agents. The company could even use a combination of direct marketing methods and the traditional middlemen. Whichever marketing channel(s) is selected, the company is usually committed to a long-term decision as channels are not easily changed. However, the company must be prepared to modify the channel if market and environmental conditions dictate so, therefore, the channel must be capable of adaptation.

In recent years, a number of progressive companies have set up direct marketing operations selling to the end-users and ignoring the traditional marketing channels used by other firms in the industry.

Direct marketing

Dell Computers[1]

Dell Computers Corporation, (which was in 1993 the world's third largest manufacturer of IBM-compatible personal computers) in 1984 became the computer industry's first ever direct marketing operation, selling computers through mail-order.

Products are advertised in trade magazines and through an in-house catalogue called Dellware. Dell has being extraordinarily successful with this unique distribution strategy. In 1992, annual revenue was $2 billion with net profits generated of $102 million. Freephone telephone numbers are listed to enable the customer to receive advice and place orders. Dell also offers the customer the opportunity to tailor the product, e.g. to choose the disk drive, the chip, the software and additional peripherals. The finished product is shipped out within a few days of receiving an order.

Using this distribution approach, Dell has acquired a competitive advantage made up of high quality service, tailored products, low prices and award-winning end-user support. Overheads are kept to a minimum to keep prices low, e.g. factories are leased and headquarters rented. The company has one of the lowest R.&D. budgets in the industry preferring to use the peripherals and components of the industry's leading technology specialists – software from Microsoft, chips from Intel, etc. and instead investing resources in ease-of-use systems, user interfaces, set-up systems, training and processes which help customers solve their problems. Dell also uses discount stores and mass merchants for the atypical shopper but after-sales service is provided by Dell.

The leading computer manufacturers – Apple, IBM and Compaq – also developed direct marketing operations of their own in response to Dell's success.

FURTHER REFERENCE

Chapter 4, Marketing Research, Information, Forecasting and Measurement: Databases (pp. 64–68)

Direct Line Insurance

Direct Line Insurance, a UK wholly owned subsidiary of the Bank of Scotland set up in 1985, was one of the first motor insurance companies to cut out the traditional broker middleman and use telesales techniques to interface directly with customers. In its first year of operation, it secured 300,000 new policyholders. Over the same time period, the established UK insurance companies using brokers generally came nowhere near the success achieved by Direct Line. This distribution strategy has secured a strong competitive advantage for Direct Line and to date, the company remains extraordinarily successful.

Finding an alternative to the channel arrangements used in an industry can provide an individual firm with a distinct competitive advantage, as we have seen with the direct marketing examples above.

Vertical marketing systems

Vertical marketing systems (VMS) are distribution entities that consist of intermediaries, e.g. manufacturers, wholesalers, retailers, working together to achieve operating economies and maximum market impact. They include:

1 Retailer co-operative

ADM-Londis

The emergence of the supermarkets in Ireland posed a threat to the large number of small independent retailers throughout the country. Groups of retailers organised themselves and developed a new business entity to carry on wholesaling and some production. This retail co-operative is called **ADM-Londis** and is Ireland's largest retail co-operative. It offers its members buying economies that enable them to stand against the huge buying power of the multiples. It also conducts group advertising, offers merchandising help and own-label products for its members.

2 Wholesaler sponsored voluntary chain

Spar

Spar is an example of a wholesaler sponsored voluntary chain, where the wholesaler has taken the initiative in defending its customers – small independent retailers – against the supermarkets and has developed a merchandising strategy for them. The retailers join the wholesaler voluntarily and agree to purchase. The benefits to the retailer are the same as those in a retail co-operative and the wholesaler gets an assured customer. Super Value Stores and VG are also wholesaler sponsored voluntary chains.

3 Franchising

Franchising is a contractual VMS. This consists of independent distribution intermediaries co-operating on a contractual basis to obtain greater economies and /or market impact than they could achieve alone.

Franchising is where a person wishing to start their own business, called a franchisee, signs a contractual agreement to use the brand name and established method of doing business of an existing company, called the franchiser. The franchisee receives promotional and other support (e.g. training, marketing, technical, financial services) from the franchiser. The franchiser gains wider market coverage without increased capital costs and risk and still retains tight control over the marketing of its product or service. Franchisees, although self employed, are required to work within an existing framework and standards laid down by the franchiser. The franchisee usually pays an initial fee and an on-going royalty (percentage of sales usually) to the franchiser.

Dragons[2]

Dragons, a UK manufacturer of exclusive handmade children's bedroom furniture founded in 1976, used franchising to expand abroad in the 1990s. Their product range includes, for example, hand-painted beds, toy boxes, chairs, fabrics, soft toys and wallpaper. Its products can also be personalised by painting on children's names.

By the end of the 1980s, Dragons was exporting its products all over the developed world. In 1992, the idea of setting up a European franchise operation was considered. It was recognised that this route to expansion would increase its high street presence with minimum capital investment and allow Dragons to retain control over quality and standards. By 1993, with the help of a marketing consultant, Dragons had opened two European franchises in Oslo and Stockholm.

Laura Ashley

The Laura Ashley group designs, manufactures and retails its own clothes, home furnishings and related products world-wide. Laura Ashley has hundreds of shops, the majority of them owned by the group with a small number of franchised outlets. Franchisees are required to adhere to particular standards, e.g. store layout and presentation of merchandise that is consistent with company-owned shops and echoes the individual style and design of Laura Ashley.

British School of Motoring (BSM)

BSM driving instructors are franchisees. BSM provides a dual-control car (which it repairs, services, replaces regularly and taxes and insures) and training materials in return for a slice of the fees received by the 2,000 or so instructors. Instructors pay for their own petrol and pay their own National Insurance and tax.

BSM also provides the franchisees with learner drivers who are attracted by the well-known brand name.

MOTIVATING CHANNEL MEMBERS

Dealer incentives

As a manufacturer, developing an innovative dealer incentive scheme is important in standing out from other suppliers.

Hewlett-Packard[3]

In the UK in 1992, Hewlett-Packard, the computer manufacturer, developed an incentive package for its dealers called the Diamond Edge Support Package. Customers were offered a three-year service package providing next day on-site service at a fixed premium, through Hewlett-Packard distributors.

The service package offered a good margin to the dealers and did not create any complex administration for them as service agreements were returned by customers directly to Hewlett-Packard. The success of the incentive scheme led to its extension to Hewlett-Packard dealers all over Europe.

Anheuser-Busch

The US brewer Anheuser-Busch, the world's largest brewing company with the famous Budweiser brand, gives its independent wholesale distributors a very high level of corporate support to motivate them. The support provided also serves to dissuade them from carrying competing product lines. Every three years, the company throws a huge wholesalers' convention with appearances by such celebrities as Paul Newman and Bob Hope. The company is willing to back special promotions for its wholesalers (often providing up to half the cost of the promotion), including sporting events and festivals and often 'loans' headquarters' personnel for such events.

Zanussi CLV Systems   This catering equipment manufacturer launched its MD 700 range of heavy duty equipment in the UK and it used air miles as the principal incentive for its dealers to push the new range. Dealers were awarded air miles in proportion to the size of the order.

The following two examples illustrate the importance of developing effective and motivating discount structures for dealers.

Canadian publisher[4]

A Canadian publisher developed a new four volume set of encyclo-paedias which were forecasted to be a market success. The Canadian market consisted of a combination of independent book shops and chain stores, two of which controlled a large proportion of the market. The publisher's retail price was $175 per set, a price which all appeared to be happy with. However, discounts increased rapidly with increased volumes resulting in the chain stores quickly being able to purchase at huge volume discounts and much lower than the independents at a price of $75 to $80. They anticipated that the books would be in great demand and could afford to place only a relatively small mark-up on the set due to the large forecasted demand. The chain stores' final retail price was placed at $99 a set. The independent book shops had already paid $125 per set due to the small quantities they could order. The large price difference between the independents and the chain stores resulted in large quantities of unsold stock in the former stores which was sub-sequently shipped back to the publishers. Much bad feeling was generated towards the publishers with the result that the independent book shops boycotted a number of later books.

FURTHER REFERENCE

Chapter 9, Pricing: Setting prices (pp. 155–158)

QMS Inc.[5]

QMS Inc., a US manufacturer of high quality moderately priced laserjet printers, was reputed to be offering its retail dealers discounts which were inconsistent with the costs dealers were incurring in stocking, selling and promoting the printers. This resulted in dealers simply not ordering equipment from QMS. As a result $71 million of inventory accumulated at QMS, and the company lost $5 million in 1988 after making a profit of $9 million in 1987. This was a direct result of the company failing to develop a suitable discount structure for its dealers.

CHANNEL LEADERSHIP

Within a channel there is usually a dominant member, the one who leads it in trying to ensure the various intermediaries act in a co-ordinated way to ultimately achieve customer satisfaction and mutual profitability.

The dominant member is not always the manufacturer. For example, McDonald's is the most powerful firm in its channel and exerts a powerful influence over suppliers and its franchisees. In grocery retailing, a large UK multiple like Sainsbury's would be the dominant member in the channel able to influence its suppliers, often huge manufacturers themselves.

The car industry provides an example of channel leaders who are manufacturers. For example, BMW exerts powerful, if not total control over its dealers, specifying showroom design and layout, discount levels and quotas of models.

CHANNEL CONFLICT

Channel conflict is sometimes inevitable in a channel with independent intermediaries.

Honda's Acura Legend[6]

One of the most famous cases of channel conflict arose in the USA in 1985 when Honda started marketing the upmarket Acura Legend. Honda set up a new division with a dealer network separate from the regular Honda dealerships to sell its Acura luxury cars. Honda wanted the Acura dealers to specialise in the more luxurious cars and the regular dealers to specialise in small cars. The separate dealer network would distinguish Acura and Honda brands. Honda's strategy initially caused an outcry from the regular dealers who protested that it would take sales away from them but after some time, Honda had reassured the regular dealers and the conflict was resolved.

CHANNEL CO-OPERATION

Channel co-operation between manufacturers, wholesalers and retailers or whatever type of intermediaries make up a specific channel is necessary for both customer satisfaction and mutual profitability.

Lithonia Lighting[7]

Owned by National Service Industries, a clothing-to-chemicals conglomerate, Lithonia is the world's biggest maker of lighting equipment. That means everything (except bulbs) from fluorescent office-lighting to lighting-control systems.

In America lighting equipment is usually sold through a web of contractors, distributors and agents. For a new building, 'specifiers' draft the basic facts about the lighting system needed for the project, then put the job of installation out to tender. The winning contractor orders the system's components from an electrical distributor, which tends to sell several manufacturers' products. The distributor buys from an independent sales agent. These are usually linked to a single manufacturer: Lithonia follows industry practice by letting its agents stock complementary, but not competing, products.

At the start of the 1980s Lithonia was market leader, but its competitors were catching up. How could it remodel its business, become more competitive and turn itself into the world's lowest-cost, highest-quality maker of lighting equipment?

Mr Charles Darnell, a senior vice-president at Lithonia and architect of the firm's change, felt that exploiting the industry's dispersed structure and ditching Lithonia's conventional organisational hierarchy would give it an edge. He put Lithonia's independent agents at the hub of a spoked network. Grouped around the hub were the specifiers, contractors and distributors, plus Lithonia's various decentralised product divisions, its field warehouses and its headquarters' team.

This process made Lithonia rethink its business links. It was not, as it had supposed, at the top of a hierarchy, with strong links only to its agents (the second tier of the hierarchical 'pyramid'). In reality, the lighting-equipment business revolved around the agents. These had the local knowledge and customer relations necessary to get Lithonia's products chosen for lighting projects. A plan emerged: help make the agents more efficient and more profitable, break down the boundaries between Lithonia and its partners in the network, and business would boom. Lithonia has spent $20 million turning that plan into practice.

Computers now link each bit of Lithonia's network, from specifiers to agents to Lithonia's own factories. Computer-aided design and artificial-intelligence systems help specifiers to design a lighting layout to suit any project. Automated, flexible manufacturing systems (linked into the overall computer network) mean that Lithonia can swiftly modify its product lines; feedback from customers and agents help design new products. Product catalogues can be tailored to show specific ranges and prices for individual customers.

Contractors, distributors and agents check the availability of products and order them from Lithonia on-line. The company's software automatically directs the various components of each order to the relevant Lithonia product division. The progress of each order can be tracked throughout the system. Even Lithonia's delivery trucks will eventually be linked into the computer network so that customers will know exactly when their orders will arrive.

All told, Lithonia's system has cut the lead-time on orders from up to nine days to under a day. None of the firm's competitors (principally Cooper Industries, Genlyte, Kidde and USI, the last two owned by Britain's Hanson) has such an integrated system. They also sell their products through specifiers, distributors and independent agents. Developing a Lithonia-like computerised information network would take them at least five years. But do they need one?

Lithonia reckons that its networked structure has contributed greatly to a close-to-doubling of sales (to $717 million in the year to August 1990) over the past six years, and a more-than-doubling of profits, to $59.5 million. It also encourages agents to be loyal – and agents are at the hub of Mr Darnell's network. The efficiency of Lithonia's system increases the agents' profits and ties them more closely to Lithonia by providing them with a plethora of computer systems and software to help them run their own businesses with fewer support staff. Defecting to another manufacturer would rob them of those benefits overnight.

Harley-Davidson

After years of losing market share to the Japanese, Harley-Davidson in the 1980s successfully embarked on product innovation, improved its quality and styling and began targeting up-market riders. The company realised as part of its new image and positioning, it was necessary to change the image of its dealers so that a consistent picture of the company was presented to its new target market. Harley-Davidson sought their dealers' co-operation and showrooms were brightened up and modernised with new display equipment and cabinets advertising Harley's range of clothing and accessories.

The strategy has helped Harley-Davidson return to the dominant position in the heavyweight (over 750cc) motorcycle category.

FURTHER REFERENCE

Chapter 14, Market status and competitive moves: Competitive moves (pp. 233–235)

CHANNEL COMPETITION

Channel competition can take a number of different forms. For example, a manufacturer selling products to similar but competing outlets (for example, Heinz selling to UK multiples Sainsbury's and Tesco) where the competition is between the retailers. Another type of channel competition is between two or more different channel types. An example of this is Compaq in the USA which sells computers in the discount retailer Wal Mart and by mail order.

Channel competition is healthy and from the customer's point of view opens the way for a wider range of products, prices and services.

RETAILING TYPES

Department stores

Department stores emerged as an alternative to the small speciality retailers. They became a one-stop shopping centre for almost all personal and household goods offering a wide variety of merchandise and depth of product lines. Department stores are distinguished by the high degree of departmentalisation, where related products are organised into separate departments, for example, housewares, cosmetics, men's clothing, and women's clothing. Each department acts almost as a separate business within the store with buying, selling, promoting and other functions conducted entirely or at least in part at the department level.

Department stores originally started out as high-volume, low-cost operations and over time began adding extra services such as credit and delivery which in turn increased their prices. Famous department store chains include House of Fraser and Debenhams. Harrods is the largest department store in the world.

Discount superstores

The move upmarket by the department stores opened the way for the discount superstores which pose a serious threat to department stores today.

Discounters are attracting customers particularly in the areas of consumer electronics, linens, home furnishings and automotive supplies. They are usually located on the edge of town in large purpose-built warehouses either on their own or grouped with complementary discount retailers together in what is termed 'retail parks'(see below).

Companies such as Comet (consumer electronics), Texas (home-wares) and Wickes (DIY) operate discount superstores. Department stores chains are increasingly developing superstores of their own, e.g. Debenhams.

Category killers

There are specialist discount superstores (category killers) which deal in one product category, e.g. toys by Toys 'R' Us, and video rental and sales by Blockbusters which because of their buying power, resulting from product specialisation, can undercut department stores and smaller specialist retailers in their product category. Their ability to destroy much of the competition in their market sector explains their name.

Retail parks

Over the 1980s and 1990s, retailing has witnessed the growth of edge-of-town superstores in, for example, groceries, electronics, furniture, DIY and carpets. Often, these giant purpose-built warehouses are located together in retail parks. Their growth has been fuelled by many factors including the rise in city centre rents, the shortage of large city-centre sites necessary to display the increasing proliferation of product lines, the relaxing of planning laws in the green belt and the increase in car ownership.

Retail parks are composed primarily of discount retailers operating in large purpose-built warehouses on the edge of town. These discount superstores complement one another providing one-stop shopping for car owners, e.g. DIY, gardenwares, consumer electronics, carpets and home furnishings. A grocery superstore and a speciality shopping mall is also usually located in one of these retail parks.

Lakeside at Thurrock in Essex, Gateshead's MetroCentre and Sheffield's Meadowhall, all in England, are examples of retail parks. These out-of-town shopping complexes provide extensive parking facilities (12,000 spaces at Lakeside), attract millions of shoppers every year (25 million per annum to Gateshead's MetroCentre) and have enormous turnover – the MetroCentre pulls in well over £0.5 billion per annum. These retail parks have become a 'great day out' for many people, with their multi-level shopping malls containing speciality stores, restaurants and cinemas.

Variety stores

In contrast to department stores, variety stores are often more specialised offering a reduced range of merchandise. Woolworth's is an example of this type of store, offering records and tapes, children's clothing, housewares, gardenwares and confectionery. Marks & Spencer is also a variety store with its emphasis on clothing and food. Other variety store chains include BHS and Littlewoods. Variety stores are increasingly posing a serious threat to department stores as they add product lines.

Speciality shops

Speciality shops deal in a narrow line of products but offer great depth. As such, they are a threat to department stores who don't have the same great depth of product lines.

Examples include footwear shops (e.g. Saxone), specialist hi-fi shops, clothing (e.g. Tie Rack, Benetton), children's clothing (e.g. Adams, Benetton 012). Benetton shops possess a particular format and image which is laid down by the Benetton company. Store layout and merchandise display are important factors in positioning the company and creating the desired ambience within the store.

Catalogue retailers

Catalogue retailers, for example, Argos, offer a limited number of lines from each product class at low prices. Product classes include toys, luggage, small electrical appliances and jewellery. Catalogues are mailed to customers who can order direct, or else customers may shop in one of their retail outlets. In the retail outlets, a small number of goods are displayed. Customers find what they want in catalogues on the shop counters. A large storeroom behind the shop holds the merchandise.

Supermarket chains (or multiples), discounters and warehouse clubs

In the UK, supermarkets rose to prominence after the second world war with rapid expansion in the 1960s, 1970s and 1980s. The late 1980s in particular witnessed a considerable expansion in the number of super-markets, particularly huge edge-of-town superstores, located on their own or in retail parks with non-food discount retailers. The grocery superstore is simply a large diversified supermarket that sells a broader range of food and non-food items, e.g. gardenwares.

Retailing is increasingly becoming more concentrated, particularly grocery retailing, i.e. few very large retailers now account for a large proportion of the retail market. In the UK 'the big three', the super-market giants Sainsbury's, Tesco and Argyll (owner of Safeway and Presto), account for nearly £23 billion of the UK's annual grocery bill. The growth of the large supermarket chains and the discounters has seen the decline of more traditional types of retailers, the small independent retailers and co-operative societies.

In the 1990s, the major supermarket chains like Tesco, Sainsbury's and Safeway showed signs of a slowdown in growth, mainly because of the tougher economic climate and the emergence of European price-cutting discounters like Aldi and Netto.

A number of the major chains have cut back on further expansion plans for the 1990s although some others have not. Price-cutting among the large chains became the norm in 1994 as the grocery discounters emerged in the UK. The supermarket chains increasingly shifted their focus to areas the discounters ignored such as fresh foods (e.g. fish, meat, in-store bakeries), non-food business such as petrol sales and photo-processing, and to providing additional customer facilities such as child care and on-site banking, all to keep their customers from shopping with the no-frills discounters.

The early 1990s witnessed the emergence of another type of dis-counter known as the warehouse club. Costco and Cargo Club opened their first UK outlets in late 1993 and early 1994 respectively and sell bulk groceries and electrical goods at prices well below those of supermarkets. Customers must buy club membership in order to shop. The warehouse clubs provide an alternative to the cash and carry for the small trader.

Independent retailers

Independent retailers have fought to survive against the supermarket chains and discounters by forming retailer co-operatives, and engaging in wholesaler-sponsored voluntary chains and franchising. There are some 20,000 small independent grocers in the UK and some 35,000 small specialist traders – butchers, greengrocers, etc.

Convenience stores

Convenience stores are typically compact, self-service retail outlets that operate outside traditional shopping hours and sell mainly essential groceries. They are designed along the lines of their larger competitors, the supermarkets. Convenience stores may also sell fast-food, alcohol, and may even have a video-rental facility. Prices are high to pay for the increased costs of longer opening hours.

They are usually franchised or part of a national chain or symbol group. 7–Eleven stores are franchised and the symbol group Spar has its convenience stores known as Eight Till Late.

NON-STORE RETAILING TYPES

Direct selling

People set themselves up as agents selling to their family and friends, to contacts they have made/referrals they have been given, and sometimes sell door-to-door.

Examples of companies engaged in direct selling include Avon Cosmetics, Amway and Encyclopaedia Britannia.

Party plan

Party Plan is a form of direct selling where an individual agrees to invite family and friends to their house where an agent of the company demonstrates the product range. The individual holding the party receives a commission on the value of sales generated at the party. Ann Summers (lingerie and erotic toys) and Tupperware (housewares) operate this form of direct selling.

Mail order/catalogue selling

Mail order selling is where mail order houses post catalogues targeted to appropriate households. Freemans, Grattan, and Littlewoods are well known mail order houses in the UK.

Catalogues generally had a low quality downmarket image until 1987, when the high street retail fashion chain Next launched its upmarket catalogue. Next set a trend which other upmarket catalogues followed including Land's End, Racing Green and Jake. Products sold through catalogues include clothing, computers and DIY. A variation of mail order/catalogue selling is pursued by Betterware in the UK.

Betterware[8]

The development of DIY superstores and the decline of the traditional local hardware shops, have meant that consumers usually have to travel longer distances to purchase their hardware/DIY products. This has made the purchase process particularly difficult for non-car owners, especially elderly people. One company which is capitalising on the gap left behind by the 'out-of-town' superstore is Betterware, which sells products primarily through its sales catalogues. The catalogues are distributed by self-employed 'distributors' who simply deliver the catalogue to the potential customer without any selling involved. They return at a later date to pick up the customer's order form. The delivery of the order is made within 72 hours.

The distribution strategy is supported by a computerised mapping system which is based on a combination of census and postcode data, and ordinance survey mapping. Betterware claims to reach 45 per cent of the population. In 1992 the company had a product line of around 400 items, with sales of £8 per customer. Sales are measured on a per household basis and catalogues are distributed to match this. The driving force for sales is the catalogue, of which four are produced each year. The catalogues have a price of £1.50 printed on them, but are not sold. The price discourages customers from disposing of them. Once the order has been placed the catalogue is passed on to another customer by the distributor.

In 1992 sales in Betterware's home shopping division increased from £8.3 million to £23 million with operating profit rising to £5.85 million. By early 1993 door-to-door household goods sales were £56 million.

Home shopping

In October 1993, QVC (Quality, Value, Convenience), the UK's first 24-hour home shopping channel was launched. The channel, a joint venture between QVC in the USA and British Sky Broadcasting is broadcast by satellite as part of the Sky multi-channels subscription TV package. For 24 hours a day there are hourly shows, each dealing with a separate product category, e.g. clothing, leisurewear, electrical. The product details, price and freephone number are displayed on the screen. Customers can pay by credit card, cheque or postal order and the goods are delivered to the customer's door. QVC buys the products directly from manufacturers or agents.

THE WHEEL OF RETAILING

The wheel of retailing is a well-known theoretical concept put forward by Malcolm P. McNair[9] which describes institutional evolution in retailing. The theory describes a continual cycle in retailing where retail innovations begin as discounters aiming at the low-end of the market offering low price, limited product lines and low profit margin requirements. Over time the company aims to increase sales and its customer base and begins upgrading product lines, facilities and services. This increases costs and results in increased prices. The move upmarket by these discount retailers creates a gap at the lower end of the market and new low-price retailers emerge to take advantage of the price conscious consumers who are left behind. Again, over time, these discount retailers move upmarket creating a continual cycle.

Not all retail innovations follow this path beginning as low-cost operations, for example, suburban shopping centres and speciality chains such as the Body Shop.

Macy's[10]

Macy's, the famous New York department store, illustrates the wheel of retailing in action. The store originally started as a low-price/limited product line operation. Over time, Macy's expanded, added new more expensive product lines, introduced services such as credit and moved to a more upmarket location. Macy's move upmarket with its higher prices left a gap in the market for a discounter and the Gimbels department store opened near Macy's with its low prices/limited product line strategy. Gimbels closed in 1986 after years of rivalry between it and Macy's.

Tesco[11]

The wheel of retailing can be observed in the UK with reference to Tesco, the giant UK supermarket chain.

In the 1970s, Tesco was a low-price downmarket retailer with a 'pile it high, sell it cheap' philosophy. During the 1980s it moved into the premium end of the market alongside the other two giant upmarket retailers – Sainsbury's and Safeway – by adding product lines and upgrading its facilities and customer service. With many of the major supermarket chains appealing to the premium end of the market and the recession making people more price-conscious, a gap emerged for discounters in the 1990s – companies such as Aldi and Netto. For example,

Aldi, the German discounter and one of Europe's largest grocery retailers, provides a limited range of cut-price staple groceries which are displayed in their cardboard boxes in the stores. Minimum expense is devoted to store design and fittings.

The established upmarket retailers have reacted to their low-price competitors who are particularly popular in the north of England where the effects of the recession tend to be more pronounced. The 1990s has seen the major upmarket retailers reducing prices on a wide range of merchandise. In late 1993, Sainsbury's launched a price war, indefinitely cutting the prices of 300 of its most popular own-brand labels. In August 1993, although committed to the premium end of the market, Tesco launched Tesco Value, the name for a range of seventy product lines that are around 50 per cent cheaper than their branded counterparts in a move designed to offset the power of the discounters.

FURTHER REFERENCE

Chapter 6, Segmentation and Positioning: Repositioning (pp. 107–108)
Chapter 9, Pricing: Price wars (pp. 158–159)

WHOLESALING

The word wholesaling usually brings to mind an organisation that buys goods in bulk from manufacturers and sells them to a host of different retailers at a profit. However wholesalers also sell to other wholesalers (e.g. primary fresh fruit wholesalers selling to secondary fresh fruit wholesalers who then sell to greengrocers), to industrial users, to exporters, and may even sell to the general public.

Wholesalers are not always necessary. For example, many manufacturers deal directly with the large retail multiples such as Tesco and Sainsbury's. Wholesalers, however, are necessary for many producers and retailers. Wholesalers offer producers many benefits including storing, assembling/grading, and distribution of the goods. Wholesalers have contacts and know-how in the market place.

For small independent retailers who lack the buying power of the multiples, wholesalers provide several important functions including stockholding (the retailer does not have to have space and capital tied up), breaking bulk (assembling assortments to match retailer's requirements), credit facilities and delivery of the goods (with the exception of cash and carry wholesalers).

In grocery retailing, wholesalers have reacted to the growing threat of the multiples in many ways. For example, wholesalers have organised small retailers into voluntary groups (see p. 165), developed private branding, formed cash and carry operations, turned to advanced systems of material handling, billing and shipping, all to reduce costs and keep prices low for the retailers and so help them compete with the multiples. The most common wholesaling forms found in the UK are discussed here.

Cash and carry wholesalers

These buy, take title to (ownership), and resell goods on behalf of manufacturers. They do not offer credit or delivery to the small independent retailers they serve. Because they offer fewer services, prices are lower.

In groceries, Booker, and Nurdin and Peacock operate cash and carry outlets. Nurdin and Peacock opened the first cash and carry in the UK in 1963. There are cash and carry buying groups which consist of a consortia of wholesalers, for example, Sterling, Today's Super Group and Landmark.

Full-service wholesalers

These buy, take title to, resell and offer credit and delivery on goods. Examples of this type in groceries include Booker, Amalgamated Foods, DBC, and Londis.

In pharmaceuticals, AAH Pharmaceuticals and Unichem are the major players. Retailers need a frequent and speedy service and it would be impossible for manufacturers to provide this service to the huge number of independent chemists in the UK.

THE DISTRIBUTION STRATEGY

Choosing the intermediaries between manufacturer and user involves strategic decisions of a crucial nature that if properly conducted can make long-term relationships through the level of customer service that they afford and also present opportunities for distinctive competencies relative to competitors.

Canon

An interesting example of a company that challenged conventional industry wisdom and set up a channel arrangement that was unique and successful is provided by Canon's entry into the UK photocopier market.

Canon designed a cheaper, simpler copier than market leader, Xerox. The simplicity of the copier allowed the company to sell through office products retailers instead of using a sales force – the traditional method of selling copiers in the industry. Xerox prided itself on its sales force which was now effectively side-stepped. This new market discovered by Canon grew at the expense of the traditional market and Canon dominated the new market.

Intensive distribution

Intensive distribution, where the manufacturer seeks to stock his product in as many outlets as possible is used for high volume low-value products in mass demand, for which the typical buying behaviour is one of habit and convenience. Coca-Cola aims to distribute its products intensively in every possible retail outlet and device (e.g. vending machines) to create maximum brand exposure and convenience.

Exclusive distribution

Exclusive distribution, where a manufacturer limits the number of outlets to one per geographical area, is used in the UK by Lamborghini, the car manufacturer based in Italy. Portman Concessionaires are the sole UK importer/sales agent of Lamborghini cars. In this way, Lamborghini exercises great control over image and price. Portman also benefit from the enhanced image associated with exclusive distribution. This is particularly important in the market for second-hand Lamborghini cars, where a number of dealers may have Lamborghinis for sale. The exclusivity factor inspires confidence from car buyers.

Selective distribution

Between the two distribution policies of intensive and exclusive distribution, lies selective distribution. It is used by manufacturers wishing to develop good working relationships with selected outlets and secure better then average selling effort. It allows the manufacturer to gain adequate market coverage with more control and less cost than intensive distribution. Sony appoints its agents selectively.

A selective distribution strategy may be used to support an upmarket brand image. Church Shoes in the UK only sells its shoes in upmarket men's clothing shops that sell classic apparel. Church is concerned about image control and thus steers clear of the mainstream shoe stores.

CONCLUSION

Marketing channel decisions are complex and include some of the most challenging decisions facing a firm due to the host of alternative distribution options. This chapter has provided examples of companies successfully using some of the distribution options available. Once an option is chosen, the channel then needs to be managed, calling for great skill as a firm usually has to forge and maintain relationships with outside parties. Successful marketing channel management carries with it rewards for all the parties in the channel.

It is almost certain that the large multiples and discounters will continue to account for the bulk of retailing, although there will always be a need for the local convenience store. The concentration of retailing in out-of-town sites or 'shopping cities' will likely continue and traditional shopping centres in towns will inevitably suffer. Town centres will need to adapt, for example, by changing the range of shops, improving car parking and increasing pedestrianisation making shopping in towns a more enjoyable and less stressful experience. Wholesalers will continue to be important in serving the smaller retailers now that the growth rate of the multiples has slowed down somewhat from the 1980s. Wholesalers will also continue to be important in certain industries such as pharmaceuticals, where there are many small chemists requiring frequent and rapid delivery of large numbers of product lines.

NOTES

1 Dell Computers section based on information supplied by *Marketing Business* magazine.
2 Dragons section based on information supplied by *Marketing Business* magazine.
3 Hewlett-Packard section adapted from Colin Lazaro, 'Finding the right incentive buttons to push', *Business Marketing Digest*, 1993, third quarter, vol. 18, no. 3, pp. 11–17.
4 Canadian Publisher section adapted from Alan J. McGrath, 'Ten timeless truths about pricing', *The Journal of Consumer Marketing*, winter 1991, vol. 8, no. 1, pp. 5–14.

5 QMS Inc. section adapted from Alan J. McGrath, op. cit.
6 Honda's Accura Legend section adapted from: 'The selling of Acura – a Honda that's not a Honda', *Business Week*, 17 March 1986, p. 93; Stewart Toy, 'This isn't the legend Acura dealers had in mind', *Business Week*, 28 November 1988.
7 Lithonia Lighting section reprinted from 'Lighting the way', *The Economist*, October 1990. © *The Economist*.
8 Betterware section adapted from: Charles Darwent, 'Knock knock! Who's there? Betterware', *Management Today*, July 1992, pp. 55–56; Jane Fuller, 'Betterware leaps to £6.3m in first half', *Financial Times*, 10 November 1992, p. 22; Catherine Milton, 'Betterware's 21 per cent rise fails to impress City', *Financial Times*, 27 October 1993, p. 22; Allan Piper, 'Knock! Knock!, Who's there?', *The Mail on Sunday*, 6 February 1994.
9 Malcolm P. McNair, 'Significant trends and developments in the postwar period', in A.B. Smith (ed.) *Competitive Distribution in a Free, High-level Economy and its Implications for the University*, Pittsburgh: University of Pittsburgh Press, 1958.
10 Macy's section adapted from: Nan Birmingham Tillson, *Store*, New York: Putnam, 1978; Nina Darnton, Todd Barrett, Margaret Nelson, Patricia King, John P. McCormick, 'Shop till they drop', *Newsweek*, 11 December 1989, pp. 76–78.
11 Tesco section adapted from the following: Timothy Harper, 'Revamped image pays for Tesco', *Advertising Age*, 28 April 1986; Helen Slingsby, 'Tesco Gets a Cheap Frill', *Marketing Week*, 13 August 1993, pp. 22–23; 'Aldi Arrives', *Marketing*, 9 May 1990, p. 3; 'Changing the face of Tesco', *Management Today*, September 1985, p. 11; Sandra Hogarth-Scott and Stephen P. Rice, 'The new food discounters', *International Journal of Retail and Distribution Management*, 1994, vol. 22, no. 1, pp. 20–28.

Chapter 11

Advertising

INTRODUCTION

Advertising is one of the major elements of the communications mix and is generally inextricably linked with overall marketing objectives. The starting point for developing advertising campaigns is to establish advertising or communication objectives. The simplest of these is that of informing the market of the availability of a product or service. But advertising also provides a strong medium for persuading potential purchasers to buy the product or service.

The use of advertising in achieving the aims of the overall marketing strategy flows from prior decisions on target market, positioning, messages and the objectives of the other elements of the marketing mix. Setting advertising objectives is therefore the first step in developing an effective advertising programme. Their identification develops out of the marketing decision makers' understanding of the target market and the needs of the organisation itself.

The advertiser may use different types of appeal to develop the advertising message, among the most powerful of these being rational, social, sensory and ego satisfaction.[1] Once the objectives have been set it is then necessary to establish the advertising budget. The available budget, along with the objectives, will determine the media vehicles to be used. Finally, advertising should be evaluated for its effectiveness.

COMMUNICATION OBJECTIVES

Bristol-Myers[2]

Many organisations also face the problem of differentiating their product/service from those of their competitors. The Bristol-Myers

Company in the USA faced this problem with their pain relief drug Nuprin. In tests their Nuprin brand achieved greater pain relief results than the most popular brand, Tylenol. It appeared that consumers believed one painkiller was the same as any other and the performance of Nuprin was not getting through to them. The company then sought to differentiate the product by focusing on a particular characteristic of the product – its yellow colour. Advertisements were produced in black and white, with only the Nuprin tablet in colour. The advertisements resulted in a more favourable attitude towards Nuprin and its sales began to grow faster than other brands.

FURTHER REFERENCE

Chapter 7, Products: Product differentiation (pp. 117–118)

National Dairy Council[3]

The National Dairy Council (NDC) embarked on a promotional campaign in 1991 to halt the decline in demand for milk delivery services. Milk deliveries' share of the market had declined from 82 per cent in 1986 to 65 per cent in 1990. The main reason for this was competition from the supermarkets which sold milk at a cheaper price. The NDC decided to carry out television advertising aimed at those customers who had begun to purchase some of their milk from retailers. One of the reasons for targeting this group was that they were not strongly influenced by the price factor and therefore it was expected that they would respond to advertising. Such customers were still using the milk delivery service but often purchased milk from the supermarket for the weekend or in emergencies or other unforeseen circumstances. When this situation continued, people became more and more aware of the price difference between the two sources of supply, increasing their purchases from supermarkets and eventually cancelling their milk delivery after a period of time. It was concluded that it was easier to try to keep these existing customers than to recruit new ones.

The objective of the campaign was to slow down the decline in the milk delivery service's share of the total market. The period of transition into consistent purchasing from retailers was a crucial part of the cancelling process. If existing customers could be prevented from entering this phase this would go a long way in achieving the objective.

The creative brief for the campaign was as follows:

Target audience:	Housewives with a milkman who occasionally buy extra milk from the shops.
Who are they?	25–45-year-old housewives, with children, heavier purchasers of milk.
Objective:	Persuade them to continue buying from the milkman (or buy more from him) rather than drifting into the habit of regularly stocking up at the supermarket.
Proposition:	Don't forget how helpful and convenient your milkman is.
Support:	(i) The archetypical lovable friendly milkman – they've forgotten how wonderful he is.
	(ii) He delivers low fat milks.
	(iii) His returnable glass bottles are friendlier to the environment.
	(iv) He's more convenient for weekend extras than carrying heavy, bulky milk home.

It was accepted that the campaign resulted in a halting of 'drifting' in 1991 and a halt to the decline in the milkman's volume share of the market during the period of advertising. However, the rate of cancellation continued in 1991, but began declining in 1992. This was due to the reversal in drifting achieved in 1991. A further outcome was an increase in the quantity of milk purchased from the milkman by loyal customers.

FURTHER REFERENCE

Chapter 7, Products: Product line extension (p. 112)

MESSAGE GENERATION

Eurotunnel[4]

The decision on how to market the Channel Tunnel was an important one for Eurotunnel. In France the tunnel is promoted on its achievement, as a grand project and in a celebratory triumphal manner. Advertisements feature Queen Victoria, Napoleon and Churchill, thus emphasising the advent of the tunnel as a momentous event in history. This appears to be the significance of the tunnel for the French.

In Britain, however, the perception seems to be different. The British appeared to be adopting a more questioning approach. Market research carried out for Eurotunnel demonstrated that potential customers needed to be reassured about tunnel travel, and the triumphal approach was not appropriate. Advertising also needed to emphasise the benefits of the tunnel. This led to the development of advertisements portraying a friendly, reassuring relaxed image using cartoons, thus minimising the fears which customers may have. Cartoon-like images portrayed users in a relaxed mode while using the tunnel. Press advertising was primarily informative and relatively low-key. Direct mail was also used to explain the service to the British.

By utilising market research in this way Eurotunnel was able to generate a message which they hope will encourage potential customers to use the tunnel. Essentially the tunnel will be promoted as a travel service and not as the eighth wonder of the world.

COMMUNICATION STRATEGY

Pull strategy

A pull promotional strategy by a manufacturer is aimed at the ultimate customer or end-user, and attempts to stimulate demand for the manufacturer's product in order to persuade distributors to carry the product.

Intel[5]

Intel, the world's largest and most successful manufacturer of microprocessors provides an example of a company that successfully used such a pull strategy to encourage computer manufacturers to use their microprocessors.

The company pioneered the development of the 386 and 486 microprocessors which they successfully marketed to computer manufacturers. The chips soon became the industry standard and were initially identifiable as an Intel product. During this period the manufacturers were the primary target market for the company. At the beginning of the 1990s imitators became more and more prevalent and also began using the 386 and 486 terminology to describe their own products. In 1991 Intel lost a court case against one such competitor who had adopted the 386 number to describe its microprocessor. As a result Intel was faced with direct low cost competition. This led Intel to develop a pull strategy targeted at the end user.

In the early 1990s, Intel began running an 'Intel inside' advertising campaign aimed at persuading computer buyers that the important feature is not the brand of PC they buy, but the chip within. At this stage computers were heading towards commodity products with price becoming the major factor in the purchase decision. By branding the 'ingredients' of the computer, Intel was attempting to differentiate their product and the computer itself. Up to then, what really sold computers was the brand name, be it IBM, Apple, etc. In attempting to influence the final consumer, one of Intel's objectives was to exert a 'pull' pressure on manufacturers to use Intel chips, i.e. persuading end users to buy computers with an Intel chip and therefore forcing manufacturers to use the chips. It was also a response to the decision by Microsoft to lessen its dependence on Intel by making its software compatible with several of the new rival processors, as well as the emergence of microprocessors as consumer products for those who wanted to upgrade their systems. In 1994 over 1000 manufacturers used Intel chips, with the added incentive that they receive co-operative funding from Intel for co-brand advertising.

It is estimated that Intel spent around $100 million on their campaign in the first two years. Intel's 'Red X' campaign was the first to directly target PC users in encouraging them to purchase computers with 386SX processors. The advertisement featured the number 286 crossed out with a red X and the number 386 with the letters SX in red underneath. The advertisement was run in newspapers, magazines and on billboards. Promotion of Intel also includes network TV commercials. One of the objectives is to build awareness of the Intel brand among PC buyers.

More recently Intel has extended its campaign to the newer and more powerful Pentium chip. The promotion of the Pentium was stepped up in 1994 with the release on to the market of the Power PC by Apple followed by IBM. The Power PC is based on a chip jointly developed by IBM, Apple and Motorola. Intel is utilising a wide range of media in promoting the Pentium, from magazine inserts to TV. It even targeted traditional Macintosh users by taking out four-page inserts in the Macintosh magazines – *MacUser*, *MacWeek* and *Macworld* – in an attempt to induce switching.

FURTHER REFERENCE

Chapter 6, Segmentation and positioning: Target marketing (pp. 102–105)
Chapter 7, Products: Branding – Ingredient branding (p. 115); Product differentiation (pp. 117–118)

TYPES OF APPEAL

Rational appeal

Death cigarettes[6]

A new brand of cigarettes introduced into the UK market in the early 1990s was initially promoted on the attribute of the adverse effect smoking can have on a person's health. Called 'Death', the advertising campaign for the cigarettes claimed 'Cigarette smoking will not make you attractive . . . it will make you dead'. Advertisements also featured an x-ray image of a cancer affected lung with the headline 'The Shadow of Death'. Death Cigarettes claim they are simply telling the truth about cigarettes, and letting people know the possible consequences of smoking. This approach in effect demonstrates a rational approach to advertising a product which is more often promoted on an emotional basis.

Despite its straightforward approach the company, the Enlightened Tobacco Company, found it extremely difficult to attain outdoor advertising space. It claims this was due to the outdoor advertising site owners wanting to avoid alienating their other cigarette company customers. Nevertheless the product achieved sales growth, and the company's aim is to build the brand name through advertising.

Ernest Shackleton

> Men wanted for Hazardous Journey. Small wages, bitter cold, long months of complete darkness, constant danger, safe return doubtful. Honour and recognition in case of success.

This advertisement appeared in newspapers in London in 1900, placed by the polar explorer Ernest Shackleton. The response to the advertisement was extraordinary. Whilst providing realistic probabilities, the advertisement also appealed to the sense of honour and glory which would inevitably come with success on the expedition.

Sensory appeal

Benetton[7]

Benetton advertisements are noted for their controversial nature. The advertisements in general have greater sensory effect. A number of advertisements appeared in recent years with the following titles:

1   The new-born baby
2   The military cemetery
3   The Zebra and parrot
4   Three children of different ages

The advertisements were designed to have the following meanings as described by the company:

1   *The new-born baby*:
    Love, the force from which life itself is born
    A baby is the most permanent form of love
    Holding on to the warmth and security of a mother's womb
2   *The military cemetery*:
    A military cemetery.
    Human beings of different races and religions die for common ideals or opposing causes.
    Nobody wins a war.
3   *The Zebra and parrot*:
    The creative forces which nature possesses
    The striped zebra and brightly coloured parrot demonstrate that man's artistic attempts appear to be nothing more than imitation
4   *Three children of different ages*:
    Three different races (black, yellow and white)
    Sticking out tongues – an expression common to all children
    The faces are different colours but the tongues are the same

The meanings as advocated by the advertiser, however, are not always the meanings understood by the receiver. A study carried out by researchers at the University of Glamorgan and the Leeds Business School sought to examine the reactions of different European nationals to the images.

The study's sample group consisted of groups of students from a British business school aged between 20 and 25, and of four different nationalities, German, French, Norwegian and British.

In the case of the new-born baby image the first theme, that of 'love, the force from which life itself is born', generated greatest agreement among British students. The German and French in general disagreed that the intended message was that portrayed. Disagreement was most pronounced among the French. Norwegians in general neither agreed nor disagreed. The second theme, 'a baby is the most permanent form of love', had greatest agreement among British students with the others remaining indifferent that this message was being transmitted. A similar finding was made for the final theme of 'holding on to the warmth and security of a mother's womb'.

In the case of the military cemetery image, respondents in general understood the meaning to be simply one of death, and not the one intended by Benetton. The children image was generally interpreted as one of friendship and equality as well as innocence and happiness.

The results of the study indicated that the desired messages were not those received, and in many cases were totally different. Furthermore differences in interpretation may occur among different nationalities.

EVALUATING PERFORMANCE[8]

Electronic equipment is currently being used to measure the response of consumers to advertising. While watching television advertising, individuals are provided with an electronic handset containing button sensors which record positive and negative reactions to the advertisement. The responses from different individuals are then collated to produce a line graph (or equivalent) representing the reaction of the individuals as the advertisement runs. The technology can be particularly useful in determining the reaction in different countries to the same advertisement. A London research company, Pegram Walters Associates (PWA), carried out a survey to determine the reaction in five countries to five different commercials for five household brands – Coca-Cola and 7-Up soft drinks, Gillette, Biactol facial cream, and Levi's jeans. The countries chosen were Great Britain, Spain, Germany, Canada and the United States. The sample size was 50 in each country and the sample universe teenagers between 12 and 18, with half of each sex.

The findings showed that Spanish teenagers were more susceptible to emotional messages or atmospheric advertising, while German teenagers displayed less reaction to emotional messages. Female teenagers in Britain were averse to images of girls' hands caressing a boy's face after he had used Biactol facial cream. German and North American teenagers reacted more positively than others to demonstration advertisements for the same product.

This method is particularly suited to comparing responses to advertising among different markets or countries. Similar technology has been used to monitor public response to political campaigning.

Anheuser-Busch

Anheuser-Busch carried out experiments to determine the effectiveness of advertising by estimating its effects on sales for different advertising expenditures. The findings were such that the advertising had a positive effect on sales up to a threshold level and above this level the effect was less, or even negative. The company concluded that it was spending too much on advertising its Budweiser beer brand and therefore reduced expenditure with no resultant effect on sales.

AUtel

A market research company, the AUtel Company, conducts advertising effectiveness tests by means of cable television hook-ups. A number of different similar sample groups are selected from different areas, with each individual agreeing to expose themselves to the advertisements carried by AUtel. If the company wants to determine the effectiveness of a particular advertisement then it exposes a particular group(s) to the advertisement while screening the other(s) from it. The effectiveness is then measured through purchases by each group.

It must be stressed however that many difficulties exist in controlling this method of monitoring.

ADVERTISING REACH

Millward Boon[9]

Research carried out by Millward Boon in 1990 on readership among a group of 1,883 women indicated that a significant amount of the readership of a number of women's monthly magazines does not occur until long after they go on sale. In some cases, the magazine may not be read until a few months after its publication. This has major implications for seasonal advertising campaigns which aim to influence their target market before or during a particular purchasing season, e.g. Christmas. Advertising carried out in the months leading up to Christmas may not achieve the desired impact due to the magazine not being read until after the Christmas period. Therefore the projected advertising reach may be out of phase with the readership.

POINT-OF-PURCHASE ADVERTISING

Actmedia[10]

Supermarkets in the USA are an important location for point-of-purchase advertising. It is estimated that up to 80 per cent of purchase decisions are actually made in the store. Actmedia Inc. recognised this and began offering advertising space on message boards which can be attached to supermarket shelves and shopping trollies. The power of such point-of-purchase advertising is that customers are already in the stores. Actmedia agreed to achieve a minimum 8 per cent increase in sales within a four week period during which the advertisements ran in the store. The supermarket receives 25 per cent of Actmedia's advertising revenue. Other point-of-purchase media introduced to varying degrees of success by players in the field were in-store TV and radio channels, coupon machines which dispensed coupons offering price discounts or free products and scented displays that emitted the odour or scent of a product.

In 1993 Actmedia sold advertising space in around 27,500 stores in the USA and Canada. It is estimated that the industry's turnover in the USA will reach US$ 1 billion by 1997 where point of purchase advertising has been growing at much faster rates than radio or TV advertising. However, not all point-of-purchase advertising is successful. In Australia Point of Purchase Media (now majority owned by Actmedia) tested the concept of mounting calculators on shopping trollies with advertisements alongside them. The concept was withdrawn because shoppers either ignored the calculators or stole them.

COMPARATIVE ADVERTISING

Qualcast Concorde[11]

One of the first major comparative advertising campaigns in the UK was that by Birmid Qualcast in relaunching their cylinder grass mower in 1980. Cylinder mowers had traditionally been used in Britain and dominated the market for many years. The development of the hover rotary mower by Flymo in the mid-1970s, and its subsequent positioning in the lightweight electric segment, posed a serious challenge to the lightweight electric cylinder mowers, dominated by the Qualcast Concorde.

The hover was perceived more positively than the Concorde, because the latter was based on the cylinder principle, which was now regarded as being out-dated. The hover, on the other hand was regarded as a 'modern' product and demand for these machines began increasing in the late 1970s. In contrast to this, Qualcast product trials resulted in findings on the superior performance of the cylinder mower. They therefore decided to embark on an advertising campaign with the aim of informing consumers of the benefits of the cylinder mower so that they understood the advantages; concentrating on the non-price aspects of the product, and revamping the company's image in the distribution network.

Market research indicated that for the Concorde's primary target, the uncommitted gardener, ease of use was the major benefit sought. In this respect the Concorde had a major advantage, in that it collected the grass as it was cut. Their trials indicated that after having tried the product most people switched from having a preference for the hover to a preference for the Concorde. This indicated that trialing was important and had to be simulated in some way through advertising. Also the perceptions and image of the hover as a modern and superior mower had to be challenged.

It was decided that television advertising would be best in presenting the case for the Concorde. Its visual images would have greatest impact on the consumer and allow them to decide for themselves. This was also backed by press advertising. The slogan emphasising ease of use, 'Much less bovver than a hover' encapsulated the comparative nature of the advertising. The advertising message suggested that hovers were not as easy to use as people thought, and when collection of grass is considered this makes the Concorde easier to use. The evidence from the product trials also allowed the campaign to emphasise the superior cutting results of the Concorde over the hover.

Advertising showed a lawn being cut with a hover and the subsequent collecting of the grass with a rake, and then grass cutting with the Concorde in neat tracks followed by the garden owner sitting on a deck chair. The potential negative aspects of leaving the grass uncollected were also emphasised, i.e. the encouragement of weed growth and earthworm proliferation.

The campaign was a major success from the strategic aspect, in that it took the major competitor, Flymo, by surprise, and resulted in an over 50 per cent increase in sales. Qualcast Concorde did not engage in serious disparagement of their competitor, but sought to undermine some myths associated with the hover mower. In effect it could be argued that the campaign resulted in educating the consumer in certain aspects of grass cutting. The campaign targeted the uncommitted gardener and focused on one of the major benefits of the product which was the collection of the grass.

After the campaign had been running for a number of years Flymo made a deputation to Parliament to protest at Qualcast's allegedly unfair advertising. Qualcast, however, maintained that tests proved the superiority of their conventional cylinder machine, and their case was upheld.

FURTHER REFERENCE

Chapter 6, Segmentation and Positioning: Positioning – positioning by association (p. 106)

CONCLUSION

Advertising can be one of the most powerful elements of the marketing mix. It often represents the ultimate means of executing the plans generated through the other parts of the marketing process. Market research or feedback may be necessary to generate effective advertising messages as in the case of Eurotunnel or to identify communication objectives as in the case of Nuprin. The type of appeal is also important; in this respect advertising is also inextricably linked with positioning. Ultimately advertising must also demonstrate its effectiveness.

In this chapter we have presented examples of how these steps have been carried out in different campaigns.

NOTES

1 John C. Maloney, 'Marketing Decisions and Attitude Research,' in George L. Baker Jr (ed.), *Effective Marketing Communication*, Chicago: American Marketing Association, 1961, pp. 595–618.
2 Bristol-Myers section adapted from the following: Laurie Freeman, 'Nuprin breaks advertisement campaign', *Advertising Age*, 9 July 1984, p. 62; 'A power mistake, a healthy choice and a soaper star', *Advertising Age*, 23–30 December 1991, p. 12; Patricia Winters, 'Excerdin bangs Tylenol: a new aspirin-free product claims it's better', *Advertising Age*, 13 August 1990, pp. 3–4; Rebecca Fannin, 'The pain game', *Marketing and Media Decisions*, February 1989, p. 34; Bob Garfield, 'Nuprin ads uphold tradition', *Advertising Age*, 15 September 1986, p. 28; 'Color Nuprin's Success Yellow, ' *Advertising Age*, 31 October 1988, p.28.
3 National Dairy Council section adapted and partly reprinted from 'National Dairy Council – the Milkman Relaunch', in Chris Baker (ed.), *Advertising Works 7*, NTC Publications Ltd, 1993, pp. 3–22.
4 Eurotunnel section adapted from the following: Penny Kiernan, 'Smooth operators push the boat out', *Marketing Week*, October 1993, p. 23; Charles Batchelor, 'Softly, softly approach', *Financial Times*, 10 February 1994; Joshua Levine, 'Chunnel vision', *Forbes*, 14 February 1994, p. 146; Stephen Downer, 'Digging that Eurotunnel', *Advertising Age*, 17 January 1994, p.3.
5 Intel section adapted from the following: Nick Hasell, 'The intelligence of Intel', *Management Today*, November 1992, pp. 76–78; 'Intel – The Coming Clash of Logic', *The Economist*, 3 July 1993, pp. 23–25; Nancy Arnott, 'Inside Intel's Marketing Coup', *Sales and Marketing Management*, February 1994, pp. 78–81; 'Leixlip benefits from Intel's chips', *The Sunday Business Post*, 31 October 1993, p. 33; David Kirkpatrick, 'Intel

goes for broke', *Fortune*, 16 May, 1994, pp. 52–57; Gerry Khermouch, 'Pentium bytes off $20m plus', *Brandweek*, 21 February 1994, p. 4; 'Intel's insider plugs into future', *Advertising Age*, 15 November 1993, p. 8; Tim Clark, 'Inside Intel's marketing machine', *Business Marketing*, October 1993, pp. 14, 16, 19; Donald G. Norris, 'Intel inside: branding a component in a business market', *Journal of Business and Industrial Marketing*, 1993, vol. 8, no. 1, pp. 14–24.

6 Death cigarettes section adapted from the following: Daniel Tilles, 'Death cigarettes haunt UK billboards – new cigarette brand plays the devil's advocate', *Adweek* (Eastern Edition), 15 February 1993, vol.34, no.7, p.12; 'Enlightened Tobacco Company makes light of death', *Marketing Week*, 18 March 1994, p. 8; 'Puffed up', *Time Out*, 20 April 1994, p. 25; Marek Kohn, 'Death and a salesman', *Arena*, May/June 1994, pp. 82–87.

7 Benetton section adapted and partly reprinted from Ian G. Evans and Sumandeep Riyat, 'Is the message being received? Benetton analysed', *International Journal of Advertising*, 1993, vol. 12, pp. 291–301.

8 Evaluating performance section adapted from Philip Kleinman, 'Ad test system points up national differences', *Admap*, November 1990, pp. 11–12.

9 Millward Boon section adapted from Philip Kleinman, op. cit.

10 Actmedia section adapted from the following: 'Satelite Programs Enter In-Store Act', *Advertising Age*, 20 March 1989, p. 54; 'An Upstart is Upsetting Actmedia's Shopping Carts', *Business Week*, 7 September 1987, pp. 28–29; Neil Shoebridge, 'High Hopes for the Cinderella Seller', *Business Review Weekly*, 21 February 1994, pp. 64–65; Patricia Sellers, 'Winning over the new customer', *Fortune*, 29 July 1991, pp. 129–137; Michael Burghi, 'The next phase in coupons', *Mediaweek*, 12 July 1993, p. 9; Alison Fahey, 'In-store insider spots growth areas', *Advertising Age*, 19 August 1991, p. 28; Dan Frost, 'TV takes on tabloids at checkout line', *American Demographics*, April 1991, pp. 9–10; Karen Singer, 'Life in the supermarket fast lane is a family affair', *AdWeeks Marketing Week*, 15 June 1987, pp. 33–34; 'An idea that moves: ads on shopping carts', *Business Week*, 26 May 1986, p. 47.

11 Qualcast Concorde section adapted from 'The Qualcast Concorde' in Simon Broadbent (ed.) *Twenty Advertising Case Histories*, Toronto: Holt, Rinehart and Winston, 1984, pp. 160–172.

Chapter 12

Personal selling

INTRODUCTION

Personal selling is the term used to describe the process of interaction between a buyer and a seller designed to match the needs of the buyer to the benefits offered by the product or service. The management of the personal selling process involves the setting of the overall selling strategy, the adoption of a suitable sales force structure and size, recruiting, training, supervising, and rewarding and motivating the sales force. Like all other elements of the marketing mix, the sales function must be consistent with overall marketing objectives. Sales force strategy and structure are key factors in determining effectiveness.

The productivity of the selling team is an issue which is coming under increasing scrutiny and more sophisticated methods such as the use of computers are being used to improve effectiveness. By maximising the sales person's time on the actual task of face-to-face selling and by passing other tasks such as order taking to other personnel, productivity can be improved. This is seen in the example of Kodak below. The structure of the sales force is dependent on the characteristics of the market. The decision to use a market/product or geographic based structure may depend on the nature of the product, the size of the market or the nature of the customer, as well as other factors. In general the more standard the product line and the fewer segments being served, then the more suitable is a geographic based structure. On the other hand the more segments and the more complicated the product line then the more appropriate is a market/product structured sales force. Personal selling is also equally important in the case of retail selling as demon- strated by the example of Home Depot in this chapter.

The question of sales force size is determined by factors such as the total number of accounts, the desired call frequency and the target number of calls per sales person. Recruiting and selecting sales representatives, training, setting targets, supervising and motivating are other important management tasks. The sales people themselves must also carry out the key tasks of prospecting, negotiation, presentation and demonstrating, and closing a sale.

In this chapter we present examples of many of these aspects of personal selling.

SALES FORCE STRATEGY

Kodak Canada[1]

The consumer imaging division of Kodak Canada Incorporated markets film, cameras and videotape to the retail trade, and paper and processing chemicals to photographic developers. In an attempt to increase the productivity of its sales force the division began examining the way its sales team was performing. The company found that sales people spent only half their time actually selling, with travel and administration taking up the rest. It was also found that sales people were performing a merchandising role. Many representatives carried out stock rotation for customers and were often asked to replace damaged stock, and maintain point-of-sale advertising.

In 1992 Kodak introduced its 'strategic sales plan'. This new sales force strategy incorporated the following elements:

1   each sales representative was given a new portable computer with the capacity for utilising electronic mail and producing automatic sales administration forms;
2   a greater use of telemarketing;
3   independent merchandisers to serve retailers;
4   the elimination of duplication of technical and retail sales representatives calling on retailers with photographic development facilities.

The objective of the use of computers and appropriate software is to allow representatives to transmit sales reports to a central network. This also eliminates the need for administratives to enter data from the representatives. Kodak also encouraged customers to make greater use of its improved telemarketing capability in sales servicing such as stock replacement, sales promotion information etc. To encourage this, the company gave customers photographs of its telesales personnel and organograms of its telesales department. The independent merchandisers took much of the mundane work of stock rotation and updating, and point-of-sales advertising maintenance away from the sales representatives.

One of the objectives of the strategy was to increase the overall productivity of the sales department, with reductions being made in expenditure on travel, entertainment and demonstration materials in the first eight months of its operation.

Push strategy

A push promotional strategy by a manufacturer is aimed at distributors and attempts to encourage the stocking and display of products so that the ultimate customer or end-user receives the maximum exposure to them. Dealer incentives, point-of-sale (POS) display material and sales force incentives are instrumental to the success of this strategy.

Creda, Dimplex

In the UK, Creda and Dimplex, manufacturers of electric space and water heating products, pursue a push promotional strategy. Over the years, these companies have forged close links with electrical wholesalers and plumbing merchants using a sales force to visit them on a regular basis and keeping them up to date on new product developments. The shops are fitted out with attractive POS display material and distributors are motivated to sell through generous incentive packages. Competitions are regularly run to reward the distributors who sell the most of the manufacturer's products. Also, distributors are regularly entertained and invited to company functions, particularly at Christmas and Easter.

Creda and Dimplex have also forged close links with the regional electricity companies whose heating engineers are often asked to recommend a brand of electric heating when designing a heating system for new building developments and refurbishments. Regular visits keeping engineers up to date with products and providing sales and technical material forms the majority of the push effort from the heating manufacturers.

Standard Fireworks   The leading UK manufacturer of fireworks provides an example of a company that uses this strategy because of the difficulty of advertising a product that is only sold for three weeks of the year. Wholesalers and retailers are the primary target market.

SALES FORCE STRUCTURE

Territorial and market based

Redland Roof Tiles

Redland Roof Tiles, part of the Redland group of companies, organises its sales force on a geographical and market/customer basis. The company sells roofing tiles in the construction market and secures sales by two different but often interconnected methods. First, sales are secured by ensuring the product is specified by the architect who is designing a building. Such a specification is written into the 'bill of quantities' (document listing materials, cost and application specifications) or the architect's drawings for the building project. The tiles are then purchased by the roofing or building contractor employed on the project. They may be purchased through an independent building materials distributor who also stocks roof tiles. In cases where a particular brand of tile is not specified it is often the roofing contractor who determines which brand is used.

The construction process therefore produces a number of different decision makers who may determine which brand is utilised. First, the architect can specify the brand and type of tile to be used on the project. Second, in cases where a particular brand of tile is not specified by the architect, it is normally the roofing contractor who determines which brand is finally purchased. The Redland Roof Tile Company employs one 'direct' sales force to deal with roofing contractors and builders merchants and another 'technical' sales force to deal with architects. The former sells the product directly to the purchaser in return for a financial payment, while the latter attempts to secure specifications but does not actually 'sell' the product in exchange for money.

The reason for structuring the sales force on this basis is the difference in the characteristics of the customers. Architects are more concerned with aesthetics, appearance, texture and other intangible qualities. Roofing contractors on the other hand are more concerned with price, quality, delivery, etc. The technical sales force are required to have a greater technical knowledge of the product and the selling approach must be more subtle and less of a 'hard-sell'. Roofing contractors are more amenable to a bargaining approach and generally seek favourable trade terms.

Both sales forces are organised on a geographical basis. Each sales representative is allocated a specific territory and reports to an area manager. Area managers report to a regional manager and the total market is managed by a national sales manager. One of the objectives of this structure is to allow the representative to develop a relationship with the customers in his or her area. This is particularly important for the technical sales representative, as it may take a considerable period of time to develop a relationship with a particular architect or specifier. Travel time is also kept to a minimum and territories are easy to administer.

FURTHER REFERENCE

Chapter 15, Organisation Structures: Adapting the organisation structure (pp. 252–258)

SALES FORCE COMPENSATION

Digital Equipment Corporation (DEC)

The Digital Equipment Corporation traditionally paid its sales representatives on a straight salary basis. Part of the reason for this was the professional nature of the purchaser who was generally technically competent and therefore, it was assumed, required product information and not a hard sell. With the rapid increase in the range of applications for computer equipment, it is no longer left to the technical specialist to choose hardware, many decision makers or members of the decision making unit do not possess in-depth computer knowledge. As a result DEC has now introduced sales commissions as part of its remuneration package, with different ratios for different products. For example high-volume, low-value transactions will receive different commissions than sales of complete systems where the rep will normally have to build up a long-term relationship with the customer.

Building materials manufacturers Manufacturers who influence architects and other specifiers on building projects, normally provide a salary based remuneration with part commission (see Chapter 5, p. 90). It is important for the representative to build a longer-term working relationship with the architect or other specifier who is generally averse to the 'pressure-sell' approach. In general, architects believe they possess sufficient product knowledge to make an informed decision, and therefore feel a pure sales approach would infringe on their professional integrity and judgement.

RECRUITING AND SELECTING SALES REPRESENTATIVES

The Registry Inc.[2]

The Registry Inc., in Newton, Massachusetts, USA acts as a type of employment agency for computer programmers, software engineers and technical writers. The Registry places selected professionals in client companies from a database of over 50,000 specialists. The Registry may be required to provide one specialist or a team of specialists to customers from as little as a few days to over a year. The Registry employs over 50 direct sales representatives and the solution which the company provides requires its sales representatives to understand the client's business and needs.

The recruitment and selection process is therefore very important for the Registry Inc. The process consists of a series of interviews which include meeting representatives who have recently joined as well as longer standing representatives. One of the purposes of these meetings is to ensure that applicants understand the requirements of the job in practical terms and receive a realistic view of the position. The company also recruits representatives in groups of three or four so that they can give each other support in the new job. The personnel employed to identify and recruit the programmers, engineers and technical writers are recruited using a similar approach.

The Registry commenced operating in 1987 and by 1993 had sales of $40 million, and projections for 1995 are in the range of $100 million.

TRAINING

General Motors Saturn[3]

General Motors carries out week-long training sessions for those sales people whose job it is to sell its Saturn model. The course identifies 40 critical 'moments of truth' in the process of making a sale. The approach to selling the car is more subtle than the traditional 'hard sell' once employed. Part of the training involves individual participants falling backwards from a height into the arms of the other participants. The objective is to build trust and teamwork in carrying out the sales process. The classes also encourage dealers to provide a better service for their customers, such as washing customers' cars free of charge. Trainees are also taught the Saturn cheer, which is employed at meetings, and to send customers on their way when they purchase a new car.

In 1993 sales of the Saturn reached almost 230,000 in the USA and is estimated to have broken even on its investment. However, the division must compete for investment funds with other GM divisions and demonstrate its worth.

Home Depot[4]

Home Depot, the US hardware/DIY chain store, emphasises product knowledge among its staff and trains them in the practical application of many of the products it sells, such as laying tiles, electrical installations, plumbing, etc. The company often employs experienced trades people such as electricians or carpenters to work in the branches. Those who are not experienced in dealing with customers are initially trained over a five-day period covering issues from company history to greeting customers. This training is supplemented by a three-week period where new employees work alongside a departmental manager learning how to make orders, stock the store and sell products. Sales personnel embark on ongoing training by attending seminars on products such as paint, electrical products, etc.

Top class service is at the heart of the company's philosophy and employees are also trained to help customers obtain the best value for money, even by informing them of cheaper ways of doing a do-it-yourself job. Store attendants are encouraged to build relationships with regular customers and to educate them on home repairs. Home Depot's chief executive, Bernard Marcus, and President Arthur Blank adopt a hands-on approach to management. They regularly walk round stores and also hold a 'Breakfast with Bernie and Arthur' programme on the company's closed-circuit TV network, which is broadcast to employees. This is designed to motivate employees and also train them further in the ways of the company. Employees are also motivated by being allowed to take stock options in the company and many are stockholders as a result.

Home Depot had over 200 stores in 1993 and is planning further expansion. The high quality level of service and low prices have made it the most successful DIY retailer in the USA.

SETTING TARGETS

Barclays Mercantile Business Finance[5]

Barclays Mercantile Business Finance offers lease and lease purchasing services to the corporate sector in the UK. When the company opened a new branch in Wolverhampton it applied a method of matching its own internal customer base with an external database of all customers in the available market place. Barclays Mercantile identified the character-istics of company, age and size, SIC code, and status of the unit such as head office, subsidiary etc., as a basis for segmenting their market. Using the internal and external database comparison it was able to make an estimate of the potential business that could be generated by the new branch office. When sales representatives were allocated to the area, they were also given a prospect list based on the database.

Traditionally sales targets were determined on an historical basis; however the company could now determine targets on the basis of the potential sales for an area using the databases. The potential sales for each prospect could be estimated based on the level of sales to existing customers within the particular market segment. This provided a basis on which the branch and its sales representatives could be allocated targets.

FURTHER REFERENCE

Chapter 12, Personal Selling: Prospecting (pp. 205–206)

SUPERVISING/DIRECTING SALES REPRESENTATIVES

Hewlett Packard [6]

In analysing how its sales people spent their time, Hewlett-Packard monitored 135 of its representatives. The company then issued each person with a portable computer under a six-month pilot programme. The objectives of the programme included the improvement of sales productivity through more efficient account management, order tracking and planning. The tasks which the representatives began to perform with the computers included sales monitoring and forecasting, storing account histories and checking the status of customer orders.

Initial results were promising with an increase in the proportion of time spent with customers and reductions in travelling time and time spent in internal meetings. However the project was not completely successful due to insufficient computing power of the HP Portable Plus, the lack of computer literacy of much of the sales force and the failure to adapt successfully to a new way of working. This was not helped by the weight of the machine, at over 5 kilos. In 1993 the company revamped the programme by issuing its sales force with Toshiba notebook computers backed with more training and administration support.

Chrysler[7]

In some companies the traditional methods of commission based remuneration for motivating sales personnel is being reassessed. The Chrysler Corporation has started to use customer satisfaction as a measure of the performance of their dealers, by carrying out customer satisfaction surveys. Chrysler now pays dealers more for achieving higher scores on these surveys. Such methods reward sales personnel for the longer-term objective of retaining customers.

PROSPECTING

Construction industry

In the UK permission for the erection of buildings must be given by officially appointed planning authorities. Any person or organisation wishing to build a building must apply for planning permission to the local planning authority. These applications are available for public inspection usually through local government offices by anyone who requests them. At any one time there may be thousands of planning applications awaiting approval. The planning applications are of enormous interest to those companies who supply products and services to the construction industry as they provide them with vital information on building projects. Such information includes the project sponsor (client), the appointed architect, quantity surveyor and other professionals, the size of the project by floor area, the location and type of building. A number of companies, such as Glenigans, collate this information and sell it to building materials suppliers and building contractors. The information is then used by materials suppliers and contractors in prospecting for potential customers.

These customers include the building sponsor (client), architects and other professionals who constitute the decision making unit for procurement of the materials or services. The information from the planning applications is recorded on computer disk and either sent direct to the building materials suppliers, contractors, etc. or printed on summary sheets. The company's sales personnel use the information to prospect for customers through telephone calling or physically calling on the potential customer.

Many companies use the information and as a result potential customers may receive numerous calls regarding particular projects. This is one of the drawbacks of using the source, as potential customers (often architects) may become unco-operative if they receive an unending stream of calls. It is therefore important for prospecting sales people to reach their target before anybody else does. Another potential drawback of the method is the 'liveness' of the project. Some planning applications take years for approval and may lie dormant for long periods without any design work being carried out. Such projects are therefore of little use to sales people in the short term. However, the planning applications are often used as a means of monitoring architects with whom a sales person may already have a built a relationship. Despite these potential drawbacks of the information, the planning applications are sometimes the only means a sales person has of identifying potential projects and customers.

FURTHER REFERENCE

Chapter 5, Buyer Behaviour: Decision making unit/Buyer chain (pp. 91–93)

Laser Vision Centers[8]

Laser Vision Centers, a small US company involved in the sale of laser equipment and other services in the medical health market, uses independent sales representatives or other contacts to prospect for potential clients. Such representatives sell complimentary or associated products/ services (to Laser Vision's products/services) to clients in the market which Laser Vision targets. When dealing with their own customers the representative will attempt to set up an appointment for Laser Vision and receive payment for a successful sales meeting. This referral system generates between 20 per cent and 25 per cent of Laser Vision's sales leads, and the conversion rate of appointments to sales is around 40 per cent.

This method is a more definite way of prospecting for potential customers, and it overcomes one of the difficulties in personal selling which is the task of securing an initial appointment. However it costs the company more per sale than if its own reps did all the work.

PRESENTATION AND DEMONSTRATION

Lotus Development[9]

In presenting their products and services to potential customers, some companies are turning to seminar-type selling. In the Canadian market Microsoft, Lotus Development Ltd and IBM all use seminar selling as a means of presenting their products/services. In the case of Lotus, seminars are rolled out in a series of different locations. These are pre-advertised in each area and a toll-free number is provided for potential delegates to obtain further information. Audiences for the seminars can be as many as 700. Different series of seminars are targeted at different customer types. The 'Evaluators Series' is aimed at managers of management information systems and software purchasers from organisations. The 'Consultants Series' is targeted at consultants and systems specialists. The Consultants Series is held monthly at Lotus offices in Toronto and quarterly in Vancouver and Montreal offices. In the course of these events delegates sign a confidential agreement and are shown products still at the development stage.

Lotus has not built up a large sales force as it traditionally relied on retailers to sell its main product, the Lotus 1–2–3 spreadsheet product. However with the development of network products for business the traditional route was unsuitable. The presentation and selling of products through seminars proved to be cost effective, reaching a large number of customers for minimum outlay in comparison with a direct sales force.

CONCLUSION

The personal selling function is usually more important in business-to-business markets, but as we have seen above it is also becoming increasingly important in retail situations, particularly where quality service is important. Because of the high cost of a sales force it is important that the company maximises the time each sales representative spends in face-to-face contact with the customer. The achievement of this goal should be planned for right from the start by adopting an effective sales force strategy and structure, implementing training, supervising and rewarding representatives. The sales force itself should also have the necessary back-up and information to make maximum use of their time, and possess the ability to achieve company sales targets.

NOTES

1 Kodak Canada section adapted from Mark Stevenson, 'The lean, mean sales machine', *Canadian Business*, January 1994, pp. 32–35.

2 The Registry Inc. section from Jack Falvey, 'Coming attractions', *Sales and Marketing Management*, July 1993, vol. 145, no. 8, pp. 16–17. Reprinted with permission of *Sales and Marketing Management*, 355 Park Avenue South, New York NY 10010–1789.

3 General Motors Saturn section adapted from the following: David Woodruff, 'May we help you kick your tires?', *Business Week*, 3 August 1992, pp. 38–44; 'Planet falls to earth', *The Economist*, 12 March 1994, pp. 76–77; Fara Warner, 'Donald Hudler Saturns marketing VP; 1992 marketer of the year', *Brandweek*, 16 November 1992, p. 21; Hugh Filman, 'Long term strategy drives GM in 1993', *Marketing* (Maclean Hunter), 12 October 1992, p. 2; Kathleen Kerwin, 'Meanwhile, Chevy is skulking in the garage', *Business Week*, 17 August 1992, pp. 90–91; D. Cottrell, L. Davis, P. Detrick and M. Raymond, 'Sales training and the Saturn difference', *Training and Development* (US), December 1992, vol. 46, no. 12, p. 60.

4 Home Depot section adapted from the following: Walecia Konrad, 'Smart selling – cheerleading, and clerks who know awls from augers', *Business Week*, 3 August 1992, pp. 38–44; Mary McKenzie Dixon, 'One on one: Nathan Morton; ready for prime time', *Dealerscope Merchandising*, November 1993, pp. 12–13; Patricia Sellers, 'Companies that serve you best', *Fortune*, 31 May 1993, pp. 50–59; 'Blank fills out the niche for Home Depot growth', *Advertising Age*, 1 February 1993, p. S5; Steve Weinstein, 'Masters of their universe', *Progressive Grocer*, September 1992, p. 95; Seth Lubove, 'A chain's weak links', *Forbes*, 21 January 1991, pp. 76–77.

5 Barclays Mercantile Business Finance section adapted from 'Microsegmentation's role in maximising rep performance', *Business Marketing Digest*, 4th quarter 1991, vol. 16, no. 4, pp. 65–70.

6 Hewlett Packard section adapted from 'If only Willy Loman had used a laptop', *Business Week*, 12 October 1987, p. 75; Thayer C. Taylor, 'Hewlett-Packard gives sales reps a competitive edge', *Sales and Marketing Management*, February 1987, p. 39; Edmund O. Lawler, 'Sales force rearms with portables', *Business Marketing*, July 1993, p. 47; Thayer C. Taylor, 'The tough get going – computers and office equipment', *Sales and Marketing Management*, September 1993, p. 59.

7 Chrysler section adapted from 'Smart selling – how companies are winning over today's tougher customer', *Business Week*, 3 August 1992, pp. 38–44.

8 Laser Vision Centers reprinted from Susan Greco, 'Prospecting: using others to sell your product', *Inc.*, August 1991, vol. 13, no. 8, p. 81. Reprinted with permission, *Inc.* magazine, August 1991. Copyright 1991 by Goldhirsh Group, Inc., 38 Commercial Wharf, Boston MA 02110.

9 Lotus Development section adapted from Mark Stevenson, op. cit.

Sales promotion and public relations

INTRODUCTION

Sales promotion consists of mostly short-term marketing inducements to encourage consumers to purchase a product or service. It is used more in consumer markets than in business-to-business markets, particularly for fast moving consumer goods, and may be tied in with public relations and/or advertising. There is a multitude of methods and tools for implementing sales promotions which include free samples, coupons, contests, etc., but not all are mentioned in this chapter. The objective of sales promotion is usually to increase the sales of a product; however, it may be used for other reasons such as market research or to generate advertising messages.

Sales promotion may be linked in with public relations activities, as we shall see in the case of Rollerblade (p. 210) and Perrier (p. 215). Public relations is particularly important in building awareness of the organisation and its products or services. It is also used to promote a better image and understanding among the various publics an organisation may wish to influence. Other important uses include countering negative reactions against an organisation, as in the case of Perrier, and many companies have contingency plans for dealing with crises. There are numerous tools which may be used in implementing a public relations programme, ranging from telephone information services to speeches at important events, a selection of which are presented in this chapter. The decision sequence in managing the public relations function is similar to other elements of the marketing mix. Objectives are identified, target markets chosen, a suitable positioning for the activities selected and finally the strategy formulated and implemented.

SALES PROMOTION

Rollerblade[1]

The development of the market for 'Rollerblade' skates can largely be attributed to a combination of sales promotion, public relations and other promotional activities by the company which began marketing them, Rollerblade Inc. in the USA. The skates are similar in principle to traditional roller skates, but contain the important difference of the wheels being placed in line, instead of in parallel as in the case of traditional roller skates. The company was the first to produce the product in 1980, but it wasn't until 1987 that it began making a significant impact on the market. The objectives and methods of its sales promotional activities were as follows:

1 Objectives

A more aggressive approach to marketing was adopted, and the first objective was to increase awareness of the product in the target market nationally and generate word of mouth communication. Other objectives included building brand image. A limited budget was available, so a considerable amount of free publicity needed to be generated.

2 Methods

The first step in this process was to attempt to secure high profile advocates for the product. This was carried out by giving free samples of the skates to successful individuals in their respective fields of activity – from media celebrities, journalists and courier services, to surfers, footballers and ice-skaters. This created good exposure for the product and stimulated word of mouth communication. Rollerblade Inc. estimates that the equivalent of around $250,000 worth of advertising was generated as a result.

Another means of building awareness and brand image was joint promotion with products from other companies to the mutual target market. In 1987 Rollerblade conducted a joint promotion with General Mills featuring that company's Golden Grahams cereal product. The cereal was aimed at families and teenagers and had a healthy image which was ideal for Rollerblade. Under the promotion 1000 pairs of skates were given away and the product was exposed on around 6 million cereal boxes.

Rollerblades were also featured in a video film on activity sports sponsored by Swatch and in TV advertisements by Procter & Gamble and Pepsi Co. Videos for in-store displays were also commissioned. The company allowed potential users to trial the product through the use of roving trial vans which set up in parks and community areas and at events which attracted potential customers, such as marathons, etc., throughout the USA. Other forms of promotion included sponsoring skating races and camps, books, videos and Team Rollerblade, a group of top class skaters which performed at events such as the Super Bowl.

By 1991 Rollerblade held around 70 per cent of the market with sales of $100 million per annum.

FURTHER REFERENCE

Chapter 13, Sales Promotional Public Relations: Sales promotion – joint sales promotion (pp. 212–213)

Objectives[2]

Objectives for sales promotional campaigns range from simply trying to obtain market feedback to the objective of increasing overall sales.

Competitions

Competitions are another form of sales promotion and many include a request for the participant to sum up what the product or service means to them, often in the form of a slogan or catchphrase. Such slogans can be examined by psychologists to determine consumers' perception of the product or service. Some slogans may also be used in future promotion. The slogan used by Vauxhall 'Once driven, forever smitten' came from a competition.

Promotions

Promotions may also be used to maintain awareness of a company's product or service. Their objective may be to stimulate recall of the product when the consumer is in a position to make a purchase decision. Examples of promotions which can provide this stimulus include company diaries, calendars, etc. This stimulus can also come into play in the case of deferred purchases or in cases of cross selling. For example the Milk Marketing Board produced a diary containing milk recipes, thus encouraging users to increase their consumption of milk and align this with seasonal recipes to reflect milk supply throughout the year.

Guinness   This company direct mailed customers with an offer of 50p off its canned draught beer in return for answering a short questionnaire. One of the objectives of the promotion for Guinness was to identify its main competitor in both the pub and carry-out market.

Strategies[3]

Sony

Up to the mid-1980s the traditional time for introducing new products on to the hi-fi market in the UK was September, in time for the Christmas sales period. However when Sony introduced their 'Compact 7' mid I hi-fi series in 1985 they decided to break convention by introducing it in June. They named the launch 'The Sony Compact Challenge' and offered a free high-performance Sony tape mailed to customers who had listened to the system in a store. Customers were also asked to fill in a test report comparing their existing system with Sony's. The intention of the comparison exercise was to show the customers' existing system in a bad light in relation to the new Sony system, which was expected to be superior, thus inducing the customer to purchase. The promotion effort also offered the dealer with a good selling opportunity. A further aspect of the promotion consisted of a trade offer of prizes for dealers based on the number of systems sold and quality of displays. A point-of-sale display was also introduced to participating dealers consisting of window displays, test report form dispensers and shelf strips. Dealers were also included in a free draw held by Sony. As a result of the promotion Sony's share of the mid I market increased from 15 per cent to 36 per cent in 1985.

FURTHER REFERENCE

Chapter 10, Marketing Channels: Motivating channel members (pp. 167–168)
Chapter 11, Advertising: Point-of-purchase advertising (pp. 192–193)

Joint sales promotion[4]

While some companies such as Procter & Gamble in the USA are cutting back on their sales promotion strategies, others are seeking to gain more cost effective promotion through teaming up with other products or services. In the UK, joint promotions have become more popular as part of a company's promotional plans. The major benefit of joint promotions is greater value for money, and this is particularly important during a recession.

A similar target market and similar image positioning are factors which many joint promotions have in common. This was the case with Mills and Boon, the romantic fiction publishers, and Old England Sherry. Mills and Boon novels were offered as an incentive to purchase Old England Sherry. The image of sherry is one which is also likely to appeal to Mills and Boon readers, being a conservative, traditional but also aspiringly sophisticated drink. In other cases the products may complement each other such as videos and take-away food as with a joint promotion between CIC Video and Kentucky Fried Chicken. In this case it is the occasion of use criteria which make the two products complement each other. Banks also regularly target young customers with promotions which include freebies such as CDs or jeans.

Agencies and services now exist for matching companies in joint sales promotion activities. However, it is not all plain sailing for joint promotions or sales promotions in general. P&G in the USA has reduced sales promotion activities in favour of an everyday low pricing strategy and more advertising. This was because they were finding sales promotions to be less and less cost effective with shoppers taking the best offer in the sales promotion auction. Companies must therefore be wary of brand image depletion through an endless stream of sales promotions.

PUBLIC RELATIONS

Cause marketing[5]

A scheme to provide computers for schools was launched in 1992 by Tesco, one of the major supermarket chains in the UK. The objective of the scheme was to build links with schools at the local level, to enhance Tesco's image as a retailer which caters for the family and to build customer loyalty. The scheme entitled 'Computers for Schools' provided customers with a computer voucher for every £25 spent in the store, which was then passed on to the local school. About 200 vouchers were required for a standard software package. It was administered in conjunction with Acorn, the largest supplier of computers to schools in the UK.

The scheme appealed to many of the stores' customers, about one-third of whom have children. It also served to raise Tesco's image in the local community, an objective which is part of the job for each manager of a Tesco store. Clearly this is allied with increasing customer levels of spending, with a standard software package being equivalent to £5,000 spent in the store.

Research indicated that consumers were more likely to purchase from a company that supports the community. The 'Computers for Schools' campaign was therefore designed to provide a mutually beneficial outcome for both the community and the company despite the £3 million outlay by Tesco. This is also an example of the more focused approach being used by companies as opposed to the wider mass-marketing type techniques.

It is estimated that companies spent almost $1 billion on cause-related campaigns in 1993 in the USA. In 1994 Sears & Roebuck sponsored a concert tour by the singer Phil Collins covering 40 cities in the USA with $1 million going to the homeless. Other companies which have used cause marketing include Avon cosmetics in contributing to research into breast cancer, Kraft General Foods who donated $0.25 on certain products purchased for the education of African American college students. Cause marketing is another means of differentiating a company's product or service from competitors. This can be particularly important when the offer is similar to those of its competitors, and can give additional benefits of satisfaction to consumers making them feel better about purchasing the products or services. As identified above it can also help to develop brand loyalty. In this way it can also serve to attain the more traditional goals of marketing such as increased sales, greater market share, etc.

FURTHER REFERENCE

Chapter 7, Products: Product differentiation (pp. 117–118)

Texaco   The government's road safety campaigns were supplemented by a similar campaign by Texaco. The campaign included the slogan 'Children should be seen and not hurt', and contained a run of television advertisements. It is estimated that Texaco sales increased and the number of road accidents fell in the period following the campaign.

WWF   On the charities side, the World Wide Fund for Nature (WWF) is active in raising funds for its cause. The Fund's approach is to market itself as a 'partner' to commercial organisations. Its partners include Cadbury Schweppes and National Westminster Bank. The bank has been donating £1 for every junior account opened.

Crisis management

Perrier[6]

During the week of 10 February 1990 the mineral water manufacturer Perrier had to withdraw its product world-wide due to minute traces of benzene (6 parts per billion) being found in the product. The traces were found by a test carried in North Carolina in the USA. There was no danger to health from the traces, but the company decided to withdraw the product to protect its name. Perrier UK already had a crisis management contingency plan in place in the event of such catastrophes. The UK division took the following steps:

Saturday p.m. 10 February	First meeting of Perrier Crisis Management Committee which informed the company's hydrologists, Hydrotechnica, that it wanted testing of its UK supplies carried out on the following Monday morning. The Ministry for Agriculture Fisheries and Food (MAFF) were also contacted immediately and asked to carry out their own tests.
Monday a.m. 12 February	Ten emergency telephone lines were in operation. Company officials met with MAFF.
Wednesday a.m. 14 February	First results of Hydrotechnica tests (due to minimum of 48 hours needed to carry them out) confirmed traces of benzene. Unofficial contamination theory hypothesised by a spokesman in the parent company, which suggested the source of contamination may have been the accidental splashing by an employee of incorrect cleaning fluid on bottling machinery. This resulted in wild speculation in the press. The British subsidiary wanted to withdraw the product immediately, as allowed for in its contingency plan, but this was vetoed by the HQ until a statement was issued in Paris. However the Parisian press conference failed to ease the situation. The situation was

not helped by the initial reluctance of the parent company, Source Perrier, to provide information until this press conference.

Thursday 15 February

In the UK full page advertisements ran in every national newspaper informing of the withdrawal of the product. MAFF tests confirmed presence of benzene. Marshall Foster (Chairwoman and Chief Executive of Perrier UK) met with journalists individually, thus giving the company more control over the meetings and avoiding the barrage of questions experienced in the Paris press conference. A relatively sympathetic reaction was solicited from the British press as a result. Source Perrier announced the withdrawal of world stocks of 160ml bottles of the water. This was seen as a way of eradicating the blemish which the contamination caused to the Perrier image, and the company portrayed it as a demonstration of their commitment to the quality of their brand.

Tuesday 20 February

Full page advertisements in the UK press informing that the technical problem causing the contamination had been solved, new quality control procedures were in place and bottling had restarted. The British and French health authorities had declared the water safe.

The true cause of the contamination turned out to be a filter used for purifying carbon dioxide at the bottling plant. The estimated cost of the recall was in the region of £125 million.

In March 1990 a £4 million promotional campaign was launched in the UK. The product was sold in a 750ml bottle with a label declaring 'New Production'. By May of the same year Perrier had regained 17 per cent of the sparkling water market from a position of 36 per cent before the crisis. Competitors could not fill the gap left by Perrier because they simply could not expand production fast enough, operating as they were at maximum capacity already. Furthermore it was highly risky for any producer of mineral water to attack Perrier because the Perrier name was almost synonymous with mineral water and by attacking Perrier they ran the risk of weakening the image of mineral water in general. However, the experience was one which Perrier would have preferred not to have had.

Handling complaints

British Airways[7]

The adage that it is much easier to keep an existing customer than it is to gain a new one, certainly holds true in the service economy. British Airways have recognised the importance of dealing effectively with customer complaints in ensuring that such customers stay with the airline. They are essentially treating the matter of a complaint as an opportunity rather than a chore which puts the company on the defensive.

BA have installed a new computer system which it calls 'Caress', especially to deal with complaints. The old approach was paper based and took a significant amount of time before any reply was actually made. Monitoring of the complaint was particularly difficult as the process often involved numerous departments and individuals with little means of co-ordinating the different inputs in dealing with the complaint.

Under the new system, when a complaint is first received the customer is ranked according to their value to the company in a 'lifetime' in terms of potential future business. Complaints are also categorised into one of 23 types and assigned a classification for their degree of urgency. The problem of involvement of different departments and functions within the organisation is handled by linking them together through the new system. Such functions may include booking, information, catering, baggage handling, in flight service, etc.

At the heart of the system is a workstation with two screens, one for displaying the customer's actual complaint (letter etc.) and another for monitoring progress on the complaint and producing the reply, as well as recording the different inputs into the complaint. The system allows access to information from other functions within the organisation such as booking, etc., and replies are often built using this information which can be transferred from the source system to the Caress system.

BA tries to ensure that the overall level of service is improved by feeding back the information from the customer service function to the other functions involved in the process. The success of the complaints handling procedure is high and the company claims that almost three quarters of those who make complaints use BA again. In this way the complaints process can be used to reverse customers' sense of dissatisfaction by impressing them with the speed and quality of the response and therefore creating an improved perception of the company among complainants. These indeed are the objectives of the complaints handling process.

FURTHER REFERENCE

Chapter 6, Segmentation and Positioning: Types of segmentation and positioning – Behavioural – user-status segmentation (pp. 98–99)

PR tools – telephone information services[8]

Procter & Gamble, Flora Margarine, Burger King, Coca-Cola & Schweppes Beverages

Companies are increasingly using telephone information services as a means of providing more information about their products, gaining information on the market and countering negative publicity. One of the more celebrated use of a telephone information service was that of Procter & Gamble in the USA, when it was alleged that their logo included images which were associated with the devil. As part of the strategy to dispel the rumour the company set up a telephone information service to reassure the public that there was no foundation to the allegations. Thousands of calls were received by a bank of operators. Similarly in the UK the suppliers of Flora margarine used a telephone information service to counter allegations that their product contained pig fat. Such an allegation would deter Jewish consumers in particular from purchasing the product. The answering service contributed to the countering of false allegations.

Telephone information services are included on product packs as a matter of course and not just used in times of crisis. They are more common in the USA where surveys have shown that over three quarters of brands carry service numbers. They are however less common in Europe with 8 per cent of brands carrying them in the UK and about one third of all brands in France. The lines can help contribute to building customer loyalty and establishing customer databases. Reactions to existing or new products can also be recorded and new product or service ideas generated. Burger King in the UK also offers a service line, through which customer feedback led to the inclusion of a breakfast menu.

There can however be a downside to telephone service numbers. Coca-Cola & Schweppes Beverages, a joint venture company, introduced a service line in 1992, and consumer complaints have doubled since then. Around 5000 calls are received per week, about half of these being prank or nuisance calls. Ten per cent of the genuine calls are complaints and the remainder are mostly enquiries about the product or the company.

Evaluating PR results[9]

Public Relations Consultants Association

The evaluation of public relations activity is particularly difficult due to the relatively subjective nature of the process. The process may involve setting measurable objectives such as quantitative sales targets or qualitative perception of image, establishing criteria for measurement and methods for monitoring and finally conducting the evaluation. To improve the evaluation of PR in the UK the Public Relations Consultants Association helped set up a computerised press scanning system for its members called Precis, owned and operated by Computerised Media Systems Ltd. Applications of the system include competitor intelligence, sponsorship assessment, product launch evaluation, issue management and advertising tracking and evaluation.

One of the benefits of the service is that media planning connected with the National Readership Survey can be carried out prior to a campaign and evaluation conducted during and after the campaign. BMW uses the service to evaluate its coverage in about 60 publications. The coverage obtained by its competitors can also be tracked to determine the frequency, type and reasons for the coverage, e.g. the features which are focused on. This contributes to the development of its own strategy. Precis has also been used to evaluate the coverage of the political parties during the 1993 election campaign. It is estimated that the Conservatives may have received publicity worth a possible £55 million against Labour's £18 million. Other systems are available which use criteria such as article size, message quality and headline size to evaluate effectiveness.

Other methods for evaluating effectiveness are tracking studies and target audience audits. Large organisations often carry out their own opinion research or tracking which may include recognition of particular messages and market profile. The comparative performance of competitors is another factor taken into account in evaluating PR. Infopress Communications in the UK provides a service called 'Impact' under which an organisation's competition is evaluated in PR terms. The service provides analysis of the required target market, media and messages, according to the brief given. The researchers are not told who the client organisation is, thus minimising potential bias in the process.

Lobbying/influencing specific target groups

Ratcliff Tail Lifts[10]

The development of a professional or seemingly impartial image for a company can be an important objective for many organisations. This can be partly achieved by building links with groups responsible for policy making in the sector in which the company operates. Ratcliff Tail Lifts, based in Welwyn Garden City, manufactures hydraulic lifts for loading and unloading which are attached to vehicles. The company recently developed a new application for its technology by entering the market for lifts for disabled persons to enter and disembark from vehicles.

Social policy within the European Union and in many European countries has focused on increasing concern for accessible transport for disabled people. The emergence of pressure groups to campaign for rights for the disabled and the socio-political nature of the issue, has meant that forums which debate and influence policy development in the area are particularly important. Such forums include events on public transport where decision makers from local and national government officials to campaigners for disabled rights can be found. Committees established to shape and make decisions in the area of public transport are also important forums. Ratcliff recognised the importance of such forums and began attending events and participating in committees. One of their objectives was to obtain first-hand knowledge of the processes which would shape the development of policy in the area. The company now attempts to link itself with independent people or groups and avoids the selling approach.

Ratcliff's potential contribution to a solution to the disabled transport issue enabled them to contribute to the various forums where decisions are shaped. The company began contributing to conferences on public transport by speaking at such events. This made people in the area aware of the company and also allowed its representative to develop contacts with decision makers (including potential customers) in the field of public transport. Delegate lists for conferences also provide useful potential contacts for the company and these form a database used to disseminate information on the company and its products. The company aims to establish itself as a credible and impartial source of information whose views will be sought on the issue of passenger lifts for vehicles.

As a result of its links with decision makers Ratcliff developed a prototype lift for the Rome City Transport Authority. An order for lift equipment for twenty trains for Swedish Railways was also won by the company, and led to a further order from Dutch railways. However, equally as important is the knowledge which the company gains on the potential direction of policy in this area, particularly in relation to whether vehicles produced are already equipped to cater for disabled people by having low floors, or whether lifting equipment is attached to a standard vehicle. Clearly the latter presents a major opportunity for Ratcliff.

FURTHER REFERENCE

Chapter 3, The Marketing Environment: Environmental factors – Regulatory (pp. 44–45); Social (pp. 52–53)

CONCLUSION

Sales promotion is often used to boost sales for established products or to introduce new products. It is more commonly used for fast moving consumer goods and a multitude of methods may be employed. In this chapter we have selected a number of examples which demonstrate the uses of sales promotion. The over-use of sales promotion, however, should be avoided. Over-saturation may result in increased clutter in the market and may adversely affect brand equity and reduce loyalty.

In the area of public relations, companies have introduced cause marketing in an attempt to enhance their image, build brand loyalty and differentiate their product. Public relations in general is used to communicate with the multiple publics which the organisation deals with. It is also necessary for many organisations to have strategies in place to deal with adverse publicity, as in the case of Perrier. In some cases adverse publicity or negative reactions can actually be turned to the company's advantage, if the organisation has an effective contingency strategy in place. This was demonstrated by British Airways and to a lesser extent by Perrier.

NOTES

1 Rollerblade section reprinted from *Working Woman*, December 1991, vol. 16, no. 12, pp. 23–24. Written by Annetta Miller. Reprinted with permission of *Working Woman*. Copyright © 1991 *Working Woman*.
2 Objectives section adapted from Mark Davies, 'Sales promotions as a competitive strategy', *Management Decision*, 1992, vol. 30, no. 7, pp. 5–10.
3 Strategies section adapted from Hugh Davidson, *Offensive Marketing*, London, Penguin, 1975, pp. 250–252. Reproduced by permission of Penguin Books Ltd.

4 Joint sales promotion section adapted from: 'Romantic read for Old England drinkers', *Off-licence News*, 1 July 1993, p. 8; Louella Miles, 'Perfect Partners', *Marketing Business*, September 1992, pp. 37–38; Cathy Bond, 'Marriages of Some Convenience', *Marketing* (UK), October 1991, pp. 23–26.

5 Cause marketing section adapted from: Tesco's Computers for Schools promotional material; Diane Summers, 'Rewards for the loyal shopper', *Financial Times*, 2 December 1993, p. 14; Geoffrey Smith and Ron Stodghill, 'Are good causes good marketing?', *Business Week*, 28 March 1994, p. 54D–E; Nancy Arnott, 'Marketing with a passion', *Sales and Marketing Management* (US), January 1994, pp. 64–71; Tom O'Sullivan, 'School projects: could do better', *Marketing Week*, 3 December, 1993, pp. 23–24; Helen Slingsby, 'Time to stimulate the feel-good factor', *Marketing Week*, 3 April 1992, p. 14.

6 Perrier section adapted from the following: Stewart Toy and Lisa Driscoll, 'Can Perrier purify its reputation?', *Business Week*, 26 February 1990, p. 18; Ali Qassim, 'Lady of the first water', *Marketing Week*, 2 March 1990, p. 35; Alan Friedman, 'Perrier water production halted', *Financial Times*, 12 February 1990, p. 1; Patricia Sellers, 'Perrier plots its comeback', *Fortune*, 23 April 1990, pp. 277–278; *Fortune*, 23 April 1990; Alix M. Freedman, 'Perrier finds mystique hard to restore', *The Wall Street Journal*, 12 December 1990, pp. B1 B6; Laura Bird, 'Perrier's launch stalled – again – over health concerns', *Adweek's Marketing Week*, 30 April 1990, pp. 5–6; Daniel Butler, 'Perrier's painful period', *Management Today*, August 1990, pp. 72–73; William Dawkins, 'Perrier counts the cost of contamination', *Financial Times*, 13 February 1990; William Dawkins, 'Perrier to destroy world stocks after benzene find', *Financial Times*, 15 February 1990, pp. 1, 26; William Dawkins, 'A tres bitter pill to swalleau', *Financial Times*, 15 February 1990, p. 30; Paul Abrahams, Paul Betts, William Dawkins, Alan Friedman and Ian Rodger, 'Putting Perrier back together', *Financial Times*, 17 February 1990; various reports in British national press, February 1990.

7 British Airways section adapted from Claire Gooding, 'A caress for the customer', *Financial Times*, 24 February 1994, p. 19.

8 PR tools – telephone information services section adpated from Diane Summers, 'Show your customers you care', *Financial Times*, 13 January 1994, p. 11.

9 Evaluating PR Results section adapted from: Joan Plachta, 'Valuing the PR industry', *Marketing*, 21 March 1991, p. 25; Computerised Media Services Ltd. company literature; 'Tabloid help "worth a possible £37 m"', *Guardian*, 26 January 1994.

10 Ratcliff Tail Lifts section adapted from 'How Ratcliff feels its way into uncharted markets', *Business Marketing Digest*, vol. 16, no. 2, 2nd quarter 1991, pp. 17–25.

Chapter 14

Market status and competitive moves

INTRODUCTION

In many competitive situations, there are typically four types of players:

1 The market leader – the firm with the largest market share.
2 The market challenger – the runner-up firm that is actively trying to expand its market share and replace the market leader.
3 The market follower – another runner-up firm with a smaller market share than the market challenger that is seeking to maintain its market share and not upset the applecart.
4 The market nichers – small firms that serve small market segments, ignored or overlooked by the larger players in the market.

This chapter provides examples of companies that assume these roles. The chapter continues with a description of the competitive moves undertaken by US motorcycle manufacturer Harley-Davidson when trying to defend itself against the onslaught of the Japanese motorcycle manufacturers, particularly Honda, into the US market in the 1960s. The competitive moves undertaken by both Caterpillar and Komatsu in the fight for market share in the USA are also presented.

Companies do not, however, always enter into confrontational situations with competitors to achieve their goals. The very fact that markets are becoming more competitive and the importance of scale of operation are leading companies to seek strategic alliances in some industries. Such co-operation is an important part of competitive moves. Companies in the automotive, computer and airline industries are increasingly adopting this approach. The chapter ends with some examples of such alliances.

MARKET LEADER

Motorola [1]

Motorola, the US multinational manufacturer of products including cellular phones, pagers, two-way radio and semconductors, is world market leader in cellular phones (45 per cent of world-wide market) and pagers (85 per cent of world-wide market). Motorola's dominance of these product-markets has been due to many factors including the relentless pursuit of quality in all operations and the fostering of a company culture characterised by strong management–labour co-operation, teamwork, decentralised decision making, a commitment to increasing productivity from both blue-collar and white-collar employees, and technological leadership.

Motorola is a marketing oriented outfit and recruits from companies who lead the field in marketing. The company is developing markets abroad including Japan, Eastern Europe, Latin America, Asia and the developing countries. The developing countries, many of whom lack a traditional telephone infrastructure, are good prospects for cellular phones. In cellular phones, Motorola faces a formidable competitor – Nokia – the Finnish company which holds the number one position in Europe and is number two in the USA after Motorola.

Another element of the company's strategy is the development of strategic alliances with other companies. Motorola, along with Apple and IBM, developed the new microprocessor chip for the new generation Power PCs. In today's competitive environment many companies are finding it no longer possible to serve more than one global market simply by themselves. Strategic alliances allow the company to achieve synergy in markets with other organisations, providing mutual benefit.

To maintain its market leadership position the company aggressively pursues total quality management (TQM) with objectives including reducing defects and cycle time, cutting costs and increasing productivity. Motorola's success at TQM allows it to reduce its prices on its products thus further strengthening its market position. It was one of the first major companies to win the prestigious Malcolm Baldrige National Quality Award in the USA. Motorola has also increased sales per employee by around 100 per cent in the five years to 1993.

Regular meetings are held where management and professional staff from divisions within the Motorola group get together and swap best practices in several areas including manufacturing, quality, and cycle time reduction. Staff are highly trained and motivated and the company recognises the contribution of these factors to its own competitiveness. The electronics industry is one which demands a high level of innovation and fast product development. To this end Motorola also invests significantly in research and development.

FURTHER REFERENCE

Chapter 2, Marketing Strategies: Intensive, integrative and diversification growth strategies – Backward cooperation (pp. 31–32)

Ford[2]

Ford, the largest car manufacturer in the UK, provides an example of a market leader just hanging on to market dominance over Vauxhall, its closest rival. Ford's dominance had been slowly eroded since 1987 when it held 28.8 per cent of the market and Vauxhall trailed in second place with less than half that figure. By 1993, the gap had closed and Ford held 22 per cent of the market with Vauxhall holding 18 per cent. In fact, in July 1993, Vauxhall overtook Ford in sales although July is traditionally the slowest month for car sales, and nearly toppled Ford from the top position. Vauxhall's wider product range was the reason Ford nearly lost market dominance.

A five-year plan was developed by Ford to overhaul the whole product range in an attempt to halt the market slide. In 1994 the new sports coupé and replacement for the Capri, the Ford Probe GT, and the four-wheel-drive Maverick were launched. Ford also announced plans in 1994 to launch a small car to bolster its competitive position in the small car market segment. Ford had an advertising spend of £45million in 1993 and advertising expenditures remain huge. Continual improvement of product quality is a cornerstone of the Ford strategy.

MARKET CHALLENGER

Compaq[3]

In the two years since Eckhard Pfeiffer became CEO of Compaq Computer, he has engineered such a stunning turnaround that it's surprising the company still has the same name. Pfeiffer, 52, mandated that Compaq transform itself from a supplier of PCs to corporations into something far broader – a maker of machines for every market, from pocket communications to home computers, and at a blisteringly competitive price.

IBM and Apple, look out: Since Compaq changed course, it has more than doubled its share of the $35-billion-a-year PC and workstation market, from 3.8 per cent to 10 per cent, according to BIS Strategic Decisions in Norwell, Massachusetts. Compaq made more money last year than both rivals combined. No wonder that when Pfeiffer declared in September that Compaq intends to be number one in PC and work-station market share by 1996, few people scoffed.

Traditionally, Compaq has focused on selling to corporations through 'resellers', middlemen dedicated to that purpose, but when surveys revealed that consumers thought Compaq products hard to find, Pfeiffer added thousands of retailers to the distribution scheme.

Take the Presario, a line of home computers introduced last August. The machines are designed to attract technophobes, with friendly features like factory-style software and a built-in telephone answering machine. Compaq's hottest new PC ever, the Presario quickly became mass merchants' top selling computer under $1,500.

The Presario demonstrates how fundamentally the company has changed. Compaq is in the vanguard of a trend towards designing computers for specific market segments and advertising them aggressively.

After three years with no TV advertising, Compaq launched a $12 million dollar campaign last fall. It included a Presario advertisement that shows a training class being forced to parrot computer terms like gigabyte and wysiwyg. The tag line: 'Instead of sounding smart about computers, you can *be* smart about computers'.

Compaq has quintupled the number of North American outlets from 2,000 to 10,500 in just two years: retailers now account for more than 20 per cent of Compaq's shipments vs. only 5 per cent in 1992. This March, Wal Mart will join the ranks of Compaq retailers.

In 1993, as volume doubled from 1.5 million to 3 million computers, total manufacturing costs fell by almost $10 million. Under pressure from Pfeiffer, manufacturing executives decided that to save money Compaq would have to abandon its practice of assembling every nut and bolt itself. This was a wrenching change in a company that built a reputation on the Made By Compaq label. Compaq began giving sub-assembly work to contractors in 1992. To help safeguard quality, it instructs them on how to put the components together.

It has its eye on a potentially juicy market Apple helped pioneer: hand-held personal digital assistants, or PDAs, like Apple's over hyped Newton MessagePad. Compaq's first PDA will appear this year and will be priced at less than $1000. But it won't serve the same functions as Newton and won't be called a PDA. Compaq has introduced the term 'mobile companion' and hopes competitors will adopt it for their hand-held devices.

Unlike the Newton, which works mainly as an electronic Filofax, Compaq's device is intended to serve as a wee, featherweight notebook computer. While not in use, the companion will rest in a cradle designed to attach to the side of any Windows-equipped PC and recharge its battery. When you are ready to go, up pops a menu on your PC screen that lets you copy the necessary files from your computer to your companion. If you forget to transfer a file before you go on the road, you can fetch it via phonelines and the companion's built-in modem. The product uses a stylus as its main pointing device and has an optional plug-in keyboard.

Compaq is developing the mobile companion with Intel and Micro-soft, which is fine-tuning a version of its Windows software for the machine. Such alliances are a key weapon in Compaq's war with IBM for the top spot. Working closely with Microsoft and networking king-pin Novell, for example, Compaq has become the biggest maker of servers, high powered PCs that anchor office networks. The machines, which account for some 17 per cent of Compaq's sales and 30 per cent of profits, appeal to customers because they replace costly minicomputers.

Compaq hasn't lost its fondness for price warfare. Its latest move is the release this month of the Contura Aero subnotebook – a category of highly portable PCs that weigh less than four pounds and have no floppy disk drive. A fully equipped Aero with a monochrome screen costs under $1,500 – about $500 less than its IBM counterpart, the Think-Pad 500.

FURTHER REFERENCE

Chapter 9, Pricing: Pricing strategies – Penetration pricing (pp. 149–150)

Fuji [4]

For years, Kodak dominated the photography market in film, packaged in its famous yellow boxes, and easy-to-use 'point and shoot' cameras. Films were premium priced giving Kodak healthy profits. Then Fuji Photo Film Company of Japan began offering high-quality lower priced film in a direct head-on attack on Kodak's leadership position. Kodak began losing market share and profits also fell during the 1980s. Fuji proved to be very innovative and introduced fast-colour film products, always ahead of Kodak, in some cases by years. For example, in 1984,

Fuji introduced 1600-speed colour film and Kodak was not able to match it until 1990. Kodak, faced with such an aggressive market challenger, increased its responsiveness. When Fuji introduced a professional slide film, Velvia, that offered super-saturated colours, Kodak quickly responded with a competitive product. In the 1980s, Fuji's relentless pursuit of market share paid off and the company managed to capture 10 per cent market share in the USA.

Its confidence was increased as well as its visibility when it beat Kodak for the prize of official photographic sponsor of the 1984 Olympics. This was an important victory for Fuji at that early time in its growth and helped its sales to take off. Kodak, however, still dominates the US market, helped by its distribution clout where its products are well-entrenched in supermarkets and drugstore chains. Kodak also has agreements with 40 of America's largest amusement parks which guarantee to sell only Kodak film.

Lipton's Tea[5]

In 1993, Unilever's Van den Bergh Foods set a target to be number two in the Irish tea market within two years with its Lipton brand of tea, thus effectively promising to displace Barry's Tea from the number 2 position where it had held a 29 per cent market share. The market leader, Lyons, had a 51 per cent share of the tea market spending approximately £2 million annually promoting its labels. Lipton planned to spend £2 million on a major promotional campaign starting on new year's day 1994 using TV and poster advertising. The blend and the slogan 'big leaves, bigger taste' emerged from consumer research when Lipton discovered that many consumers still erroneously believed tea bags were made from tea factory floor sweepings. Lipton tea bags contain larger leaves, the unique selling proposition for the product.

MARKET FOLLOWER

The story of ERF, in 1993 Britain's biggest remaining home-grown heavy truck maker, provides an example of a company avoiding intense competitive retaliation from the major European truck manufacturers yet attacking target markets to which it can bring distinct advantages, entering new markets that are opening up, keeping R.&D. costs and manufacturing costs low and product and service quality high. ERF defined its own path to growth in a fiercely competitive market that avoided head-on clashes with the majors.

ERF[6]

It is 62 years since Edwin Richard Foden stomped out of a board meeting of his family's lorry company at Sandbach, Cheshire, because he disagreed with their assessment that the future of road haulage lay in steam power. Astonishingly, both ERF, the company he founded two years later with Dennis, his son, to demonstrate his belief in the diesel engine, and Foden, now owned by Paccar, the American truck maker, are still in business.

But it is ERF that flies the flag as Britain's biggest remaining home-grown heavy truck maker. And it is ERF that will live or die by its belief that an American-style assembly operation can out-manoeuvre the rumbling advance of the huge, vertically integrated European truck builders.

It is a David and Goliath battle of heroic proportions. On the one side, companies such as Mercedes-Benz, Volvo, Renault and Iveco, with multi-billion pound product development budgets, scale economies, plants round the globe and entrenched international dealer networks. On the other, Peter Foden, ERF chairman, and 700 employees, making perhaps 3,000 lorries a year and with £14 million to spend on designing and introducing a new truck that must win back defectors among British customers and win over European hauliers. Impossible odds? Apparently not. This May ERF launched its new tractor unit, the EC. In July, the company sold 124 trucks, up from 98 a year ago and maintaining a strong surge for a second month. ERF believes the fight back has begun.

Not before time. A three-year recession of unprecedented severity has played havoc with Britain's truck industry. From an unsustainable 1989 peak of 55,000 vehicles a year, sales slumped to 30,000 a year and now, in their first year of slow recovery, are on course to perhaps 35,000 in 1993.

The slump drove AWD in Dunstable, Bedfordshire, out of business, and fragmented what had been Britain's biggest producer, the Anglo-Dutch Leyland DAF group. A management buyout team has taken over the Leyland plant in Lancashire, but the hiatus has enabled Iveco to seize market leadership.

During the first seven months of 1993, the number of trucks sold in Britain was up year-on-year by 5.7 per cent at 17,482. But the number of trucks made in Britain fell 638 to 9,359. In twelve months, foreign-built vehicles have increased their market share from 39.5 to 46.5 per cent. Given that Britain had a hefty trade deficit on trucks, spending £506 million on imports in 1992, but selling only £330 million of British-built trucks overseas, the figures should be a cause for concern.

Britain has joined the European truck market without an effective national champion. The January–July UK sales table shows Iveco at number one, followed in descending order of volume by Mercedes-Benz, Leyland, Renault/Volvo, Scania, MAN, and ERF.

But among the Europeans, only Iveco and Volvo assemble vehicles in Britain. Mercedes, Scania and MAN do not. Every extra truck they sell displaces British jobs and cash overseas. Iveco is not just UK market leader: it is also the largest volume truck builder in Britain through Iveco Ford, a company jointly owned by Fiat of Italy and Ford of America, and a niche player through ownership of Seddon Atkinson. Here is a perfect demonstration of the impact intensifying competition is having among Europe's lorry manufacturers.

Iveco was formed in 1975 by a merger of the truck-making activities of Fiat and OM in Italy, Unic in France and Margirus Deutz in Germany. A decade later, Iveco, now a Fiat subsidiary, moved to strengthen its United Kingdom presence by acquiring a half share in Ford's British lorry making business, based at Langley, Hertfordshire.

Iveco Ford has invested £400 million in modernisation and the introduction of a new light- and medium-weight truck, the Cargo, with a SuperCargo model available for heavier jobs. UK sales from Langley rose 10 per cent during the first seven months, to reach 3,105 vehicles. Trucks were also exported to Scandinavia. But sales of Iveco imports from Italy and Germany were up faster still, as the company, traditionally a weakling at the heavy end of the UK market, introduced other new models generated by its £2.5 billion model replacement programme.

New products are only part of the Europeans' success. Another is their desperation to sell trucks. Manufacturers left with hefty surplus capacity and rising losses have thrown themselves into the British market. Huge discounts are offered on list prices. Fair competition or predatory pricing? The line is thin.

Amid this maelstrom, ERF's survival is a source of wonder. Thirty years at the company's helm have given Mr Foden a knack of steering the company through the industry's storms. John Bryant, the managing director, recruited from Volvo two years ago, has reorganised the plants at Sandbach and nearby Middlewich to make them leaner, more flexible, more efficient.

ERF's battle for market share is more than a tussle between truck makers. It is a trial between two manufacturing systems. The continentals have built their success upon vertical integration, developing their own engines and drive trains at huge cost, but selling standardised trucks in large volumes. ERF, like its American peers, has chosen instead to buy components from world-leading specialist manufacturers: engines from Cummins and Perkins, gearboxes from Eaton and ZF, axles from Rockwell, and so on. Together, Rod England, sales director, says, ERF's suppliers spend $1 billion a year on research and development, and achieve economies of scale that even the Europeans cannot achieve.

So ERF's £14 million investment in the EC range was concentrated on developing the new cab and vehicle suspension and on tooling-up for production. The new cab is available in three trim levels, on a variety of chassis. An ERF customer is thus offered an extraordinary pick 'n' mix range of options from which to select a truck to suit his requirements exactly, albeit at a somewhat higher price.

The market verdict on this strategy is encouraging. ERF trucks are operated by many of Britain's leading distribution groups, including oil companies, BOC, Wincanton and Exel Logistics. Since Britain's distribution industry is supposedly the world's best, that is an important badge of quality and a reflection of competitive through-life cost.

Among the smaller operators who account for 60 per cent of UK heavy truck purchases, ERF reckons sales are on an upswing. Mr England is now attacking behind enemy lines, appointing distributors in France and Spain with overnight parts distribution from Sandbach by express carrier.

The battle among truck makers for survival is intensifying. For the past two decades, vertical integration has proved the best formula for success. But the 1990s are demanding a new agility from manufacturers. Like his heirs, Edwin Richard Foden would have relished the challenge.

MARKET NICHER

Rover[7]

In the mid-1980s, Rover Cars was making fewer than ten cars per worker a year, one of the worst productivity records in the world industry. At the time, survival was a real issue for Rover. Since then, Rover has been transformed from a poor performing volume car maker, struggling hopelessly to compete across the board with the industry giants like Ford and General Motors, into a streamlined producer of niche vehicles at the upper end of each market segment. In 1993, Rover outperformed the majority of car makers in Europe, increasing sales and returning to trading profitability. The Motor Industry Research Unit (UK) forecast profits of £201 million for 1995.

It was under the stewardship of Graham Day, Chairman of Rover, in the mid-1980s that the shift to a niche player began. Day realised that Rover, to be a successful player in the car industry, had to become a specialist manufacturer and move upmarket. Rover simply lacked the volumes to be a low cost producer. Day embarked on a drive to cut the company's break-even point from its mid-1980s level of more than 500,000 cars a year and to improve product and service quality. Honda engineering is used for many of the models (Honda owned 20 per cent of Rover before the BMW takeover) which has been the key to improving Rover's quality. Financially, the company has become lean. Labour costs were reduced by redundancies and component price rises have been minimised and reliability of systems increased by working in partnership with a handful of key suppliers. By the end of 1993, it was expected to break-even down to Rover's target of 400,000 cars.

Avon Tyres [8]

The 1970s witnessed dramatic changes in the market for tyres – the oil crisis and the switch from cross-ply to radial tyres by the car manufacturers in the original equipment market (OEM) precipitated change. Demand for remoulds and second-hand tyres also began to increase further reducing the market for the tyre manufacturers.

Faced with these changes, one of the world's smallest tyre manufacturers began to realise its survival depended on it finding market niches. Avon identified two niches: high performance motorcycle tyres and high performance car tyres.

Avon has concentrated on developing high quality tyres for these segments. It succeeded in becoming an original equipment supplier to Rolls Royce, Bentley and Aston Martin. Avon still manufacturers conventional tyres but is not dependent on this market. Its quality image no doubt helps sales of its conventional tyres.

Bugatti

As one of the world's handful of producers of supercars, the Italian car company Bugatti occupies a small but very profitable niche in the car market.. Bugatti's high-price high performance car, the EB110, whose competitors include the McLaren F1 and Jaguar's XJ220, carries with it the history and flawless pedigree of the Bugatti name.

The Bugatti EB110, with a price tag of approximately £350,000, is aimed at the super rich. Bugatti first began making its sporty performance cars in the 1920s and today these old cars are collectors' items. Bugatti ceased production in 1952 but the company was revived in 1992. The cars are superbly engineered, aided as they are by Bugatti's purchase of the UK car manufacturer Lotus with its rich engineering skills. The cars are beautifully designed and, combined with the classic image of the Bugatti name, are a 'must have' for very rich car enthusiasts.

COMPETITIVE MOVES

Harley-Davidson and Honda[9]

The classic marketing story of Harley-Davidson fighting to maintain its market share and very survival against the entry of the Japanese motorcycle manufacturers, most notably Honda, into the US market in the mid-1960s, allows us to examine the different strengths and weaknesses, objectives and strategies employed by two very different competitors.

In the 1950s big motorcycles were the norm and the US motorcycle market was dominated by Harley-Davidson which had a 70 per cent share. Motorcycles were associated with tough macho type men and the manufacturers were willing to continue to appeal to this market as it brought steady growth. Harley-Davidson took pride in its macho image and the resultant 'street cred' it gave to its products. Its products were distinct and customers were fiercely loyal to them. Even today, the name is as synonymous with the American way of life as Coca-Cola and McDonald's.

In 1959, Honda entered the US market with a range of small motorcycles and completely redefined the market so that by 1966, only seven years later, it controlled 85 per cent of the market. Harley-Davidson and the other US and European manufacturers were completely unprepared. The Japanese were never taken as a serious threat even though Honda was at that time the world's largest producer of motorcycles. Honda's size at home gave it great economies of scale in production, distribution, technology and marketing and it used its highly competitive cost position as a springboard for penetrating world markets, notably the USA, with, at first, small motorcycles.

Honda introduced the concept of the small bike for the public and used advertising featuring ordinary everyday people (including women) riding their machines with the slogan 'You meet the nicest people on a Honda'. A motorcycle was now being marketed as something to have in addition to a car. Honda had effectively found a new untapped market segment. Honda's success in selling its light-weight motorcycles was phenomenal. Its sales in the USA went from $0.5 million in 1960 to $77 million in 1965. Honda started with the 50cc motorbike and gradually introduced larger motorcycles, eventually developing high quality/low price models for the big motorcycle segment (700cc upwards).

Honda's strategy (similar to the strategies of its Japanese counterparts) was centred around taking a long-term view of the market and developing a willingness to forgo short-term profitability in favour of long-term market share. Its strategy was concerned with building volume and riding down the experience curve to lower costs and greater profitability in order to fund the further development of better and bigger models through extensive research and development. This was all supported by creative marketing.

Harley-Davidson had been caught unawares. It had believed the market was mature and to be harvested rather than further developed. The company lacked Honda's strategic vision of the market in the future.

Harley-Davidson was certain that Honda would not enter the big motorcycle sector and conceded the smaller motorcycle segments to the Japanese believing the big motorcycle segment was impregnable. This combination of a lack of strategic vision and failure to monitor and understand its competitors resulted in Harley-Davidson's share of the big motorcycle segment falling from almost total domination to less than half in 1975.

Harley-Davidson allowed its range of models to fall to just a handful when the Japanese routinely offered five times that many. Harley-Davidson, seeing market share slipping away, began accusing the Japanese of 'dumping' their products on the market. In 1977, Harley-Davidson unsuccessfully petitioned the US government for a tariff relief programme that would protect it from the pressures of Japanese imports. The response by Honda (together with Kawasaki) was to establish production facilities in the USA. In 1983, after record losses in 1981 and 1982 Harley-Davidson was successful. The International Trade Commission (ITC) imposed a five-year tariff on bikes with an engine size of 700cc or more in order to give the sole remaining US motorcycle manufacturer Harley-Davidson a chance to get back on its feet. However, by this time the market had simply matured and the sales growth rates of the 1960s were gone forever. In the early 1980s, Harley-Davidson's market share in the US had fallen to one-fifth.

Since 1981, Harley-Davidson has become committed to Japanese-style production and inventory control methods including quality circles, flexible manufacturing, JIT (just-in-time) production, employee empowerment, and a teamwork culture has been fostered within the organisation. Harley switched from making all its own components to sourcing many from outside and engineering improvements have led to greater product reliability and performance. Production costs have been reduced and the number of models increased. Small gains in market share in the over 700cc segment have been made. In 1983, Harley-Davidson returned to profitability and in 1989, its market share in the big motorcycle sector reached over 60 per cent.

FURTHER REFERENCE

Chapter 10, Marketing Channels: Channel co-operation (pp. 169–171)

Caterpillar and Komatsu [10]

For fifty years Caterpillar – makers of agricultural and construction industry machinery – had experienced consistent sales growth. The company had gained a strong quality image and was noted for its parts delivery system and dealer network. In the late 1970s, however, Caterpillar was experiencing strong competition from the Japanese company Komatsu who began to cut prices 40 per cent below those of Caterpillar. The result of this was an 11 per cent gain in US market share by Komatsu between 1981 and 1986, while Caterpillar recorded a $953 million loss between 1982 and 1985.

The choice then facing Caterpillar was either to cut price in response to Komatsu and as a result continue to make a loss, or to maintain its prices and inevitably lose further market share: i.e. it could lose more money or lose market share. The company chose the former, deciding that if it did not maintain market share it would not be able to meet the long-term challenge of Komatsu. The Japanese company's objective was to achieve a 15 per cent US market share; however it only achieved a maximum of 12 per cent by 1986 and now stands at 9 per cent. Caterpillar's strategic reaction consisted of developing new products, improving quality and interaction of advanced production techniques – lowering costs. The outcome was a return to pre-1981 levels of profitability.

STRATEGIC ALLIANCES

Philips [11]

Since the 1980s, Philips, the Dutch Electronics giant, has been developing its global competitiveness through the formation of strategic alliances (Figure 14.1). To name a few examples:

- In 1989 the company entered into a joint venture with the Taiwan Fluorescent Lamp Company in Taipei to manufacture high pressure discharge lamps and other energy saving light appliances. The rationale behind this strategy was to reduce its costs by utilising low costs of production in Asia and to capitalise on the increased concern for the environment in the form of conservation of energy resources.
- In 1986 agreements were signed with Du Pont for the production of CDs.
- In 1988 an alliance was formed between Propaganda Films (US) and Working Title Films Ltd (US) for the formation of a television production company.
- Also in 1988 an alliance was formed with John Fluke (US) which now sells Philips test and measurement equipment in North America, China, Hong Kong and Japan while Philips does the same for Flukes products in the rest of the world. This enabled Philips to supply an entire range of products on a world-wide basis, allowing it to compete with other full-line suppliers.
- In 1990 an alliance was formed with a Japanese electronics company named JVC to establish a joint venture (JV) for the production of video recorders in Malaysia. Production alliances have also been formed with East European and Chinese firms. In embarking on this JV the company was able to reduce its dependence on European markets and strengthen its position in the Far East. It could obtain a more balanced portfolio of geographical markets. Philips have also formed alliances to participate in joint research and development projects.
- In 1990 Philips and Thompson CSF (France) signed an agreement which involves joint research and development on integrated circuits, flat screens, liquid crystal displays and broadcasting equipment. This was an attempt by European companies to catch up with the Japanese and improve their technology.

VMX and Mercury Communications[12]

For Telecoms companies around the world, alliances are often an essential ingredient of corporate strategy. In the 1980s, fuelled by de-regulation of state enterprises in many countries and investment in developing countries, the industry was transformed into one of the fastest growing

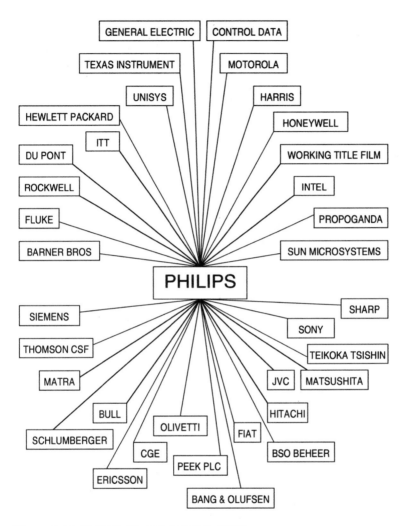

Figure 14.1 Philips' alliance network, 1990

and most competitive in the world. At the end of 1991, the world telecoms market including equipment and calls was worth a massive $300 billion. The UK telecoms market in particular was radically transformed in the 1980s with the privatisation of British Telecom (BT) and the opening up of the call and equipment market to international competition. The US company VMX, a manufacturer of voice paging systems, forged an alliance with Mercury Communications (direct competitor of BT) in the UK in the late 1980s. For VMX, it was the only way to enter the market at minimum cost and with an automatic customer base of 10,000.

FURTHER REFERENCE

Chapter 7, Products: Stages of the product life cycle – Growth (pp. 124–126)

CONCLUSION

There is a multitude of different strategic options open to firms, whether they be market leaders, challengers, followers or nichers and this chapter couldn't possibly describe the huge number of different strategies that are being pursued by the different categories of firms. Nevertheless, the chapter has provided an interesting picture of the strategies available to firms depending on their market status.

NOTES

1 Motorola section adapted from the following: Myron Magnet, 'The new golden rule of business', *Fortune*, 21 February 1994, pp. 28–32; Ronald Henkoff, 'Keeping Motorola on a roll', *Fortune*, 18 April 1994, pp. 51–56; William Echikson, 'How Nokia wins in cellular phones', *Fortune*, 21 March 1994, pp. 38–40; John Morkes, 'How Motorola keeps beating the competition', *Research and Development*, December 1993, pp. 30–32; E.B. Baatz, 'Motorola's secret weapon', *Electronic Business*, April 1993, pp. 51–53; Kevin Kelly and Peter Burrows, 'Motorola: training for the millenium', *International Business Week*, 28 March 1994, pp. 58–61.

2 Ford section adapted from the following: Tom O' Sullivan, 'Fordian slip', *Marketing Week*, 27 August 1993, pp. 22–23; 'Ford's big idea – a 90s mini', *The Times*, London, 4 February 1994, p. 5; John Lawless, 'Re-fashioning faltering Ford', *Management Today*, August 1992, pp. 42–47.

3 Compaq section reprinted from Stephanie Losee, 'How Compaq keeps the magic going', *Fortune*, 21 February 1994. © 1994 Time Inc. All rights reserved.

4 Fuji section adapted from the following: Clare Ansberry, 'New Kodak and Fuji films target advanced amateurs', *The Wall Street Journal*, 17 March 1989; Clare Ansberry and Masayoshi Kanabayashi, 'Kodak remains out of focus in Japan when it comes to key colour film market', *The Wall Street Journal*, 7 December 1990; Gale Eisenstodt and Amy Feldman, 'Sharply focused', *Forbes*, 24 December 1990, pp. 50, 53; Alex Taylor III, 'Kodak scrambles to refocus', *Fortune*, 3 March 1986; 'Now for Kodak', *The Economist*, 30 July 1988, pp. 67–68.

5 Lipton's tea section adapted from Gerry Byrne, 'Barry's rejects market threat by Lipton's to hit number two spot', *The Sunday Press* (Ireland), 9 January 1994.

6 ERF section reprinted from Ross Tieman, 'UK truck maker slips into top gear to take on the giants', *The Times*, 17 August 1993. Copyright © Times Newspapers Ltd 1993.

7 Rover section adapted from Andrew Lorenz, 'In the fast lane', *The Sunday Times*, 8 August 1993, p. 3. © Times Newspapers Ltd, 1993.

8 Avon Tyres section adapted from S.A. Crainer, 'Niche for high performance', *Marketing Business*, October 1990.

9 Harley-Davidson and Honda section adapted from the following: Robert L. Rose, 'Vrooming back: after nearly stalling, Harley-Davidson finds new crowd of riders', *Wall Street Journal*, 31 August 1990; 'Perspectives on strategy: the real story behind Honda's success', *California Management Review*, 1984, no. 3, pp. 47–72; Martin Norris, *Rolling Thunder, The Harley Davidson Legend*, London, The Apple Press, 1992; Brian S. Moskal, 'Born to be real', *Industry Week*, 2 August 1993, pp. 14–18; Kevin Kelly and Lowry Miller, 'The rumble heard around the world: Harleys', *Business Week*, 24 May 1993, p. 58; Charles J. Anderer, 'Harley-Davidson Motor Co. Inc.: defending a piece of the domestic pie', International Business Case Study Project, 1986, Center for International Business Studies, Pace University, USA; 'Harley-Davidson Motor Company Inc.', *Forbes*, 24 May 1993, pp. 45–46; 'Marketer of the month: Willie G. Davidson: born to ride (Harley-Davidson VP)', *Sales and Marketing Management*, April 1991, pp. 26–27; Charles J. Anderer, 'Global competition – motorcycles 1955–1985', International Business Case Study Project, 1986, Center for International Business Studies, Pace University, USA; Thomas Gelb, 'Overhauling corporate engine drives winning strategy', *Journal of Business Strategy*, November–December 1989, vol. 10, pp. 8–12; John A. Conway, 'Harley back in gear', *Forbes*, 20 April 1987, p. 8; Vineeta Anand, 'Japanese management style puts Harley-Davidson on the road again', *Global Trade Executive*, May 1986, pp. 66–68; Daniel Seligman, 'Ganging up on motor-cycle gangs', *Fortune*, 16 May 1983, p. 101; Michael Kolbenschlag, 'Harley-Davidson takes lessons from arch-rivals' handbook', *International Management* (European edition), February 1985; Steve Kichen, 'Thunder road', *Forbes*, 18 July 1983, pp. 92–93; Rod Willis, 'Harley-Davidson comes roaring back', *Management Review*, March 1986, pp. 20–24.

10 Caterpillar and Komatsu section adapted from Alan J. McGrath, 'Ten timeless truths about pricing', *Journal of Consumer Marketing*, winter 1991, vol. 8, no. 1, pp. 5–14.

11 Philips section, including Figure 14.1, reprinted from Philippe Gugler, 'Building transnational alliances to create competitive advantage', *Long Range Planning*, 1992, vol. 25, no. 2. Copyright © 1992, with kind permission of Elsevier Science Ltd.

12 VMX and Mercury Communications section adapted from Matthew Lynn, 'Calling for partners', *Management Today*, July 1992, pp. 80–81.

Chapter 15

Organisation structures

INTRODUCTION

The marketing function within an organisation is closely linked with the other functions of the business, such as R.&D., production, finance, etc. In this chapter we focus on the broader organisation structures of companies, particularly those of international organisations. Organisation structures must allow the company to respond to changes within their business environment. In the case of international organisations important local differences should be taken into account while leveraging the corporate knowledge, know-how and experience across the international network. The organisation structure must facilitate the development and implementation of the selected strategies for the market.

This chapter focuses on the main types of organisational structures operated by companies. These include product, market/customer, geographic, matrix and strategic business unit based structures. Other structures adopted in the international context include the international division and network organisations. We present examples of the way in which different companies organise their businesses and some of the reasons for such structures, including advantages and disadvantages. Many factors may influence the type of structure adopted by an organisation, both internal and external. These can include geographic factors, the type of customer, type of product, the corporate culture and goals of the company, its resources and other environmental factors. These diverse factors produce a range of organisation structures in the market place and companies must develop a structure to best suit their needs.

TYPES OF ORGANISATION STRUCTURES

Product based structures

3M[1]

Partly in response to the establishment of the European single market, 3M adopted a new structure for its marketing activities within Europe in 1993. The structure has changed from one organised primarily on a geographical or country basis to one organised into nineteen product-based divisions ranging from tapes and adhesives to medical imaging systems, each having responsibility for marketing throughout Europe. Product groups are centralised in what are called European 'business centres' (EBC), with many of the groups further subdivided into 33 European business units. However the company has retained elements of the geographical organisation by organising some functions on a geographical basis. These functions include finance, personnel development, information technology and logistics. These are organised into ten new European 'regions'. There is further subdivision in the geographical structure in the form of country managers and local subsidiaries also implement marketing strategies.

The European business centres consist of a central team headed by a team leader. This team operates on a Europe-wide basis. Whilst having responsibility for the management of a particular product line, the team or its members may also be allocated certain special project responsibilities. The managers with geographical functional responsibilities are of the same managerial level as the managers of the European business centres. Part of the rationale for this is to identify any differences among national or country markets (through country managers) and ensure that the EBCs take account of this and respond to local differences if necessary.

The EBCs are normally situated in locations where the company has large manufacturing plants, found in five countries, Belgium, France, Germany, Italy and the UK. The rationale for reorganisation included the emergence of Europe-wide customers and distributors, and the need to make decisions on a Europe-wide basis, along with other aspects of the single market. Another benefit of the change in structure is the sharing of product knowledge among different national or country markets. The time taken to introduce new products or services on to the European market as a whole, has also been reduced. Marketing strategy is now more co-ordinated across Europe, particularly in terms of pricing policy. Under the geographic structure, country units could charge different prices for the same product, which in some cases led to buyers purchasing in the cheaper market. However there have been some drawbacks including in some cases the apparent reluctance for one EBC to sell the products of another. Overall the combination of a product and elements of a geographically based structure in Europe allows 3M to adopt a global strategy while responding to local differences.

FURTHER REFERENCE

Chapter 1, The Strategic Planning Process: Business portfolios (pp. 5–8)

Ciba Geigy[2]

In 1992, the Swiss pharmaceutical and chemical group Ciba-Geigy was organised into three broad business segments of Agriculture, Healthcare and Industry. These segments contained fourteen divisions in total worldwide – Agriculture with three, Healthcare with four and Industry having seven. Divisions range from Pharmaceuticals to Seeds to Polymers. Each division operates its own functional activities including marketing, production, research and development. The divisions are responsible for their own performance. The structure also contains group companies which are incorporated in countries in which they operate.

Certain functions however remain under central control, and these include corporate planning, investment planning, organisational development, environmental protection and safety, and communication policy. Research and development into more speculative technologies is carried out by the corporate research function. The central services charge the divisions for their services, and the divisions are free to go to outside suppliers for the services of the central units.

One of the objectives of this structure is to devolve greater power to the divisions and eliminate the hierarchical structure which previously existed. Individuals are now encouraged to take initiatives through the newly acquired autonomy of the divisions, as against the previous culture of the avoidance of making mistakes. This discouraged individuals from taking the initiative and encouraged an over-cautious approach.

Geographic/product based structures

IBM [3]

At the beginning of the 1990s IBM divided its operations into thirteen 'lines of business' (LOBs), consisting of nine manufacturing and development businesses and four marketing/services businesses. The objective was to devolve more autonomy to the LOBs and allow the manufacturing and development companies to 'sell' their outputs to the marketing businesses who in turn market and sell the products and services. LOBs were also given the freedom to form strategic alliances with other companies. The marketing businesses were allowed to combine other companies' products or services in providing a complete package to customers.

The four marketing businesses consisted of companies operating in four geographic regions: North America; Europe/Middle East/Africa; Asia Pacific; Latin America. In North America the marketing/sales operation contained 63 geographic trading areas further broken down into a network of branches. Two of the manufacturing LOBs – Pennant Systems (printers and printer related software) and the personal computers business – had their own marketing functions with their own sales forces.

The new structure has produced some conflict between the different LOBs, due to competition between competing offers. For example, some of the products produced by the personal systems business compete with products from the application business systems LOB. The freedom to sell products from other companies also caused conflict.

Ultimately it was expected the new business units would have greater autonomy to develop strategies, operate a sales force, and market in new ways such as mail order. R.&D. could also be pursued. The restructuring was a response to changing market conditions which saw demand in IBM's markets falling and translating into sluggish sales and profits for the organisation. Customers had become increasingly sophisticated in their requirements and knowledge of information technology, and also required suppliers to know as much about the customers' business as their own product or services.

The new business groupings were to be more entrepreneurial and aggressive, aiming to stimulate demand for the company's products rather than simply reacting to the previous buoyant demand that existed before the recession. Breaking the company down into smaller business units translates into a closer relationship with customers, greater flexibility, faster response and quicker decision making.

Account management, or looking after the needs of existing customers, was vital to the business. Market development was at the heart of the push towards a more marketing-led culture and involved researching the needs of markets and developing products for those markets. Client operations were responsible for finding generic solutions that could be applied to customers across a sector – a cheque clearing system for banks, for example. Consultancy, an area with huge potential, is one which IBM with its vast information technology expertise, is eager to exploit.

The heads of the businesses are similar to general managers of companies and are financially accountable. Huge organisational upheavals were involved, together with extensive staff training. Staff needed to be made more aware of the marketing concept and the company's commitment to a marketing orientation. Remuneration moved from being solely revenue driven to a situation in which share, profit and customer satisfaction played central roles. Customers are polled twice a year as the basis for a customer satisfaction index and everyone's pay is determined by shifts in the index. Business managers are also judged on the satisfaction levels of their individual customers.

Note In May 1993 IBM indicated it was planning to restructure its organisation once again. The expectations were that it would be based around market segments, but no details were available before publication of this book.

Matrix structure

Matrix organisations contain two dimensions of equal weight in the structure, reporting and decision making. These may be product- and geographic-based structures or other combinations. Under the matrix structure the two dimensions are separately structured but are combined through a usually complex communication network and dual chain of command.

Asea Brown Boveri[4]

In 1987 the Asea Brown Boveri group was formed by the merger of two engineering companies, ASEA in Sweden and Brown Boveri in Switzerland. In 1993 the new group evolved into a structure consisting of five business segments containing 50 business areas operated by 1,300 locally incorporated companies throughout the world. The business segments were Transportation, Industrial and Building Systems, Power Plants, Power Transmission and Distribution, and Financial Services.

At the national country level a locally incorporated ABB company for the country manages subsidiary companies and autonomous profit centres which operate within the business areas. In general the profit centres operate their own balance sheets and profit and loss accounts, own their own assets and are usually subsidiaries of the national ABB company. Generally profit centres are managed by a team of four or five.

In total the ABB organisation has three layers of management. At the top is the executive committee, next the senior executive level and then the profit centre managers. Included in the senior executive level are the managers of business areas responsible for global strategy, including marketing, within the business area. The size of the business area team can be as small as one and as large as around eleven individuals. The team operates largely as facilitator to the profit centres, and is not necessarily based in a fixed location but can move from one market to another in response to needs and opportunities. In parallel to the business area structure is the national ABB company, usually established along country lines. These companies represent ABB's interests for the particular country. The local profit centres within the country report to the national ABB company and to the business area managers under a matrix structure.

The structure contributes to the realisation of the adage 'Think global, act local'. The group expects national companies to act in the interest of the national market and meet the needs of that market. This may require taking on the identity of an indigenous company in that country, because purchasers may prefer dealing with companies from within their country. The matrix also allows a sophisticated structure of simultaneous centralisation through the business areas and ultimately the group executive management, and decentralisation through the profit centre local companies. The business area manager makes decisions on worldwide strategy, marketing, production, performance and exports and research decisions within the business area. In parallel the national companies may co-ordinate the activities of different business areas within the country.

One of the potential drawbacks of the profit centre approach is the difficulty in combining the efforts of the units in working on a large project requiring co-ordination on the bidding process and execution of the work if successful. Another potential problem is that of communication between the different elements of the group. This must be co-ordinated through the executive committee who should receive sufficient and up-to-date information. Each member of the executive committee is responsible for a business segment and/or a corporate function such as corporate communications, research & development or legal affairs and/or a business region covering a number of country markets. The group head office in Zurich contains only around 100 personnel. This emphasises the cor- porate objective of decentralisation.

Strategic business units

This structure consists of separate units which virtually operate as separate companies. Ideally each unit should serve a different market or segment and compete with separate competitors.

Sun Microsystems [5]

At the end of the 1980s Sun Microsystems, suppliers of workstation computer networks, began to establish a formal planning system within the organisation. The company had grown rapidly from its beginning in 1982, to becoming the market leader in the supply of UNIX[®6] work-stations, achieving revenues of $4.3 billion in 1993, and employing over 13,000 employees worldwide. Due to the rapid growth, the existing planning system and organisation structure had to be reassessed to take account of the changed circumstances.

The new planning process identified key target markets for the company to operate in and key objectives relating to these. It also resulted in the company adopting a more focused approach to markets, concentrating on a limited number rather than trying to satisfy all. Following from this corporate decision, another outcome of the revised planning process was a decision for the company to develop its core technologies and products in-house, sub-contract maintenance service (due to the increasing reliability of the products) and concentrate on greater value-added activities in this area such as consultancy and software support. Also the company decided to make its sales force concentrate on larger customers and to market to individuals and small organisations through retailers.

Originally the company was structured along functional and geographic lines. However, due to the range of different customer types, changes in the planning system, the sheer size of the organisation and the diversification into new business areas such as customer training and software design, the geographic and functional structure was no longer appropriate.

In 1991 it was decided to restructure the company into five strategic business units (SBUs) and establish Sun as a holding company (see Figure 15.2). The units consisted of:

1 Sun Technology Enterprises – to develop hardware and software for its own SPARC® microprocessors.
2 Sun Microsystems Laboratories – to develop new technologies and products;
3 SunSoft – to develop UNIX® software for its microprocessor operating products and others;
4 Sun Express – customer services and miscellaneous products;
5 Sun Microsystems Computer Corporation – concentrated on the supply of complete network systems.

Each SBU had its own profit targets and was responsible for achieving the corporate strategic goals appropriate to its area of activity. This was further developed by devolving strategic planning to each of the SBUs. These plans were then developed into an overall corporate strategy. The units reported to the executive management group which consisted of the president/CEO and the vice presidents of corporate functions within the company. These included finance, R.&D., corporate resources, operations, worldwide field operations, corporate marketing, general systems group, corporate development and desktop systems and graphics group.

Network organisation

A network organisation consists of a series of inter-connected organisations who co-operate to serve a particular market. The organisations within the network are usually independent companies but are dependent on each other in attaining their business goals.

Benetton[7]

The Italian fashion company Benetton sells its products through a network of shops owned by thousands of individual entrepreneurs worldwide. In each market or country the retailers are serviced by an agent who acts as the intermediary between the retailers and the company. The agents are independent and many also own retail outlets. These agents are responsible for establishing and developing the retail network in most markets. They are also encouraged to own shops, which gives them

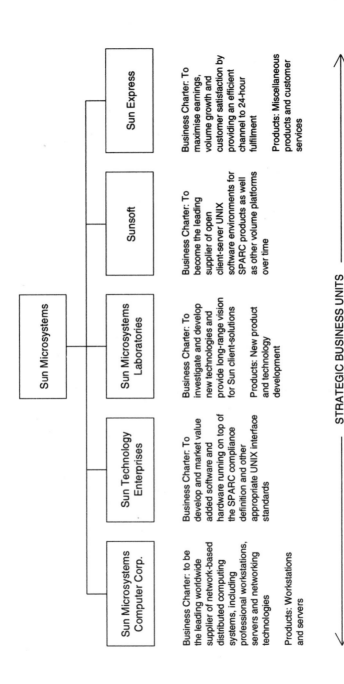

Figure 15.1 Organisation Structure of Sun Microsystems

direct experience of retail business itself. Agents offer advice on such matters as strategy, location of stores, merchandising and display and also receive much support from Benetton head office. The format and design of shops are determined by Benetton.

The advantage of this system is that Benetton can expand the network of shops worldwide without having to invest capital in the expansion. The investment in the retail facilities is made by the entrepreneurs. The company markets through more than 7,000 retail outlets worldwide. Some flagship stores are owned directly by Benetton, but most are owned by independent entrepreneurs. This reduces the risk to which the company is exposed and the Benetton brand can be built up through the network. The core functions of marketing, finance, strategy, information systems, production planning and distribution are controlled centrally. Potential drawbacks, however, can be that store owners are reticent about adopting a new strategy or approach.

Technically, the system is not a franchise, as Benetton does not require royalties on sales or payment for the use of the Benetton name. In theory, Benetton does not have direct power to force network companies to adopt what is desired by the company.

At the production end, Benetton subcontracts most of its production to a network of about 700 independent manufacturers, some of which the company partially owns. Guaranteed prices are paid to subcontractors (10 per cent margins on average cost of production). These companies often do not have marketing or sales functions, as they are provided with relative security by Benetton and have formed strong working relationships with the company. This tends to minimise overheads and duplication within the network.

Among the advantages of the system is the fact that Benetton can respond quickly to changes in the market place, and increase or decrease production accordingly. The company also minimises its own overheads and subcontractors are motivated to improve efficiency.

Activities which are key to the success of the company such as those involving high technology or specialised production processes and those for which economies of scale can be achieved, are kept in-house. These include raw materials purchasing, computer aided design and manufacture, garment colour creating chemical processes and automatic warehousing.

FURTHER REFERENCE

Chapter 10, Marketing Channels: Retailing types – Speciality shops (p. 174)

International division

Toppan Printing Co.[8]

Toppan Printing Co. Ltd is a Japanese company with its core operations in the printing business. The company is divided into a number of product divisions: commercial printing, electronics, industrial materials, information and publications, packaging, and securities printing, and a number of geographic area divisions. These divisions are co-ordinated through a system of business units on a matrix-type structure. The business unit headquarters carry out market analysis and develop strategic leadership for the unit. One of the major objectives of this structure is to provide the company with the power and flexibility to respond quickly to changes in the business environment. The result has been a decentralisation of decision making and improved integration of operations. The business unit is responsible for decisions in its own market. Any other activities that transcend the unit are handled by the company headquarters.

The various divisions have also developed certain activities which enhance their services. The electronics section of the general printing division established design centres which design electronic circuits.

The company headquarters contains the corporate marketing function which provides support and strategic direction to units. The company also established the Toppan Service Centre for the development of 'upstream' activities by the company focusing on the planning and design of printing projects for customers. In this way it began creating demand for its products and services. The Toppan Idea Centre is part of the marketing function and is involved in activities in the form of marketing and distribution aspects of customers' products. Included in the services provided are development of marketing strategies for customers, market research, sales promotional activities and media development. Packaging, distribution and direct marketing are also undertaken by Toppan.

Research and development is carried out by the Toppan Technical Research Institute (TTRI). The divisions also contain technical development centres such as the integrated circuit design centre located in the electronics division, and these work in conjunction with the TTRI. The International Department at head office is responsible for international operations.

The overall structure is depicted in Figure 15.2.

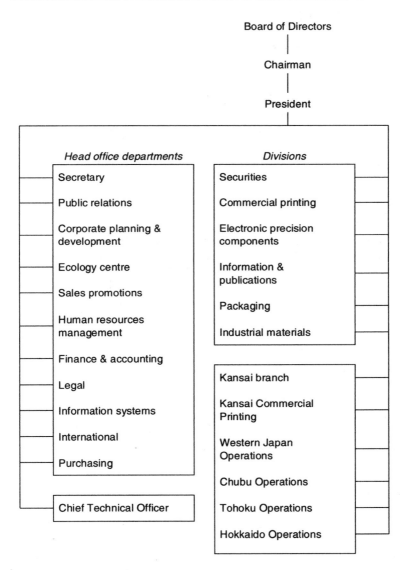

Figure 15.2 **The overall structure of Toppan Printing Co. Ltd**

ADAPTING THE ORGANISATION STRUCTURE

IBM[9]

Since the 1960s the marketing organisation structure of IBM has changed a number of times in response to market conditions and other factors. In the first half of 1960 IBM introduced a new product line, the A360. This product was so important to the organisation that it needed to establish a structure which would ensure its success. The development costs of the A360 were equivalent to the company's total sales at the time. The initial structure was product based.

1 Product based

IBM's data processing group (DPG) carried out the introduction of the product. The world trade subsidiary of IBM took on the function of international manufacturing and marketing. The DPG had its own sales and marketing unit called the data processing division (DPD) which was further broken down geographically, and then developed specialisations based on industry type, such as automobiles, financial services, etc. However the other divisions of IBM also marketed their products to industries or market segments, with some selling the same products as the DPD. These divisions included the Federal Systems Division which was responsible for the US government market and sold the same products as the DPD; the Office Products Division which marketed photocopiers and typewriters; and the Information Records Division, selling data processing consumables. Many of the divisions carried out both manufacturing and sales. In general the structure was product based, organised on a geographical frame with specialisation in industry or market segments. This structure is outlined in Figure 15.3.

The structure was further broadened to take account of customer requirements, thus incorporating customer segmentation into the structure.

2 Product/customer based

In 1969 in a response to the smaller systems that were coming on the market, IBM set up the General Systems Division (GSD). This group was responsible for developing and manufacturing smaller computer systems. GSD, however did not perform a marketing function, and the products were marketed through the DPG. In the early 1970s DPG was divided into two smaller units: the Data Processing Product Group,

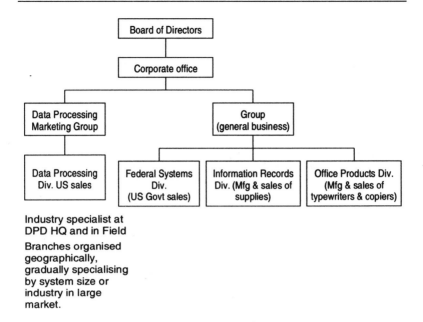

Industry specialist at
DPD HQ and in Field

Branches organised
geographically,
gradually specialising
by system size or
industry in large
market.

Figure 15.3 IBM Marketing Organisation, 1966–1972 (product based)

which looked after development and manufacture of the products, and
the Data Processing Marketing Group, which looked after sales and
servicing of all computer systems for commercial customers. One of the
reasons for this was to improve the company's technical capability in the
market. The allocation of the marketing of the new smaller systems to
the DPG meant that the market development of the smaller systems
suffered because DPG focused on the mainframe 360 product.

In 1975 the GSD took over the marketing of smaller systems with the
DPG continuing with larger systems. The Federal Systems Division
sales function was also moved to the DPG. In the 1970s the organisation
structure was as shown in Figure 15.4.

The rationale for the structure was that the GSD was responsible for
marketing smaller systems to smaller customers and the DPD was
responsible for marketing larger systems to larger accounts. It allowed
the organisation to specialise the marketing effort of its products (new
and existing) on existing and new customers. The GSD was allowed to
develop its own expertise in marketing the new smaller systems to new
customers and for new applications and maintaining the company as a

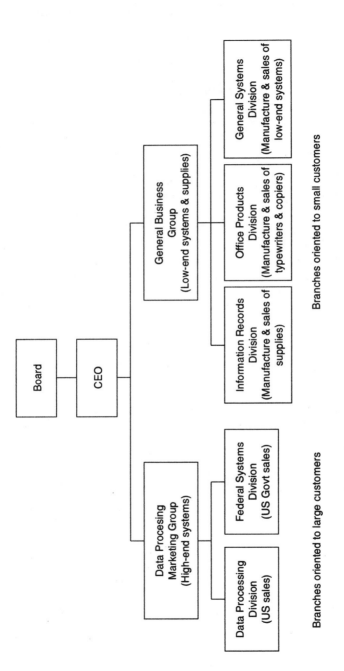

Branches oriented to large customers

Branches oriented to small customers

Figure 15.4 IBM Marketing Organisation, 1975–1982 (product/customer based)

force in the changing market which spawned new competition. The Office Products Division (OPD) and the Information Records Division still marketed their products to large and small companies. The marketing organisation, however, was fragmented. Conflict began to arise between DPD and GSD with cases occurring of both calling on each others' customers as customers began using both large and small systems. Suspicions among GSD staff of preferential treatment for DPD arose. The structure was left unchanged for the time being. The company then decided to focus on customer size as a basis for its structure.

3 Customer size

At this point markets and technologies were changing rapidly and the company's products were diversifying and increasing in complexity. In 1982 the DPD, GSD and OPD divisions were dissolved, and a National Accounts Division (NAD) catering for the 2,400 customers with the largest volume, and a National Marketing Division (NMD) targeted at all other accounts were established. Each division sold the full range of IBM products. This structure allowed IBM to develop understanding of customers' requirements and tailor the service to each customer through account management. It also provided greater opportunities for the cross-selling of IBM products to individual customers.

A National Distribution Division (NDD) was also formed. Simultaneously independent business units (IBUs) were established and the Entry Systems Division was formed as an IBU. These were given freedom to develop, manufacture and market products on a similar basis to an independent company with considerable decision making autonomy. The Entry Systems Division was responsible for IBM's PC products.

The structure was therefore based on customer size with the added dimension of the autonomous business unit to concentrate on strategic new products. The problem of conflict between different products was resolved. The structure is outlined in Figure 15.5

The new structure however also suffered from cannibalisation between the NAD and NMD divisions. Furthermore, the two divisions did not share resources which resulted in duplication and marketing issues that affected both divisions could only be resolved at a higher level. The result was that both the NAD and the NMD were dissolved in 1986 and the structure was re-established on a geographic basis.

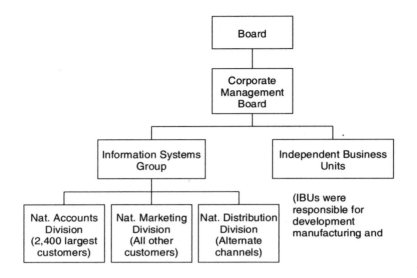

Figure 15.5 IBM marketing organisation, 1983–1985

4 Geographic structure

Two marketing units were established in their place, the North/Central Marketing Division and the South/West Marketing Division. The NDD was maintained and the Entry Systems Division was merged into the mainstream organisation. The structure was now geographically based consisting of areas, regions and districts, with each unit selling the full range of IBM products. This kept travelling and administrative expenses to a minimum and removed much of the conflict experienced under the previous structure.

Field sales personnel were now required to sell the full range of products. Because of the scope and complexity of this range individuals were unlikely to develop expertise in every line. The disadvantages of such a structure are that sales personnel are prone to concentrate on those products with which they are most familiar. To tackle this problem marketing support was placed at head office for field personnel focused on particular industries or applications. The structure was as shown in Figure 15.6.

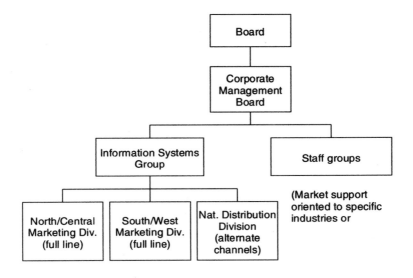

Figure 15.6 IBM marketing organisation, 1986–1987

The changing organisational structures of IBM in general have been responses to changing market conditions and the internal company environment. New structures evolved to meet new opportunities and eliminate problems experienced by previous structures.

FURTHER REFERENCE

Chapter 6, Segmentation and Positioning: Types of segmentation and positioning – Geographic segmentation (pp. 101–102)

Procter & Gamble[10] This company is organised along 39 product categories in the USA. The categories vary from soaps to laundry detergents. In this way products within the same category benefit from a co-ordinated marketing approach, furthermore each product category acts as its own profit centre. P&G use lead markets/countries to launch important global or regional initiatives. They also use 'category managers' in major national subsidiaries who control marketing, sales and manufacturing. These managers report to country managers and category managers.

General Electric[11]   General Electric consists of a range of diversified enterprises with strong central management ranging from electrical goods to jet engines.[6] The strong central management culture permeates throughout the organisation, exercising operational control of the different enterprises.

Elida Gibbs[12]   The Unilever subsidiary reorganised its marketing structure from a hierarchical marketing department into a brand development department focused on the final consumer and a customer development department focused on the retailer. Functions within this structure include a category manager whose objective is to improve total category sales and act as a key account manager and who also has responsibility for trade promotions.

Mars[13]   Mars has established pan-European operating companies for both confectionery and pet foods, with pan-European functional managers. Local managers are responsible for local activities such as production and sales force management.

Canon[14]   Canon consists of nineteen product groups covering seven business areas. About 280 subsidiaries exist worldwide. The corporation has a central research and development unit and each product group also has its own development centre. Sales and distribution in Japan are organised on a product basis, but in the rest of the world are organised on a regional or national basis. A matrix-like structure consisting of a network of 'co-ordinating committees' maintain the whole structure.

CONCLUSION

It is clear from the foregoing examples that companies often adopt a combination of different bases on which to develop organisation structures. Invariably structures are based on a combination of two or more criteria such as market, product, function, geographic etc. Organisation structures may also vary due to the culture of the organisation reflecting different degrees of control from centralisation to devolution. It is the influence of this myriad of factors which shape the structure of the organisation and help it to meet its goals.

NOTES

1 3M section adapted from: Christopher Lorenz, 'Here, there and everywhere – the lives of 3M's managers have been transformed by a Europe-wide

reorganisation', *Financial Times*, 10 November 1993; 'Facing up to responsibility', *Financial Times*, 15 December 1993.

2 Ciba-Geigy section reprinted from Carol Kennedy, 'Changing the company
culture at Ciba-Geigy', 1993, vol. 26, no. 1, pp. 18–27. Copyright © 1993,
with kind permission from Elsevier Science Ltd.

3 IBM section adapted from the following: Laura Mazur, 'Moving a Mountain',
Marketing Business, October 1992, pp. 24–27; Richard Miles, 'New model
army', *Computing*, 6 May 1993, pp.18–19; J.W. Verity, 'Out of the Big
Blue, Many Little Blues', *Business Week*, 33, 9 December 1991; J. Markoff
and John F. Ackers, 'A costly revamping at IBM', *The New York Times*, 30
December 1991, p. D8; D. Kirkpatrick, 'Breaking up IBM', *Fortune*, 27
July 1992, pp. 112–121; J.W. Verity, T. Peterson, D. Depke and E. Schwartz,
'The new IBM', *Business Week*, 16 December 1991, pp. 112–116, 118;
J.W. Verity, 'Surprise! The new IBM really looks new', *Business Week*, 18
May, 1992, pp. 124–125; J. David Lichtenthal and William Copulsky,
'How Big Blue IBM Became Black and Blue', *Industrial Marketing
Management*, 1993, vol. 22, pp. 277–285; 'IBM's search for yesterday's
glory', *Sales and Marketing Management*, July 1993, pp. 10–11; Martin
Dickson, 'A business sings the blues', *Financial Times*, 21 October 1992;
'At any price – IBM's personal-computer strategy', *The Economist*, 10
October 1992, pp. 88, 94; Elaine L. Appleton, 'Big changes going slowly',
Datamation, 15 December, 1992, pp. 39–43; 'What went wrong at IBM',
The Economist, 16 January 1993; Peter Wilsher, 'Reprogramming IBM',
Management Today, May 1992, pp. 49–52.

4 Asea Brown Boveri section adapted from the following: Tom Peters,
'ABBs prophet of smallness points the way to profit in the nineties',
Financial Times, 11 November 1992, p. 25; Ian Rodger, 'ABB managers
strip for action', *Financial Times*, 25 August 1993; Sunil Babbar and Arun
Rai, 'Competitive Intelligence for International Business', *Long Range
Planning*, 1993, vol. 26, no. 3, pp. 103–113; William Taylor, 'The Logic of
Global Business: An Interview with ABB's Percy Barnevik', *Harvard
Business Review*, March-April 1991, pp. 91–105; Asea Brown Boveri Ltd.
Annual Reports 1992 and 1993; Tom Peters, *Liberation Management*,
London, Macmillan, 1992; Carol Kennedy, 'ABB: Model Merger for the
New Europe', *Long Range Planning*, October 1992, vol. 25, no. 5,
pp. 10–17; 'Tracking customer satisfaction', Quality '93 Empowering
People With Technology, *Fortune*, 20 September 1993.

5 Sun Microsystems section, including Figure 15.2, reprinted from Sal Kukalis
and Brett Kanazawa, 'Sun Microsystems reorganises for growth', *Long
Range Planning*, 1993, vol. 26, no. 5, pp. 42–48. Copyright 1993, with kind
permission from Elsevier Science Ltd.

6 UNIX is an operating system which allows multiple user access and transfer
of information.

7 Benetton section adapted from: Fiorenza Belussi, 'The transformation of
the 1980s: growth of network companies, or the return of flexibility in large
businesses'?', *International Journal of Technology Management*, November
1993, pp. 188–189; Werner Kettelhohn, 'An Interview with Aldo Palermi
of Benetton: the early growth years', *European Management Journal*,
September 1993, vol. 11, no. 3, pp. 321–331; and *European Management*

Journal, December 1993, vol. 11, no. 4, pp. 481–484; Werner Ketelhohn, 'What do We Mean by Cooperative Advantage?', *European Management Journal*, March 1993, vol. 11, no. 1, pp. 30–37; Kenneth Labich, 'Benetton takes on the world', *Fortune*, June 13, 1983, pp. 114–119; James L. Heskett and Sergio Signorelli, *Designing Strategies for Multinational Competition*, Chapter 1.3, Case: Benetton, Raymond E. Miles, 'Causes of failure in network organisations', *California Management Review*, Summer 1992, vol. 34, no. 4, pp. 53–72; 'Why Networks may fail', *The Economist*, 10 October 1992; Fiorenza Belussi, 'New Technology in a traditional sector, the Benetton case', University of California at Berkeley, 1986, BRIE working paper no. 19.

  8 Toppan Printing Co. section, including Figure 15.2, is reprinted from Kazuo Suzuki, 'Toppan Printing: successful diversification through technology', *Long Range Planning*, 1993, vol. 26, no. 4, pp. 42–52. Copyright © 1993, with kind permission from Elsevier Science Ltd.

  9 IBM section, including figures, reprinted from Frank V. Cespedes, 'Agendas, incubators and marketing organisation', *California Management Review*, Autumn 1990, vol. 33, no. 1, p. 26. Copyright © 1990 by the Regents of the University of California. By permission of the Regents.

10 Procter & Gamble section adapted from the following: Hajo Riesenbeck and Anthony Freeling, 'How global are global brands?', *The McKinsey Quarterly*, 1991, no. 4, pp. 3–18; Douglas G. Shaw and Vincent C. Perro, 'Beating the Odds: Five reasons why companies excel', *Management Review*, August 1992, pp. 15–19; Procter & Gamble Annual Reports, 1991, 1992, 1993, 1994.

11 General Electric section adapted from: Milton Leontiades, 'The Japanese art of managing diversity', *The Journal of Business Strategy*, March/April 1991, pp. 30–36; General Electric Annual Report, 1992, 1993.

12 Elida Gibbs section adapted from: Alan Mitchell, 'Marketing's New Model Army', *Management Today*, March 1994, pp. 45–50; Elida Gibbs Annual Report, 1993.

13 Mars section adapted from Hajo Riesenbeck and Anthony Freeling, op. cit.

14 Canon section adapted from: Geoffrey Foster, 'Canon's new world order', *Management Today*, September 1992, pp. 74–76; Canon Annual Report, 1992, 1993.

Brand name index

Company name index

Subject index

advertising, communication objectives 184–6; communication strategy 186–7; comparative 193–4; message generation 186–7; performance evaluation 191–2; point-of-purchase 192–3; rational appeal 189; reach 192; sensor appeal 189–91

balanced scorecard 16
behavioural segmentation 95, 96–8; occasion of use 99–100; usage rate 100; user status 98–9
branding 111, 112–13; changing name 114–15; corporate umbrella 113; extension 113–14; family umbrella 113; ingredient 115; licensing 114
building block principle 4
business cycle 14
business portfolios 2, 5–7
buyer behaviour *see* consumer behaviour
buyer chain 91–3, *see also* decision making unit
buying decision process 90; evaluation of alternatives 91; information search 90–1

cause marketing 213–15
channels *see* distribution strategies
competitive advantage 1, 4–5, 13
competitive moves 233–5
consumer behaviour 88–9; buyer

chain 91–3; buying decision process 90–1; cultural/psychological factors 87–8; decision making unit 91–3; influencing factors 85; social/personal factors 86
corporate responsibility 12
crisis management 215–17
customer: loyalty (developing) 214; relationships 64–7; satisfaction 16–17, 18; service 14
customer information system (CIS) 67

databases 64–8; database marketing 109
dealer incentives 167–8
decision making unit 91–3
direct mail 66, 67, 104
direct marketing 163–4
distinctive competence 13
distribution strategies 107–8, 162–83; channel co-operation 169–72; channel competition 172; channel conflict 169; channel leadership 168–9; exclusive 180–1; intensive 180; motivating channel members 167–8; non-retailing types 176–8; retailing types 172–6; selecting channel type 163–6; selective 182; wheel of retailing 178–9; wholesaling 179–81
diversification strategies 34–6